Literary Meaning

Reclaiming the Study of Literature

Wendell V. Harris
Professor of English
Pennsylvania State University

NEW YORK UNIVERSITY PRESS
Washington Square, New York

PN
81
.H2847
1996

© Wendell V. Harris 1996

First published in the U.S.A. in 1996 by
NEW YORK UNIVERSITY PRESS
Washington Square
New York, N.Y. 10003

Library of Congress Cataloging-in-Publication Data
Harris, Wendell V.
Literary meaning : reclaiming the study of literature / Wendell
V. Harris.
p.   cm.
Includes bibliographical references and index.
ISBN 0–8147–3525–8
1. Criticism.   2. Literature—History and Criticism—Theory, etc.
3. Hermeticism.   4. Hermeneutics.   I. Title.
PN81.H2847   1996
801'.95—dc20   95–38306
                                                         CIP

Printed in Great Britain

Contents

Introduction

It is easy enough to make fun of the outrage and anguish expressed when the creation of a School of English was being debated at Oxford at the end of the nineteenth century. Such a School, it was contended, would either force lecturers into mere gossip about the lives and times of authors in order for them to have something to say, or else quickly become a dry philological study of the history of the language, which, by usurping the place of Latin and Greek would, in the acerbic comment of Thomas Case, Wayneflete Professor of Moral Philosophy, "reverse the Renaissance." The conservatives of course lost and the progressives entered the citadel, waving a banner reworked from Matthew Arnold that might have read, "the best that is known and thought in the world includes a good deal of English literature" (to which could later have been added "and a little American").

Well, yes, the crusty old dons, many of whom perhaps knew their port vintages at least as well as their English literature, were wrong. But in matters like these it is rare for intelligent persons to be wholly in error. Arnold himself had serious doubts about making the study of English a formal curriculum in the university, and the earliest professors of that study at Oxford and Cambridge, Walter Raleigh and Arthur Quiller-Couch, found considerable difficulty in deciding just what they were to teach. Now, a hundred years later, may be a good time to ask to what extent the old guard could have been partly in the right. Literature *does* in fact constitute an odd object of study. Reserving the question of what constitutes literature and thinking of it simply as what the ordinary librarian or book shop manager shelves under that classification, one can recognize a number of curious features. First, literary texts are singular and non-repeatable although thoroughly copiable. Such obvious features rule out a great many activities normally associated with research and scholarship. Not only is there no substratum of predictable relationships between entities as definable as electrons, quarks, or genes, but, since each poem or novel is unique, no possibility for the statistical studies (other than the most trivial) that

1

social sciences depend upon. Experiments on the texts themselves are impossible; experiments on readers' responses to texts introduce such an enormous and uncontrollable-for group of variables that the results are more anecdotal than definitive.

Even literary taxonomy is a haphazard business. One can of course produce any number of classifications of kinds of literature, or literary periods, or devices used in literature. However, nothing is in the least inevitable about any of them. The best known structure of literary classification in English is Northrop Frye's in *Anatomy of Criticism*, yet the undeniable arbitrariness of his system has been pointed out again and again. Aligning mythoi with the seasons yields interesting comparisons, but there is no necessary underlying relationship in the comparison. One can imagine four rather differently described mythoi developed out of parallels with the cardinal points of the compass. Or three paralleling sun, rain, and snow. The relationship between literary study and the physical sciences will be considered in Chapter 4, but to anticipate certain objections, let us admit that the scientists' classifications also have an arbitrary side. Nothing forced experimenters to try to reduce all physical matter to elements and then arrange the elements in the order of atomic weight. But, once this principle of classification had been found possible and useful, the arrangement had to correspond with experimentally determined atomic weights and no amount of taking thought or earnest desire on the part of a rebel chemist could move iron ahead of calcium in the periodic table. The (slight) shifts that did occur were the result of demonstrable anomalies leading to realignment by atomic number rather than weight; once this was accomplished, the assumption that there might be a new element between, say, nickel (atomic number 28) and copper (atomic number 29) became impossible. On the other hand, no principle except loose tradition controls the classification of literary texts. Polonius was only getting started in his classification of plays through the juggling of tragic, comic, historical, and pastoral; to this one could add ironic, satiric, humorous, lyric, absurd, logical, ritual, realistic, fantastic, and a good many more descriptors. Unlike chemical elements, these qualities can of course be put together in any combination and in any proportion.

There is general agreement that no amount of knowledge about an author would enable us to predict or explain that author's fiction, poems, or plays, yet no one literally supposes that if Milton, Sterne, or Shaw had not lived, *Paradise Lost, Tristram Shandy,* or

Man and Superman would nevertheless have been produced word for word. We constantly make judgments about the literature we read, but the characteristics of goodness or badness, success or failure, that we automatically assume to belong to a text correspond to no agreed criteria even within a given culture. Popularity and critical acclaim command assent only to the fact of their existence, not to their validity as critical criteria. A poem is never "wrong," though it may be judged unconvincing, tasteless, silly, irritating, or vulgar – all of which perhaps are summed up in the term "infelicitous." Although the possibility that language refers to anything outside itself and that literature can direct us toward what is true or good is now widely denied, many among those who most vigorously make these denials not only constantly announce truths about what a better society would be like but adduce literary texts in support of their propositions.

Now all these oddities can be regarded as part of the fascination of literary study. But if literature consists of unique, unpredictable events that can only be classified on an ad hoc basis and only judged by a kind of applause meter (the readings on which will vary depending on the audience whose applause is measured), *what* is there to study, and what is accomplished by that study? The peculiarities of literature necessarily imply peculiarities in writing about literature. The uniqueness, which is also the idiosyncrasy, of the individual text is necessarily a concomitant characteristic of the commentary on it.

If, when one steps back to consider, writing about literature is in essence a strange activity, the force of that realization becomes a great deal stronger when one looks at current practice. It is a considerable understatement to say that the educated reader is very likely to be puzzled, if not irritated and perhaps outraged, by the manner in which literature has been discussed for the last twenty-five years. The reader I have in mind is the adult who likes to read, has read and at times still reads literature from earlier decades and even centuries, and at least occasionally encounters essays on the literary scene in publications like *The New York Review of Books* or *The Times Literary Supplement*. Reactions of distaste are not confined to the lay reader; they are common enough among established professors in English and foreign language departments.

Elizabeth Bruss pretty well summed up the differences between the traditional literary scholarship and the new forms it was assuming in her 1982 comparison of articles by Dorrit Cohn and Henry

Sussman – I find her description all the more interesting in that she felt no hostility toward the poststructuralist revolution.

> Both critics begin with an anomaly, something unexpected or illogical in the way Kafka constructs his text, but whereas for Cohn . . . the task is to explain the incoherence and ultimately to transcend it by incorporating it as a passing stage in Kafka's overall development, for Sussman . . . it has become instead a matter to explore, a mystery that deepens as its necessity becomes more absolute. Not only does Sussman fail or refuse to use a narrative framework to give order to Kafka's career, there is a similiar fluidity and lack of a priori stages to his own argument. The proof is meandering, elements circulate and overlap; it is ultimately the density of the web thus produced on which the case must rest. Cohn's work is situated in a well-defined polemical space, between the axes of antecedents and adversaries whose opinions are explicitly acknowledged and set off from Cohn's own argument. Concepts are either attributed to particular "owners" or designated as the shared property of the community at large. There is little or no attribution machinery in Sussman's work, however, which relies on the reader's familiarity with key terms like *textuality* and *exchange* to establish its relationship to the work of other critics. Glancing blows and playful allusions replace official footnotes, making Sussman's text seem more porous than Cohn's, full of minute fissures through which concepts seep in or leak out, impossible either to claim or entirely disclaim. (7)

An esoteric vocabulary accompanied by gnomic references to what various authority figures (Saussure, Barthes, Lacan, Derrida, de Man) are seemingly presumed to have demonstrated without question, strange unargued assumptions, and arcane modes of argument cannot but seem unassimilably technical or perversely trivial to those unfamiliar with the dominant modes of poststructuralist writing. Such essays appear all the more absurd when, after endlessly turning back on themselves in demonstrating finally that something or other about the work in question is not as everyone else had thought, they arrive at the conclusion, explicit or implicit, that it all makes no difference anyway. It is no less strange how little of what is written about presumed works of literature these days entices, or seems intended to entice, its readers to seek out the work itself.

Most of what I have tried to present here has been said in many ways by many others. There are a good number of useful accounts of the ways in which certain philosophical, social, psychological, and linguistic theories led literary criticism to its present perilous state, from Gerald Graff's *Literature Against Itself* (1979) to Bernard Bergonzi's *Exploding English* (1990).[1] Deconstruction is no longer the magic word, many a recent essay and review tells us, and Derrida no longer the infallible prophet. For those of us who have felt that the trick of turning gold into lead is interesting but hardly profitable, that is good news. However, the eristic strategies and fallacious forms of argument to which deconstruction and related movements have accustomed us continue to litter the intellectual landscape. One finds the same journals that announce the decline and fall of deconstruction still cluttered by deconstructive vocabulary and tricks of argument. I make no apology then for wishing to contribute to the evidently unfinished business of pushing certain intellectual debris out of the way. Nor for rehearsing in homely straightforward language a number of points that are well known – if frequently misunderstood or ignored. Since one of the most annoying of current critical practices is to write as though the reader will be capable of taking every expression in the (unexplained and often idiosyncratic) sense it has for the author, I try to make it a rule to explain exactly how I understand the critics, theories, and terminology I cite, however unsophisticated or banal such a procedure seems.

The organization of the book reflects the view that despite the many theories that are brandished and the variety of directions from which literary texts are currently approached, the central issues around which most disagreements and debates center – often only implicitly – are the curiously yoked issues of authorial intention and extra-linguistic reference. Accordingly, I have divided the mass of critical commentary along that line. Chapter 1 provides a kind of orienting summary of what I call the Great Dichotomy: that between "hermetic" and "hermeneutic" views of discourse. While hermetic theorists and critics deny the relevance and/or possibility of determining authorial intention and, frequently, of any decidable meaning whatever, a number of others, whose efforts I have labelled hermeneutic, have dedicated themselves to the task of describing just how it is that meanings, in literature and all other discourse, are in fact communicated with what is on the whole demonstrable success. Curiously enough, the forms of hermetic and hermeneutic thought I examine developed and ramified side by side over the last three decades without substantive interaction. However, since the hermeticists have achieved much greater notice and influence, the words "literary theory" have become primarily associated with them; that is why I prefer to speak of hermeneutic principles even though such principles necessarily have their own theoretical dimension.

In Chapter 2 I seek to analyze what seem to me the major errors – perhaps excesses is the better word – of the structuralist and post-structuralist (hermetic) denials of intention and reference and critique certain of the corollary arguments. Chapter 3 is devoted to an analysis not of the conclusions of specific hermetic arguments but of the dominant fallacies and strategies that produce such conclusions. Chapter 4 is focused on certain peculiar attitudes toward physical science and the scientific method that were initiated by the advent of structuralism. A considerable amount of confusion has been produced in literary studies by a yearning toward the certitude associated with the physical sciences; somehow this continues to coexist with the explicit denial of the possibility of any such certitude. This yearning, which has been accurately enough called "physics envy," lies behind a good bit of pretentious theorizing about literature. Even though hermetic theorizing has developed what in some senses are more sophisticated patterns of argument, the first four chapters concentrate on key early essays since these have remained the prime sources of positions which are explicitly adopted or tacitly assumed in succeeding hermetic essays. Moreover, these early statements are the ones that continue to be reprinted in anthologies intended to introduce students to contemporary criticism and theory.

Chapter 5 surveys literary hermeneutics, not the philosophically oriented hermeneutics conspicuously exemplified by Martin Heidegger, but the application of a common-sense principle for seeking authorial meaning. The reconstruction of the most likely intended meaning is presented as not only a reasonable goal but the necessary first step in exploring those significances of interest to the individual reader that the author could not have intended. The chapter seeks to make clear the limits within which interpretation of intended meaning is possible and to recognize that the intellectual activity of reading rarely if ever stops with the effort to reconstruct the author's intended meaning. The constructive side of the book centers on this chapter. Although I insist that inescapable oddities accompany the academic study of literature, literary hermeneutics does not require or indeed sanction the willfully paradoxical theorizing or careless conflation of concepts that under-lie literary hermeticism. Delight in disorder need not extend to intellectual disarray.

The succeeding chapters attempt not only to point out various forms of confusion in literary studies but suggest ways of avoiding them. The meaning of the concept of theory and the ramifications of the difference between understanding and explanation are the topics of Chapter 6. Explorations of the necessity of pluralism in literary commentary and the problems of an increasingly chaotic theoretical and critical terminology make up Chapter 7. Chapter 8 considers the confusions arising from the several senses in which "literary history" is used and insists on the distinction between the facts of historical scholarship and their use. What I hope are more constructive ways of regarding the relation of rhetoric to both lit-erature and writing about literature are offered in Chapter 9. It is more than a little odd that just about the time that the concept of rhetoric had been liberated from most of the connotations of dis-honesty and trickery that had attached to it, critics and theorists began to identify literature, and indeed all discourse, with rhetoric in ways that imply that rhetorical deception (including self-deception) is a necessary part of every use of language.

The absurdities of expecting the field of English to emulate the sciences and demonstrate that its professors are up and doing through the production of something comparable to scientific knowl-edge is the subject of the final chapter.

TERMINOLOGY

It seems best to be as specific as possible about my use of certain important terms as early as possible, especially since I will cite the lack of such clarification as one of the unnecessary causes of confu-sion in the field. Except where specifically qualified, I attempt to maintain the following definitions and distinctions, the justifica-tions for which will be developed in the course of the discussion. First, I distinguish between an author's *intended meaning* and what-ever *significances* or *symptomatic meanings* a reader finds in the text. The meaning/significance contrast has been adapted from E. D. Hirsch; I also follow him to some extent in restricting the term "inter-pretation" to the reconstruction of meanings presumably intended by the author. However, I have not found it possible wholly to adopt his restriction of "criticism" to the pursuit of meanings not anticipated by the author. The difficulty is that there seems to be no term that covers the whole of the activities of literary study. Where it is not too awkward, I use "literary commentary" as the umbrella term for all writing about literature, but at times "criticism" has seemed required to do duty as the overall term.[2]

I further distinguish between *understanding* (grasping an author's intended meaning) and *explanation* (giving an account that links a phenomenon to a body of theory and allows one to make predictions of the sort possible in the physical sciences) and *application* (finding a pattern that seems to be exemplified by, or be in some way analogous to, or illuminate patterns within a text).

The term "literature" requires special notice. While the problem of defining literature is intriguing, I have avoided attempting a definition because I believe that finally what determines whether we regard something as literature or not depends on how we choose to read it, whether primarily for information or the demonstration or analogizing of a theory on the one hand, or primarily for the pleasure of the language, construction, imagination, and intellectual suggestiveness of the given text on the other. I presume it goes without saying that some texts are much more amenable to one kind of reading than the other, but a novel read solely for a favored symptomatic meaning is not really being read as literature while a witty book on etiquette might well be read as literature.[3]

Notes

1. Graff's 1992 *Beyond the Culture Wars* finds the current clash of views much less troubling, and indeed argues that the way to revitalize the teaching of literature is through teaching the very conflicts. There is much that is useful in the book, but one realizes at the end that it does not really address the question of why literature is worth teaching, or why the conflicting theories, imported as they are from other fields, ought not to be considered directly.
2. Todorov and others have used "commentary" much more narrowly.
3. Louise Rosenblatt's view that one can read almost anything either efferently (for information) or aesthetically (taking that term in a quite broad sense) seems to me essentially sound. See *The Reader, the Text, the Poem.*

1

The Great Dichotomy

It is no doubt possible to justify the most extreme 'liberty of interpreting' when criticism is frankly concerned with the practical uses to which poems may be put by readers irrespective of their authors' intentions in composing them; they can then be made to say or mean whatever is most relevant to our interest or needs; and who can rightly object if this is what we want to do and is plainly advertised as such?
R. S. Crane, *The Languages of Criticism and the Structure of Poetry*, 33.

Shared communication proves the existence of a shared, and largely true, view of the world. But what led us to demand the common view was the recognition that sentences held true – the linguistic representatives of belief – determine the meaning of the words they contain.
Donald Davidson, "The Method of Truth in Metaphysics," 168.

Nothing in the history of literary studies is stranger than the great dichotomy that has grown up in the last 25 years: that between writers who for the most part have sought either to show that all meaning is indeterminate or to somehow disconnect linguistic meaning from extra-linguistic reality, and those who have labored to show *how* intended meanings are communicated with sufficient clarity and that such meanings are connected to a reality consisting of much more than language systems. The currents making up what is generally called poststructuralism have been the dominant ones, but during the same years that the greater part of the best-known theorists and a host of epigones have played variations on the principles of indeterminacy and infinite deferral of meaning, a significant number of theorists have devoted themselves to a variety of researches into what makes possible that communication the denial of which the poststructuralists seek constantly to communicate.

Part of the oddity of the situation is that, while some publishers and professional journals have chosen sides, many have been happily indiscriminate, publishing studies based on both of these incompatible positions with fine tolerance. The situation is rather like one portion of the medical profession devoting itself to studying how viruses induce diseases while a more influential portion is denying the existence of viruses – the parallel comes even closer if we assume that the second group in practice relies on modes of treatment that assume the existence of viruses.

Although the field of literary studies is too complicated fully to fit this central dichotomy – which seems, happily, to be breaking up – the basic opposition has been so striking and continues to exert so widespread a residual force that it requires explicit statement. The difference can be described in terms of philosophical allegiances, but the usual approach to the poststructuralist view of the world from Nietzsche, Freud, Husserl, and Heidegger to Derrida tends to lose certain basic differences amid the subtleties of metaphysical speculation. For the purpose of analyzing the oppositions, it is useful simply to recognize that two different questions are being asked. The poststructuralist (or hermetic) question is this: given the theory that the system of language is divorced from extra-linguistic reality, what devices can be found to demonstrate that language is neither interpretable nor explanatory of reality? The very different question asked by what I will call the hermeneutic group is: what principle or principles make possible our understanding of individual instances of language use? My word choices in setting up these formulations have been deliberate. "Theory," "explanation," and "language-as-system" (Saussure's *langue*) as associated with hermetics are contrasted with the hermeneutic "principle," "understanding," and "language-in-use" (Saussure's *parole*).

HERMETICS

Structuralism – though it served as a convenient rubric for a variety of intellectual perspectives – was in itself so short-lived that to follow the usual practice and call the large-scale phenomena that followed it "poststructuralist" is rather like calling contemporary literature post-dadaist. That is why I prefer the term "hermetic." The appropriateness of the word was suggested to me by essays of Umberto Eco, who learnedly traces the magical tradition of hermeticism as associated with the writings of Hermes Trismegistus.[1] Eco parallels much in contemporary criticism and theory with hermeticism's suspiciousness, its search for secrets, the accompanying inclination to seize on any similarity as a clue, and, since the rooting out of more and more hidden meanings inevitably produces contradictory meanings, the belief that texts have indeterminate meanings. I find the term "hermetics" satisfying because it suggests the rather diverse phenomena behind which stand a highly esoteric, primarily occult tradition. Hermetics has always been associated with belief that the world (or reality) is very different from what it appears to be and that its nature is sealed from ordinary human understanding. Moreover, hermetics suggests the recondite, philosophically oriented theories that lie behind much of poststructuralist thought, restricting full access to a circle of initiates, the academic group within which members write primarily for each other.

The core doctrines of contemporary hermetics are well enough known to be summarized quite briefly (I give each in its strongest form):

1. The denial that language connects with anything beyond itself together with the assertion that it is meaningless to talk about a reality outside language since all we can know and speak of is linguistically formulated.
2. The denial of the possibility of determining meaning, which entails not only the denial of the possibility of saying true things about literature but of any adequate communication. The interpretation of texts and the interpretation of (attempted) interpretations both become impossible.
3. The denial of the author and the reader as thinking, willing subjects able to think about what they are thinking and willing and will what they are thinking. The notion of a discrete unitary human mind is regarded as a myth, since what appears to be a mind is an unstable collection of linguistically determined concepts. This doctrine manifests itself in two rather different ways. The first is in the denial of the efficacy of authorial intention. If there are such things as communicative intentions, so the argument runs, they can never be usefully known, necessarily embody self-contradictions engendered by the very structure of language, and in fact alter their substance in being embodied in writing since writing may function in the absence of either the author or the reader(s) for whom the text was intended. The second form of the doctrine is the assertion that what a reader finds is wholly the function of the reader's interpretive strategies.

4. The assumption of the equal validity of whatever relations or analogues any portion of the text suggests to the reader.
5. The belief that thought takes place within frameworks such that communication across frameworks is impossible. As a corollary, it is misleading if not meaningless to refer to historical fact since all such facts are the result both of linguistically determined perspectives and related culturally determined perspectives.

The five are briefly explored in Chapter 2.

HERMENEUTICS

Hermeneutics is an awe-inspiring word. It tends to scare undergraduates, light up the eyes of Ph.D. students seeking a talisman, and, often enough, annoy solid old scholars who have in fact given their days in its service. Of little help is the tendency to talk about hermeneutics in the sort of way exemplified by Paul Ricoeur's statement that hermeneutics is "to reconstruct the internal dynamics of the text and to restore to the work its ability to project itself outside itself in the representation of a world that I could inhabit" (OI, 377).

Hermeneutics is in fact one of those words that has been pressed into such various service over time that one can hardly use it without attaching an immediate explanatory gloss. It now carries about it suggestions of the search for figurative meanings in Philo, Origen, and Augustine; of Schleiermacher's canons of interpretation; of Dilthey's more definite movement toward psychological interpretation through the recreation of "lived experience"; of Heideggerian views of hermeneutics as an interpretation of the existential world, not simply of individual texts; of Hans-Georg Gadamer's view of hermeneutics as an exercise in the fusion of the cultural horizons of author and interpreter; of Paul Ricoeur's interest in opening hidden levels of meaning; of Fredric Jameson's use of negative hermeneutics as the recognition of ideology and positive hermeneutics as "the symbolic representation of a specific historical and class form of collective unity" (*PU*, 291) and of Richard Rorty's view of hermeneutics as an endless process of discussion. The history of hermeneutic theorizing is thus an extremely complicated one (a history nowhere better summarized than in the Introduction to Kurt Mueller-Vollmer's *Hermeneutic Reader*). Nevertheless, although theorizing that invokes the term hermeneutics has become increasingly philosophical, it is not necessary to import the full library of hermeneutic thought of philosophers like Husserl, Heidegger, Gadamer, and Ricoeur into the question of understanding literary meaning. The questions addressed by what has come to be called philosophical hermeneutics have finally to do with what have traditionally been regarded as metaphysical questions about truth and reality – thus Heidegger extends hermeneutics to encompass the interpretation of Being. As Mueller-Vollmer has argued, the concepts of hermeneutics formulated by these philosophers, fashionable as they are, "have become most problematic when we consider their usefulness within the context of literary hermeneutics" (U&I, 42).[2]

If we regard the core about which most of the uses of "hermeneutics" have entwined themselves – a notion that combines translation, interpretation, and clarification – we have a very useful word to which none of those three partial synonyms is quite equivalent: the human endeavor to understand the intended meaning of verbal utterances and, more especially, written texts. Additionally hermeneutics has the advantage of having always been associated not with the system of language but with language-in-use, the language we daily encounter. Much in the following exposition of the elements of hermeneutics as I employ the word will be well-known to many readers, but I wish to make my understanding of these elements as transparent as possible.

The *OED* defines "hermeneutics" as "The art or science of interpretation, esp. of Scripture. Commonly distinguished from exegesis or practical exposition." The phrase "especially of Scripture" of course refers to the difficulties of biblical interpretation that gave rise to the earliest explorations of the problem of understanding and explanation. The words "practical exposition" are of particular importance in distinguishing intended meaning from relationships to modes of thought external to the text. Such a distinction is set out by the nineteenth-century theorist of hermeneutics, Philip August Boeckh in the *Encyclopedia and Methodology of the Philological Sciences* (1877). Hermeneutics is to understand the text in itself while the purpose of criticism is "the establishment of a relation or reference to something else so that the recognition of this relation is itself the end in view" (121). But Boeckh saw clearly that nothing can be understood wholly in itself: "When we assign to hermeneutics the task of understanding the subjects themselves, we surely do not imply that anything can be understood without reference to much besides. For interpretation many auxiliaries must be used" (45).

Which brings us to E. D. Hirsch's twentieth-century adaptation of Boeckh's distinction, one which is essential to hermeneutics. Boeckh's "interpretation" is specifically defined as the construction of the author's intended meaning. Stipulating that he will use "meaning" only to designate "verbal meaning," that is, intended meaning, Hirsch states his central formulation precisely in *Validity and Interpretation*: "Verbal meaning is whatever someone has willed to convey by a particular sequence of linguistic signs and which can be conveyed (shared) by means of those linguistic signs" *VI*, 31). The second portion of that sentence – "which can be conveyed (shared) by means of those linguistic signs" is as important as the first. It is what Steven Mailloux calls the "operative intention": "the actions that the author, *as he writes the text*, understands himself to be performing in that text and the immediate effects he understands these actions will achieve in his projected reader" (99, my italics).

As for Boeckh's use of the term "criticism," Hirsch retains its designation of relationships between the text and external sources of judgment and explanation while expanding it far beyond the correction of texts that Boeckh had primarily in mind. Thus for Hirsch it includes all patterns and relationships found by the reader that cannot be attributed to authorial intention. These patterns and relationships, which in general speech are also called "meanings," Hirsch names "significances"; these, he explicitly recognizes, are of at least as much interest to readers as authorially intended meanings. Although Hirsch's constitutes the best-known statement of the difference between authorially intended and other meanings, pretty much the same distinction has been made by many others. The most sophisticated is probably that of H. P. Grice. In the statement "a temperature of 103 degrees means that the patient is seriously ill," the patient's temperature is interpreted without the thermometer or patient intending to mean anything. Grice calls this "natural" meaning (intentional meaning is "non-natural"), although the term "symptomatic" which the above example suggests is probably the more useful.[3] Depending on specific use, Hirsch's "significance" sometimes seems the most appropriate term for non-intentional meaning, while at other times Grice's "symptomatic" seems clearer. I shall employ the two as synonymous (with the warning that this use of symptomatic is much broader than Louis Althusser's).[4] If we define hermeneutics as the reconstruction of authorial intention, the recognition of significances or symptomatic meanings can be called "symptomatics."

As for *the process of finding* intended meaning, Schleiermacher, the father of modern hermeneutics, started from the recognition that speech acts and acts of understanding are correlated in that "every act of understanding is the reverse side of an act of speaking, and one must grasp the thought that underlies a given statement" (97). This was to be accomplished through the mutually supporting operation of the two tasks of understanding. In "grammatical" interpretation, "more precise determination of any point in a given text must be decided on the basis of the use of language common to the author and his original public" (First Canon, 117) while "[t]he meaning of each word of a passage must be determined by the context in which it occurs" (Second Canon, 127).

Schleiermacher's grammatical task evidently assumes that a use of words different from what the intended readers could interpret on the basis of their own competence would be somehow made clear by the author. His second task, the technical, he also called "psychological," describing it at one point as "a moment in the development of the person" (99). Many readers have thus been led into thinking that Schleiermacher was simply looking to the individual personality of the speaker. However, as Mueller-Vollmer notes, Schleiermacher's full discussion of the psychological side of interpretation evidently includes not only the author's individuality, but the particular genre and historical circumstances embodied by the text. (*HR*, 11). Hermeneutical theorizing since may be regarded as a lengthy series of attempts to determine the methods and limits of carrying out these practices.

It is perhaps an index of the degree to which our age is enchanted by the paradoxical, counter-intuitive, inexplicable, and occultly motivated that the term hermeneutics has been driven farther from its sense as the recovery of intended meaning at the very time that speech-act theory, discourse analysis and reader-response theory have been clarifying the operation of Schleiermacher's second canon. The basic problem such investigations address is simply this: granted that a knowledge of the semantic possibilities and accepted syntactic structures of the time a text was written (Schleiermacher's first canon) is not enough for full understanding, what more must the interpreter know? The question thus becomes more practical than philosophical. Unfortunately, lacking the attractions of the kind of sweeping, paradoxical speculation now in fashion, work on the answer to this question has caught the eye of relatively few literary critics. As useful as they are undramatic, hermeneutic analyses of this kind are represented by investigations as different as those by John Searle's *Speech Acts* (1969), M. A. K. Halliday and Ruquaiya Hasan's *Cohesion in English* (1976), George Dillon's *Language Processing and the Reading of Literature* (1978), Louise Rosenblatt's *The Reader, The Text, The Poem: The Transactional Theory of the Literary Work* (1978), Bach and Harnish's *Linguistic Communication and Speech Acts* (1979), and Gillian Brown and George Yule's *Discourse Analysis* (1983). In essence, all these begin by asking not about the abstract structure of language, but how it is that we get on with the processes of interpretation upon which we constantly rely. Once one asks the question in this way the characteristics of language that hermetic criticism asserts to be absolute barriers are seen not to apply to language in use. A composite answer to the question of what the interpreter of actual discourse requires besides grammatical knowledge emerges; interpretation depends on a *communicative contract* based on the total context (background knowledge, occasion, etc.) that author and reader could reasonably expect the other would take into consideration. J. L. Austin, the founder of speech-act theory, noted in 1955, "for some years we have been realizing more and more clearly that the occasion of an utterance matters seriously, and that the words used are to be 'explained' by the 'context' in which they are designed to be or have actually been spoken in a linguistic interchange" (100). (The hermetic dismissal of context is considered in Chapter 5 below.)

A good bit of confusion can be avoided by drawing on speech-act theory to sort out quite different aspects of what is generally packed together in our notion of an intended meaning. By "locution" is meant simply a string of spoken or written words (an utterance). By "proposition" is meant the combination of reference and predication that produces the bare content of the utterance. By "illocutionary force" is meant the relation of that proposition to the utterer and addressee (is the utterer promising, ordering, describing, asking?). Austin explains that the illocutionary force is that of the act performed *in* saying something as contrasted with the act *of* saying something (that is, uttering a locution expressing a proposition) (99). "Perlocutionary effects" are the effects produced by an utterance. Obviously there may be a difference between the effect intended and that produced: a proposition with the illocutionary force of an assertion intended to have the effect of convincing may in fact amuse or irritate. By "perlocutionary intent" is meant that effect which the proposition together with its illocutionary force is intended to produce. Thus, "Hermetic theories of literature are based on egregious fallacies" is a locution that expresses a proposition about hermetic theorizing; depending on circumstances it may carry any of a number of kinds of illocutionary force intended to produce any of a number of effects. For instance, it could be uttered with the force of an assertion and with the perlocutionary intent of opening an argument. Its actual effect could only be known if and when it was uttered in an actual situation. Austin explicitly confines his use of "meaning" to the sense and reference of individual words and the proposition thus expressed, preferring to distinguish illocutionary force from meaning (100); however, since the illocutionary force of an utterance is part of authorial intention, I will include it under the umbrella of authorial meaning.

Austin had noted that utterances with such conventionally understood consequences as promising or betting can be accomplished indirectly (32). "I'll be there" can be a promise; "Five pounds on Middlesex" can be a bet. In an article that has been highly influential among students of speech acts but hardly so among literary critics ("Logic and Conversation") – H. P. Grice found indirect meaning to be dependent on what he has called the Cooperative Principle. Both the speaker and the hearer know, that is, that an utterance is expected to be as relevant to the topic at hand, as truthful from the point of view of those engaged in the discourse, as appropriate in length, as suitable in manner and tone as possible. What is reasonable in each characteristic is culturally defined – within each culture one learns what is reasonable under which circumstances (for instance when it is appropriate to speak to a stranger, how detailed to be when giving directions to persons with different backgrounds, etc.). Violations of the Cooperative Principle that are obviously intentional signal that one's meaning is indirect. "I've never liked Bartok" is an indirect answer to the question "Are you going to the concert?" if both speakers know that Bartok is to be on the program.

I have omitted to mention that the terms hermeneutics and hermetics are both distantly derived from the god Hermes. As the messenger of the gods he both transmitted and translated messages; in addition he was the god of both thieves and merchants.

He was in short both a conveyor of meanings and a transmuter of them, indispensable but not wholly trustworthy. To remember Hermes' problematic character and try to distinguish the cunning and mischievous from the undistorted and valuable was essential for any mortal having dealings with him. Hermeneutic understanding being always probabilistic, always fallible, the possibility of error is never absent, but that ought to put us even more on guard against any hermetic theorizing that denies the possibility of error on the grounds that there is no alternative to it – that we are indeed in endless error hurled.

Notes

1. For Eco, see *Interpretation and Overinterpretation*. Roger Scruton uses "hermetic" to refer to criticism dependent on a professional argot in "Public Text and Common Reader," pp. 52–3.
2. Mueller-Vollmer's position on the philosophical school of hermeneutics deserves serious consideration. "Its adherents claim to have uncovered the historical and ontological roots of hermeneutics and to have laid new ground for the sciences of man. Indubitably, important new insights and a renewed interest in the philosophy of these sciences have sprung from hermeneutic philosophy, yet, from the point of view of literary studies, these claims have little value if they are held against the actual accomplishments of nineteenth-century hermeneutics." (U&I, 44).
3. See Grice's "Meaning." Although some of the subtlety of Grice's argument is lost by substituting "symptomatic meaning" for Grice's "natural meaning" and "intentional meaning" for "non-natural meaning," Grice's terms tend to be confusing when transported outside the context of his essays. Full-scale analysis of the different meanings of meaning would require consideration of at least two other of Grice's essays: "Utterer's Meaning and Intention," and "Utterer's Meaning, Sentence-Meaning, and Word-Meaning," both reprinted in *Studies in the Way of Words*.
4. Althusser's notion of "symptomatic reading" derives from the Freudian concept of repression: "I suggested," writes Althusser, "that we had to submit Marx's text not to an immediate reading, but to a '*symptomatic*' reading, in order to discern in the apparent continuity of the discourse the lacunae, blanks, and failures of rigour, the places where Marx's discourse is merely the unsaid of his silence, arising in his discourse itself" (RC, 143). Such a form of reading is of course perfectly legitimate, but it produces just one of many possible significances or symptomatic meanings as I am using those terms.
    In discussing the meanings of films, David Bordwell divides

"meaning" into four types, the first three of which (referential construction of a world, "be it fictional or putatively real"; explicit meaning; and implicit or covert meaning) would all fall within the category of intended meaning. The fourth, "repressed or symptomatic, meanings that the work divulges 'involuntarily,'" seem to be pretty much what Althusser had in mind, although this type is still somewhat broader.

2

Hermeticism

Shakespeare's Bottom is the source of much recent literary theory. It was Bottom who led the attack on illusionist realism; it was he who advocated the self-subverting, self-referential text; and it was he who founded the praxis of deconstructionism. His ideas have been widely plagiarized on the continent (by Derrida, Todorov, Macherey, Barthes, Althusser and others), and it is a scandal of literary history that British and American popularizers of his radical doctrines have repeatedly as-cribed them to his continental disciples instead of giving Bottom due credit.

Cedric Watts, "Bottom's Children . . . ," 20.

Recent criticism has made much of a discovery that elementary logic ought long ago to have clarified. It has discovered that its subject matter – the work of art – is, if not identical with, at least enshrined in, texts, scores and other semi-permanent things. Most works of art (and all significant works of art) therefore have a power to outlast their creator, acquiring a penumbra of significance which he himself might never have been able to acknowledge or intend. Many thoughts have been inspired by that simple observation, and it is a small step in delirium, although a large one in logic, to the science of "grammatology," which takes the written character of the literary object as primary, and insists that in the act of writing the author vanishes from the scene.

Roger Scruton, *Public Text and Common Reader*, 36.

THE TRANSMOGRIFICATION OF SAUSSURE

The first two of the doctrines lying at the core of hermetic theoriz-ing – the belief that language has reference only to itself and the denial of the possibility of determining the meaning of discourse – are still oddly but widely believed to be the indisputable conse-quences of Ferdinand de Saussure's analysis of language. One sus-pects that many of those who have left the world influential modes of thought about any matter of importance would be astonished to know how many of what they thought to be perspicuous observations have been misunderstood or transmogrified. But Saussure would have more reason to be surprised than most, even though he might recognize that some of the blame falls to him. After all, he never put his insights into final form but left their transmission to the uncertain mercies of those who heard his lectures. Perhaps there is a significant difference between what Saussure would like to have published and the lecture notes edited and issued as the *Cours Linguistique General*; the *Cours* may be the mere shadow of what Saussure could have given to the world. But that shadow is in most respects a very definite one whose outline, one should think, could hardly be misinterpreted.

Yet it has been so distorted that if Saussure could return, he would find it difficult to believe that what is generally thought to be Saussurian had developed from the system he set out; he would surely think the monster he encountered had grown up from a set of ideas substituted by malicious fairies for his own well-conducted offspring. Of course, the ghost of Saussure need not return to repudiate what he is so widely credited with fathering: that the hermetic version of Saussure is a caricature has been pointed out many times. However, it seems to be another part of the quirkiness of discourse about literature that such protests have little effect because the uses of a distorted version are so much greater than those of the original. Still, one does what one can; one more summary of the major ways in which Saussure has been misinterpreted can at least do no harm.[1]

Saussure could hardly have said more clearly of his paired terms signifier and signified, the combination of which is required to constitute a sign, that the "signified" designates the mental concept and the "signifier" the sound (or its written version). Nothing is better known than his statement that the two are arbitrarily linked – there is no necessary reason that a particular sound should be linked to a particular concept, a point, incidentally, equally clearly stated in Ogden and Richard's *The Meaning of Meaning* long before the general rediscovery of Saussure.[2] Unfortunately, the word "arbitrary," which for Saussure meant unmotivated, has been taken by hermetically inclined minds to mean something like "illusory." Thus where Saussure pointed to the contingent link between the sound //tree// and the concept tree, hermeticists cite Saussure's work as evidence that the concept tree has no relation to any reality outside language. Language, they seem to wish to believe, must refer only to itself – there can be no reference in the most common philosophical sense. J. G. Merquior has provided a convenient term, "the metalinguistic fallacy," for this curiously seductive mode of thought (18).

At the same time, where it has seemed useful for hermeticists to do so, Saussure is summarized as though he had stated that the relationship between the signified or concept and *that which is conceptualized*, that is the sense report to which the concept is applied, was equally arbitrary. When Catherine Belsey writes that "We use signifiers to mark off areas of a continuum" (46), she is correctly reading Saussure. However, when she goes on to say "The way we use signifiers to create differences appears in the labelling of otherwise identical toothmugs 'his' and 'hers,'" she confounds two worlds by implicitly denying the possibility of any similarity between the concept and thing conceptualized, between the world of our linguistically formed conceptions and the extra-linguistic feelings and sense reports that provided the raw material, Saussure's "indefinite plane of jumbled ideas" (112). That the mugs are identical in the physical world reported by our senses is the condition which necessitates a linguistically imposed discrimination. Moreover language is not strictly necessary for the purpose – he or she could put a touch of paint on one mug and indicate by gestures which of the now differentiated mugs was to be used by which person. To give much attention to such a point seems quite unnecessary, but the failure to pause to ask if one's explanations are really cogent is a distinguishing hermetic characteristic. That neither the source nor the accuracy of sense impressions were of interest to Saussure ought not to be taken as a denial that there is an extra-linguistic reality which our conceptions may approximate if not capture.

The meaning of "reference" is at the heart of the confusion here. The hermetic interpretation of Saussure has come to be supported by citing the problem philosophers of language encounter in seeking ideal forms of utterance that would produce statements which, regarded in and of themselves (not embedded in a larger linguistic utterance or extra-linguistic situation) would be wholly unambiguous either in what they designate or the actuality of the existence of what they designate. But that is not the kind of situation that confronts the reader of a novel or poem; a literary text has already plucked each word from the storehouse of potentialities constituting the language as a whole and placed it in a context of the sort that necessarily surrounds discourse. As Gottlob Frege put the distinction, the word "lion" as it appears in a dictionary has (at least one) sense but no reference, that is, it becomes related to time and space only in use; it thus acquires reference in an utterance such as "that lion looks dangerous."[3] The same distinction has been expressed in other terms by Charles Morris, for whom the concept to which a sign is linked is termed its designatum while an existent to which the concept is linked is its denotatum.

Logicians have much discussed the question of how to deal with a sentence like "The King of France is bald" since it seems distinctly odd to say that such a sentence as uttered in the twentieth century is true or false. One solution is to divide the proposition into two: "There is a man who is the King of France" and "The Man who is the King of France is bald." We can then state that the first proposition is false and therefore the second meaningless. But the philosophical analysis of isolated linguistic structures is one thing; the analysis of discourse is another. For the purpose of the analysis of discourse, it is enough to say that "the King of France" lacks possible reference at this time in history.

The same distinction works in the analysis of fictional discourse. In an ideal formal language sentences of the following types should be clearly differentiated by their syntactical forms:

"Sparrows are small brown and black birds." (Things that humans characterize as sparrows exist in space and time.)

"Morlocks are small whitish creatures afraid of the light." (Morlocks are fictional creatures that exist only in H. G. Wells's *The Time Machine*.)

"Unicorns have a single horn in the middle of their foreheads." (Unicorns are imaginary beasts existing only in the cultural tradition.)

However, in practice the Fregean sort of distinction usefully sorts out the differences between those words that have no counterparts in time and space and those that do. One can say of those that do not that they have "sense" without reference or, in Charles Morris's terminology, that they have "designata" without "denotata." Raymond Tallis simply distinguishes "meaning" from "reference": "Pegasus" and "manticore" have meaning without reference (*NS*, 83), "Man o' War" (an actual horse) and "platypus" in "that platypus in the zoo" have both meaning and reference. As Tallis concisely phrases it, "In reference, word and object meet in the identity of the general meaning of a particular token with one of the (general) senses of an intelligible object" (*NS*, 107).[4]

It is, of course, necessary to distinguish the kinds of reference possible for abstract concepts from those possible for concepts whose reference is to what our senses report of the physical world. Abstractions are likely to be cultural constructs or linguistic conveniences. Arbib and Hesse use "gravitation" and "embarrassment" as examples of two kinds of reference to something "that contains our schemas of the physical world" as opposed to something that "is based on how we perceive certain kinds of situations." That is, "a society in which there is no such thing as embarrassment" is conceivable (5). It is also true that words like "world," "country," "duties," and "culture" (the examples are those of Raymond Tallis, *NS*, 50) are made up of such a multitude of objects, events, and situations that they can never be pointed to or experienced in more than a fragmentary way. Indeed, as F. A. Hayek so cogently explains, such terms, which he calls "collectives,"

> do not designate definite things in the sense of stable collections of sense attributes which we recognize alike by inspection; they refer to [have as their designatum in Morris's terms] certain structures of relationship between some of the many things which we can observe within given spatial and temporal limits and which we select because we think we can discern connections between them – connections which may or may not exist in fact. (55)

But although abstractions are thus easily used ambiguously or vaguely or circularly, the opportunity for misuse does not rule out the possibility of reference for specifically defined senses. (That something may be used in a particular way is often taken by hermeticists as part of the necessary nature of a thing, but this is a fallacy: that a coin may be used to pry open a can of paint has nothing to do with the concept of coinage.)

Having dismissed the possibility of reference to anything outside language, hermeticists happily conflate Saussure's "signifier" and the word "sign" as it appears in everyday usage. Thus one reads of signifiers without signifieds – a patent impossibility in the Saussurean scheme of things, as impossible as for a piece of paper to have a single side – which is Saussure's own image. Nevertheless John Sturrock could write in 1979 of Barthes, Levi-Strauss, Derrida, Foucault, and Lacan, "what these five thinkers have very influentially done is to advance the claims of the signifier above those of the signified. The signifier is what we can be sure of, it is material; the signified is an open question" (15). As D. and J. F. MacCannell commented in *The Time of the Sign* (1982), "The question of meaning – of the signified – is deftly sidestepped by the structural critic's affection for the signifier" (108–9).

Why does one so often encounter references to signifiers without signifieds? There appear to be three answers. The expression may be intended only hyperbolically. It has been said that Swinburne's poetry consists of words that are signifiers without signifieds although what is presumably meant is that the propositions produced by Swinburne's words don't add up to much. But though the following lines seem constructed more for their sound than the expression of imaginative insight,

> It is not much that a man can save
> On the sands of life, in the straits of time,

it is easy enough to interpret them. Instead, a person writing in English and wishing to avoid signifieds would have to write something like this:

> Ot os sut mich lat eu min riu su
> Un kai sind uv het, en jai steus dai tet,

which pretty much produces the same scansion, assonance and alliteration. In order to avoid signifieds the writer must avoid signifiers.

Or the notion of a signifier without signified may be intended to mean that the sense of an individual word or the meaning of the propositions expressed is open to a variety of interpretations. This may be what Catherine Belsey means in talking about "the primacy of the signifier" (144 and see 136–7). Or the expression "signifier with no signified" may, as a result of confusing signifieds with the realm of extra-linguistic existence and signifiers with signs, be intended to mean that words are not interchangeable with things, or that nothing exists beyond language. Presumably this is what one would have to believe to speak, as does Jameson in summarizing structuralism, of the "adjustment of the *signified* to the *signifier*" (*P-HL*, 133, my italics). Of course it is always possible that the expression may just be the result of a combination of intellectual carelessness and a lust for paradox.

It is sometimes said that while language may be related to some ultimate pre-linguistic reality in that it has divided up the stream of sense reports presumably generated by such reality, there is no real correspondence between a given signified and the actual state of things outside of all human conceptions since the division of that reality is arbitrary. But it is as accurate to say that the necessity of dividing the stream of sense impressions created language as it is to say that language accomplished the dividing – that is, despite a lack of correspondence between languages, there is no more reason to assume that languages divide ultimate reality in ways that have nothing to do with the structure of that reality than there is to assume that there is complete correspondence. If there were not overwhelming evidence that our conceptions correspond well enough to allow us to manipulate whatever is "really there," hermeticists could not revel in the paradox of affirming the reality of language at the expense of nonlinguistic reality. A.D. Nuttall has made the point succinctly. "We hazard before we win, cast nets before we catch, but if we had been doing all this in a vacuum it would have felt very different. For a start, there would have been no ascertainable failures" (46). The fact is that only a very naive realism indeed would expect words in any way to resemble, or wholly describe and correspond to, that to which they have refer-ence. Raymond Tallis has put the matter very well.

> A verbal account of a piece of physical reality does not need to be shaped or structured like reality in order to be true of or to it; for what get expressed – and hence referred to – are not lumps of raw matter but the *senses* of material objects as they appear in particular situations. These senses are not the physical properties of the objects; nor do they necessarily correlate clearly with those objects; for while physical properties place limits upon plausible senses (for example feasible uses), they do not fix those senses completely. (*NS*, 110)

As Walker Percy pungently says, the pairing of word and thing may be a "cosmic blunder," but happily it makes human commu-nication possible (ML, 157). What Percy calls a symbol (he contrasts "sign" and "symbol" in a somewhat unusual way: for him a sign merely points (or indicates) while a symbol names) can function only because it is *not* the same as the thing it names. "The symbol has the peculiar property of containing within itself . . . in another mode of existence, that which is symbolized" (STK, 261). Or, in other words, what we are concerned with is not a "real identity" but an "intentional relation of identity" which involves a mutual relation between two organisms, one who names and one for whom the name is similarly meaningful.

As another example of the unhappy fate that has befallen so much of what Saussure tried to straighten out for us, every reader of Saussure knows how carefully he distinguishes *langue*, the whole system of language in which signifiers limit and signifieds define each other, from *parole*, the use of signs in a particular context. Saussure clearly stated that while language is homogeneous, speech is heterogeneous (15). Nevertheless, hermeticists tend to speak of the relations between signs used in *parole* as though they are speaking of the relationship between items in the *langue* regarded without relationship to our experience or the instance of their use. Thus, they tell us, the meaning of the word is impossible to determine since it must be pursued from word to word in an infinite regression. But while the signifieds (concepts) associated with an individual signifier are a function of relationships with other signifieds, the intended meaning of the signifier in use is limited by the context of its use. ("Context" is considered more directly in Chapter 5.)

THE DISMISSAL OF THE AUTHOR

The third hermetic doctrine – the denial of any relevance to authorial intention and/or any meaningful sense of interpretation – follows from the view that language is not linked to reality and that intended meanings cannot be communicated. Although misunderstanding of the principles of the New Critics led their followers to a curious sort of dancing around the question of authorial intention (a matter to be considered in more detail in Chapter 5), structuralists were rigorous in trying to ascribe meaning to the text, not its author. In order sufficiently to emphasize the controlling powers of language, they found it rhetorically useful to deny that, properly speaking, one can really have intentions; indeed, following Nietzsche, it was possible to deny that there is a subject (in any traditional sense) who writes. If thought is bound within the concepts expressible by language and the relationships expressible through a language's syntax, the author can be regarded as simply the outlet through which flows one set of the possibilities of what can be said.

In 1968 at the height of structuralist optimism, Roland Barthes happily wrote:

> Linguistically, the author is never more than the instance writing, just as *I* is nothing other than the instance saying *I*: language knows a "subject," not a "person," and this subject, empty outside of the very enunciation which defines it, suffices to make language "hold together," suffices, that is to say, to exhaust it (DA, 145).

Further:

> The text is a tissue of quotations drawn from the innumerable centres of culture. . . . the writer can only imitate a gesture that is always anterior, never original. His only power is to mix writings, to counter one with the others in such a way as never to rest on any one of them. Did he wish to *express himself*, he ought at least to know that the inner "thing" he thinks to "translate" is itself only a ready-formed dictionary, its words only explainable through other words and so on indefinitely . . . (DA, 146)[5]

The above quotation is taken from the best known and most influential assertion of the total separation of author and text, Barthes' "The Death of the Author." Part of the success of this essay is undoubtedly due to the coalescing of various currents important to hermeticism: a conception of linguistics that reduces all referential relations to syntactical ones (from such a point of view Martin Luther King's "I have a dream" can exhibit only a grammatical, not an existential, cogency); a reduction of J. L. Austin's concept of performatives that disregards Austin's conclusion that all speech acts are both performative and constative; a view of Saussure that remains within the system of *langue* where meaning is "infinitely deferred"; a Marxist view of the concept of the individual as a creation of capitalist ideology; and Barthes' own view of a great divide between older and modern literature, with the work or writerly (scriptible) text and author (écrivain) on one side, and the readerly (lisible) text and writer (écrivant) on the other. Barthes' distinction between author and writer, writerly and readerly, work and text, pleasure-producing and bliss-producing texts are all obviously closely associated, but the circumstances and historical moment of the change, the texts to which it applies, and the degree to which the difference inheres in the text or is induced by the reader is never made wholly specific.[6]

Another part of Barthes' success is the result of a rhetoric that gives the effect of peremptory authority which need not pause to explain itself. "Writing is that neutral, composite, oblique space where our subject slips away, the negative where all identity is lost, starting with the very identity of the body writing" (DA, 142). Powerful-sounding stuff, but in what sense is writing a "space," what is a "composite, oblique space," why must the subject "slip away" upon entering that space, and what does it mean to posit writing as a "negative"? The more exaggerated the assertion, the less, apparently, the need for explanation, not to mention proof. The situation would of course be quite different if Barthes had chosen the hypothetical rather than the hyperbolic mode. Had he written, "*If* one chooses to regard a text as authorless . . ." or "*If* we take authors like Mallarmé at their word and seek to read their poems as though they were precipitated from the language without the intervention of an author . . . ," the reading strategy Barthes advocates would have been a great deal clearer. Of course, in being seen for what it is, a particular method of reading for a particular purpose, it would have lost its claim to being the uniquely correct way of regarding (some? all?) contemporary literature.

The quotation from Barthes that opens this discussion is one more egregious example of the conflation of *langue* as a system of mutually defining words with *parole* as the specific organization of these words. Even if one accepts that the structure of language controls what can be thought and thus intended, to choose from all that could be thought a certain selection of things presented in a certain order and relationship requires an operation rather more complicated than the capacity "to mix writings." The individual words making up the language pre-exist the individual: their use to communicate something specific does not. Lumber, nails, and paint exist prior to the individual carpenter's use of them, but it is the carpenter who narrows the almost infinite possibilities of their use by deciding to build a house, or a fence, or a toy wagon. The words necessary to produce the propositions "Masses attract each other with a force varying directly as the product of the masses and inversely as the square of the distance between them" or "April is the cruelest month" existed long before Newton or Eliot.

Indeed, Barthes' essay opens with an obscurantist maneuver that one would have thought transparent. Quoting a sentence from Balzac's *Sarrasine*, Barthes asks who is speaking. "Is it the hero of the story . . . ?" "Is it Balzac the individual . . . ?" "Is it Balzac the author . . . ?"[7] The sentence is in fact an instance of free indirect discourse, one of the characteristics of which is that there is always some ambiguity as to how much of the content is attributable to the narrator and how much to the character who is presumably associated with the passage. A reader also confronts the question of the degree to which propositions expressed in indirect discourse – whether attributable to the narrator or character – agree with or are undercut by the implied author, whose view of life is projected by the text as a whole. And that determination will depend partly on what Balzac thought his readers thought about the nature of woman. Yes, it *is* all immensely complicated. However, what the reader *does* know is that, although the text was written by the flesh-and-blood author Balzac, Balzac is not "speaking" those words – he has given them to the narrator to speak.

What in fact Barthes is attacking, so far as his target is identifiable, is the attempt to see the cause of the work in information about the author found outside the text. "The image of literature to be found in ordinary culture is tyrannically centered on the author, his person, his life, his tastes, his passions. . . . The *explanation* of a work is always sought in the man or woman who produced it . . . " (143). To the extent that Barthes wished to protect the text from interpretation based on the author's life and thought as expressed apart from the text, he may well be applauded although the argument against biographically based interpretation had of course been made much earlier by the New Critics and given a particularly useful formulation through Wayne Booth's distinction in *The Rhetoric of Fiction* between the author as an individual human being and the implied author that is created by the text itself.

That Barthes' objection centers on attempts to explain the work in terms of the author's personality is made perfectly clear by his citation of the views of particular writers. For instance:

In France, Mallarmé was doubtless the first to see and to foresee in its full extent the necessity to substitute language itself for the person who until then had been supposed to be its owner . . . Mallarmé's entire poetics consists in suppressing the author in the interests of writing . . . " (DA, 145)

Presumably Mallarmé's views are quoted because he wrote poetry generally regarded as important. But Barthes is violating his own principle if he seeks impersonality in Mallarmé's poetry because the poet has said it is there; if Barthes believes impersonality to be a quality of the poetry itself, he ought to be instancing the poetry, not the author's extra-textual comments; and if the poetry does not exhibit impersonality, what Mallarmé has said is irrelevant. One assumes of course that Barthes is speaking of the authorlessness of literary texts like poems and novels – otherwise there is no point in citing Mallarmé since he, as author, could – according to Barthes – have nothing to do with what is quoted. Moreover, if it is the reader who finds the meaning – which may or may not what be Barthes means by throw-aways like "which is . . . to restore the place of the reader," "the reader . . . is simply that *someone* who holds together in a single field all the traces by which the written text is constituted," and "the birth of the reader must be at the cost of the death of the Author" – there is even less point in citing Mallarmé. The meaning we are asked to attend to must be Barthes' construction – or, to be really consistent, it belongs to us, the readers of the essay, not Mallarmé at all. In short, either Barthes is saying in exaggerated terms what many others have said – that the text is not to be understood in terms of what the author said he or she intended or what his or her life leads us to think was intended – OR the entire essay is so self-contradictory as to be meaningless.

There are reasons for leaning toward the latter view: Barthes' individual-denying Marxism seems to get in the way of "the birth of the reader" he wishes to celebrate. "The reader is the space on which all the quotations that make up a writing are inscribed without any of them being lost; a text's unity lies not in its origin but in its destination." Thus is the importance of the reader emphasized. But the Marxist in Barthes cannot accept the reader as unique, nor even, it seems, as an active mind, for the next sentence reads: "Yet this destination cannot any longer be personal; the reader is without history, biography, psychology . . . " (148). A reader without "history, biography, psychology" must be equally without syntactical or lexical knowledge, much less the ongoing cultural dialogue from which come the "quotations that make up a writing" (previously described by Barthes as "multiple writings, drawn from many cultures and entering into mutual relations of dialogue, parody, contestation"). One can imagine the reader Barthes here presents only as an empty, passive receptacle in which the text inactively lies.

Second only to Barthes in standing as the authority for the dissolution of the author is Michel Foucault, whose "What Is an Author?" appeared in 1969, only a year after Barthes' "The Death of the Author." Foucault does not, in fact, seek to banish the author as a concept, but rather transmutes the concept into a set of functions that in essence denies the relevance of authorial intention. The headlong process of Gallic theorizing, and the concomitant delight in extended play with a topic is nowhere better represented. One of the two fundamental principles of contemporary writing, the reader is told, is that "the writing of our day has freed itself from the necessity of 'expression'; it refers only to itself, yet it is not restricted to the confines of its interiority" (116). If by saying that language refers only to itself is meant that in fiction (which seems the primary, though not the only sense of writing as Foucault uses it) most words have sense without reference, one can understand the point, but how that relates to the question of the role of the author is altogether unclear. If being freed from "expression" means that we do not necessarily attribute what the narrator of a novel or voice of a poem utters to the author who held the pen, that has been a commonplace for a number of years now. Much of Foucault's argument in this essay consists of a somewhat pretentious statement of the distinction between narrator, implied author, and flesh-and-blood author already very adequately made by Wayne Booth in *The Rhetoric of Fiction* (1961).

The second theme Foucault develops is that of "the kinship between writing and death" (116). Writing used to guarantee the immortality of the hero, we are reminded, but now we have an inversion: it murders the author and cancels out "the signs of his particular individuality" (117). Aside from the sloppiness with which the idea of inversion is employed here (the disappearance of the author of the text is hardly an inversion of the immortality of the hero written about in the text), one would like examples of twentieth-century writers whose individuality has disappeared – would Barthes instance writers like Faulkner, Beckett, Genet, Pynchon, Calvino, Borges, Le Guin, Morrison? That we no longer try to identify the personality of the narrator or implied author with that of the author who was born, wrote, and died or will die is true enough, nor do we insist that every text by an author must somehow reveal the same perspective or personality, but the individuality of each text has to be attributed to something more than the conjunction of planets or vagaries of the language.

Essentially the problems that exercise Foucault arise out of an unquestioning acceptance of the Barthesian denial of the author. Foucault recognizes that there are such problems.

It has been understood that the task of criticism is not to reestablish the ties between an author and his work or reconstitute an author's thought and experience through his works and, further, that criticism should concern itself with the structures of a work, its architectonic forms, which are studied for their intrinsic and internal relationships. Yet, what of a context that questions the concept of a work? What, in short is the strange unit designated by the term, work? (118)

Foucault cogently comments that the Barthesian idea of the text as *écriture* "has merely transposed the empirical characteristics of an author to a transcendental anonymity" (120). But his creation of an "author function," which mixes together the concept of the implied author, the practices of biographical criticism, legal ramifications, and the influence of a reputation, further confounds a confusion best avoided by defining what is meant by the meaning of a text. At the end of the essay Foucault dismisses certain "tiresome" questions about the author among which is "Who is the real author?" and "What has he revealed of his most profound self in his language?" – the latter a question long ago dismissed by the main current of Anglo-American criticism. Instead, he proposes the importance of such new questions as "What are the modes of existence of this discourse?" "Where does it come from; how is it circulated; who controls it?" "What placements are possible for possible subjects?" "Who can fulfill these diverse functions of the subject?" At the same time, Foucault omits the questions, "What does this discourse mean?" and its concomitant, "What do we mean by the meaning of a discourse?" But no one would be interested in his new questions if discourse had no meaning; and once one begins to ask that question, the replacement of "author" by "subject" becomes a mere novelty.

The bizarre set of assumptions lying behind the hermetic denial of the activity of individual mind and its reduction to a "subject" that is simply a grammatical entity requires a quick look. The argument that all human thought is bounded by language so that it is more accurate to say that language speaks through a person than that a person speaks the language is often summed up as "intertextuality." The term expresses either a truism or a confusion. Intertextuality obviously exists in that language comes to us already formed, and if one wishes to be understood, one cannot stray far from conventional meanings of words or the standard syntactical structures. It is equally true that much of what anyone says in the course of a day is formulaic: in how many ways can one order a hamburger or ask the post office clerk for a book of stamps? More interestingly, whatever one has to say about major human concerns, and in particular about politics, ethics, religion, philosophy, art, or literature is likely to take the current state of discussion as a point of departure and to incorporate ideas gathered from all sorts of things one has heard or read. The more extended the discussion and the more complex the topic, the more one is likely to depend on what others have said.

What is evidently false is the implication that what the individual speaker or writer contributes is negligible. On a very obvious level, the hermetic view fails to recognize that in the case of any utterance the words selected reflect not only the situation in which they are uttered but the particular stock of memories, associations, and thoughts existing in a particular set of linkages in a particular mind. The "subject" can be conceived as that set of mental operations which on the basis of experiences peculiar to itself chooses the words that best seem to translate the concepts drawn from its unique store that seem relevant to the never wholly linguistic situation in which they are uttered. Although the ultimate ground, mechanism, or structure of consciousness can, like absolute reality generally, be assumed to be unknowable, recognition of an active, reality-related mind requires only consciousness of manifold relationships existing in addition to that consciousness and the possibility of choosing to make use of these relationships. Moreover, however much language and culture influence our understanding of sense reports, what we call experience depends on the reports received by each individual. Not even the most committed hermeticist argues that everyone speaking the same language and sharing the same general culture has the same experiences. Quentin Kraft sums this up nicely. "At the very least, each [subject] is also a history of its experiences, an historical register of the impact of the outside on the inside" (TCR, 62). It is the individual who, consciously or unconsciously, selects, groups, and modifies all that he or she has heard. Two people who read the same essay will produce different commentaries on it; if two people were to read the same twenty essays on a topic of any complexity before commencing their own essays, the results would differ not only in emphases, choices of exemplary quotations, and tone, but very likely in the conclusions at which they arrive.

The complexity with which a phrase or sentence, no matter how well worn, may be adapted to the speaker's specific intention is best illustrated by considering direct quotations. Since meaning depends on the interaction of text and context, the same words in a different situation may evidently carry different, perhaps novel meanings (a fact that seems to lead hermeticists to untoward conclusions). The original force of a quoted passage becomes secondary to its use as example, or authority, or object of satire, etc. To take a comparatively simple instance, "A policeman's lot is not a happy one," uttered by a policeman in a novel (more than one fictional detective has done it) is a complaint with the humorous overtones derived from its source in Gilbert and Sullivan's *Pirates of Penzance*, but by quoting it, the detective may suggest (depending on the context) that he is calling attention to the obvious, that Gilbert was righter than he knew when he wrote the lyric, that the humorous context of the original obscures its truth, that the speaker should indeed have considered this fact before he joined the force, that he is able to accept the unpleasant side of his work philosophically – or yet other meanings.

THE ENFRANCHISED OR ENCHAINED READER

In "The Death of the Author" Barthes proclaims, "Once the author is removed, the claim to decipher a text becomes quite futile." It is now to have no "final signified," no "ultimate meaning" (DA, 147). This can be combined with Barthes' celebration of the pleasure of the text that is possible to the reader who ignores, or perhaps welcomes, illogicality, incongruity, and self-contradiction. Such a reader is created through the "simple discard of that old spectre: *logical contradiction*" (PT, 3). In "The Death of the Author" Barthes also writes, "In the multiplicity of writing, everything is to be *disentangled*, nothing *deciphered*; the structure can be followed . . . but there is nothing beneath: the space of writing is to be ranged over, not pierced; writing ceaselessly posits meaning ceaselessly to evaporate it, carrying out a systematic exemption of meaning" (DA, 147).

All this (which, one must note, is simply asserted, not demonstrated) sounds as though readers are not only free to enjoy whatever meanings they may find in the text, but free actively to seek whatever meanings give them pleasure. But the degree to which Barthes believes readers can choose how they will regard a text is never clear.

Marxists of the Althusserian stripe see all human thought as confined by the limits of the ideology within which it takes place. Only through the action of an ideology, argues Althusser, does the individual become "subject" (in the use of which term Althusser is playing upon subject as active mind and as that which undergoes subjection, enslavement). "As a first formulation I shall say: *all ideology hails or interpellates concrete individuals as concrete subjects,* by the functioning of the category of subject" (ISA, 47). Further, "I shall then suggest that ideology 'acts' or 'functions' in such a way that it 'recruits' subjects among the individuals (it recruits them all), or 'transforms' the individuals into subjects (it transforms them all) by that very precise operation which I have called *"interpellation* or hailing . . ." (ISA, 47–8, I&ISA). Althusser is not much interested in literature *per se,* but if all understanding is ideological, the reading of literature is necessarily so. Moreover, since ideologies are transmitted and enforced by "ideological state apparatuses," the chief of which, following the decline of the Church, is the school, to read literature as one has been taught in a capitalist country is necessarily to read (for everyone but the Marxist of course) from the perspective of the capitalist ideology.

Althusser's view of ideology being based on his reading of Marx, his argument is presented in a form that presumes that one accepts Marxism generally. That is, any extended critique of it requires that one either accept the Marxist framework and center one's objections on Althusser's "clarification" and extrapolation of Marx, or enter into a critical analysis of the central tenets of Marx's thought. *Rather than embark on either,* I should like to suggest that for non-Marxists, the Althusserian view of the subjected subject is essentially the same as the one described in different terms in Stanley Fish's notion of the way readers necessarily read.

Turning to the reader envisioned by Stanley Fish, who is less interested in exiling the individual who wrote the text than in investigating the activity of those who read it, we find a very different creature from the one Barthes appears to celebrate. Indeed, Fish's version of hermetics is a militantly paradoxical one that, while content to accept the divorce of language from whatever reality exists beyond it, turns the indeterminacy of meaning on its head by arguing, in effect, that readers are always able to find whatever meaning the interpretive strategy in which they believe at the moment produces for them. One could say that here the means of deciding between interpretive strategies is indeterminate, and thus the true meaning of a text indeterminate, except of course for Fish there is no true meaning (or alternatively, all meanings found are true for those who find them). Although Fish is one of the best known, perhaps *the* best known, of the rather heterogeneous group known as reader-response critics, there is a kind of paradox in placing him under that rubric, or even in speaking, as I just did, of the "activity" of the reader as conceived by Fish. For the Fishean reader does not act, create, choose, but simply *reacts*. The heart of Fish's view is that what a reader reacts to in reading a literary text, or a judge in a rendering a decision, or presumably, a statesman confronting a difficult political decision, are only the aspects of the text, case, or situation that are made evident by interpretive strategies that have been internalized. Those strategies in essence dictate the formal properties of the text, or the judicial precedent, or the relevant aspects of the political problem, producing an interpretation or solution that fits nicely since all other aspects of the text, case, or issue have been pruned away.

Such a summary may sound over-reductive, but I hardly think it is. Thus in his key essay "Interpreting the Variorum" – almost everything Fish has written since is a variation of that essay's central themes – we find "rather than intention and its formal realization producing interpretation (the 'normal picture'), interpretation creates intention and its formal realization by creating the conditions in which it becomes possible to pick them out" (IV, 163). Or again, "In the old model utterers are in the business of handing over ready-made or prefabricated meanings. These meanings are said to be encoded, and the code is assumed to be in the world independently of the individuals who are obliged to attach themselves to it. . . . In my model, however, meanings are not extracted but made and made not by encoded forms but by interpretive strategies that call forms into being" (IV, 172–3). Unless one goes very far back in time, Fish's statement of the "old model" is nothing but a straw man, but his constant emphasis on interpretive strategies that are validated by a particular "interpretive community" is hard to fault. What is oversimplified here is the implied assignment of each individual to a given discourse community and the three-term equation of reader, the strategies belonging to the discursive community, and text. Actually Fish's formulations take into account only two terms, since the reader can hardly be said to exist apart from the interpretive community. Moreover, the context, upon which Fish frequently lays great stress, seems to be reduced to the interpretive community as well. The great gaps in Fish's account (particularly his failure to differentiate intentional and symptomatic meanings and his impoverished notion of context) can be much better discussed later, after the hermeneutic perspective has been developed, but one point ought to be made here: the lack of congruence between Fish's account of interpretation, including the kinds of judgment associated with interpretation, and our own experience. For Fish, the process of interpretation is pretty much automatic: the strategies of the interpretive community to which we belong simultaneously determine what we find in the text and construct the meaning of what is found. But part of the fascination of reading, or attending plays, is the process of trying out different strategies, of emphasizing different parts of the text and drama, of changing our attitudes as we read or watch, and, most important, of discovering something so recalcitrant to our favored modes of interpretation that we are forced to rethink the whole.

Of course, Fish has long been interested in the way we change our interpretations of certain aspects of a text while in the actual process of reading, but there is no reason to believe that upon completing the text we are locked into an interpretation. How is it that, thinking back on a novel or play, we suddenly see the importance of an event or speech that we had overlooked? How is it that we stage an internal debate about two or more possible meanings to a poem? Or, to move beyond the reading of literature, is it true that judges never agonize over their decisions? Do we as individuals never argue with ourselves? Fish asserts in a number of places that our public accounts of our actions are rationalizations after the fact, designed to fit the view of the prevailing interpretive community as closely as possible. Perhaps so, and in our internal debates about our own actions we evidently take into consideration what others will think of our possible decisions and how we might meet their objections, but the very term "rationalization" we give to such public accounts implies that they are not necessarily accurate reports of the internal debate preceding our decision. The comments of Ch. Perelman and L. Olbrechts-Tyteca are apposite here.

It is a common, and not necessarily regrettable occurrence even for a magistrate who knows the law to formulate his judgment in two steps: the conclusions are first inspired by what conforms most closely to his sense of justice, the technical motivations are added on later. *Must we conclude in this case that the decision was made without any preceding deliberation? Not at all, as the pros and cons may have been weighed with the greatest care, though not within the frame of consideration based on legal technicalities.* (43, italics mine)

In short, the reader does depend on a repertoire of interpretive strategies and does tend to notice those things which fit most easily into those strategies. But the reader of any experience has a range of strategies and the author has not a little to do with guiding the choice of strategies, just as the individual's personal experience is as likely to assign importance to certain aspects of the text, to certain patterns, as are the communally approved strategies.

FRAMEWORKS ALL THE WAY OUT

The fourth doctrine of hermetic thought is the belief in the inviolability of the frameworks within which we think. This is another notion that no one really holds in any strong form – if it were radically true we would have no way of accounting for the notion itself having appeared on the intellectual scene since we would have no way of accounting for change, nor is it easy to see from what vantage point we would be able to contemplate the fact that our thought is confined by a framework. Of course our primary framework could be the thought that all thought is confined in a framework – but if that were true it would make no sense for anyone who believed that it is true to say that is true, except to indulge in a version of the liar's paradox.

But such counter-arguments in fact serve only to strengthen the hermeticists' belief in the doctrine of the impermeable framework, since they give it the mysterious paradoxicality which is presently accepted as the imprimatur of all truly sophisticated thinking. Belief in the power of the mental framework is also hard to battle because of the number of forms this argument takes, all of which at least sound similar and mutually supporting. The version of the framework argument easiest to dismiss is the hoary recognition that humans cannot know if there are aspects of whatever there is that humans cannot know. Hardly arguable, but hardly important – wherever else the Logical Positivists may have gone astray, they were clearly right in saying that we needn't worry about the effects of that which has no discernible effects.

A second, related version argues that since thought depends on language, and language is only arbitrarily related to reality, the language we habitually employ imprisons us within a particular structure of thought from which we could break out only if we had access to an unmediated reality. As noted above, this version of the framework argument results at least partly from a confused reading of Saussure. But the argument in fact collapses in and of itself. Since experience is constituted by sense reports of brute reality as well as the frameworks that interpret these, a knowledge of unmediated reality is not required for one to change one's beliefs, including the sort of large-scale beliefs thought of as frameworks; neither is it needed to lead toward greater accuracy in our beliefs about broad aspects of experience. Beliefs about death are pretty clearly the result of at least one framework, but the belief that in what is described as death plants and animals undergo a change into a very different physical state, however explained, is based on universally similar sense reports. A framework that led to the belief that the virtuous, or the members of a particular religious sect are immune to physical death could not long exist. The confusion occurs when the human sensory apparatus is regarded as dependent on a framework no different from the frameworks imposed by thought and language.

A third version of the framework argument moves from the view that there is no way to correlate what our language allows us to think and say with what exists independently of our thinking and saying to an insistence that thought is bound to the particular language in which the individual thinks. But is it? Suppose a newly captured Abominable Snowman, in whose icy language there are for evident reasons no words for distinguishing one flower from another, confuses tulips and roses. Can anyone doubt that he could be taught to tell them apart? The difference between the two flowers does not result from the fact of our having different words for the two; our having different words results from the fact that the two flowers look different and in fact grow in quite different ways. Although persons with very different experiences, cultures, and languages may not be accustomed to noting the same distinctions, there is no reason to assume that they cannot learn to make them, so long as we assume that the percepts they receive are the same as ours. We assume, because there has never been a reason not to assume, that the great majority of humans experience very similar sense reports. That these may not faithfully reflect whatever it is that stimulates our senses produces no bar to communication. Neither are differences in language finally a bar because these are always practically translatable, however awkward the process of translation may have to be. Language does draw lines to divide what our senses report of an extra-linguistic reality, but it does so not arbitrarily but in accordance with the distinctions we find useful and often inescapable.

We constantly and easily assimilate distinctions that we had never noticed before. If for some reason I notice that the needles of some evergreens grow from the branch singly and others in clusters of from two to five, I can ever after keep the distinction in mind, and perhaps begin to associate other properties with the differences in the way the needles are attached even if I never learn the names "spruce" and "pine." Raymond Tallis sums up the matter nicely:

> If we do dissect nature along the lines laid down by our native languages, it would appear that we are not always obliged to do so. Direct experience would seem to be able to bypass – and one assumes, reform – linguistically mediated knowledge. . . . Moreover, the classification of an object is always provisional. . . . This is connected with the fact that no real object can be classified, or described without remainder. (*NS*, 52)

That there are infinite possibilities for describing an object is not to be taken as the result of some mystical property that makes objects forever unknowable. What we notice, what we call attention to, depends on our purposes. Whether I identify a book by describing it as "*Silverpoints* by John Gray," or "that handsome green book with the elongated S design," or "that book of decadent poetry we were talking about," or "that book propping open the window" will depend on the context in which I am speaking.

Abstract terms pose greater but not insuperable difficulties. "Sprezzatura" may not be translatable by any single word in English, and perhaps it may never carry the same emotional value for an Englishman as for an Italian, but the concept can be conveyed. What, then, is untranslatable from one framework to another? Experience? Well, yes, each person's experience differs from every other person's – which in itself is one of the reasons it is folly to deny that there is a self or subject. Either we do not remember and are not affected by our experiences, or there is something produced by the sequence of our experiences which is unique. But the very fact that we share a language and a culture means that we can share the fact of differing experiences even if not the precise way those experiences affect us.

Yet another version of the framework argument moves from an emphasis on the limits of one's native language to the modes of thought, attitudes, and even senses of words acquired from the particular discourse community to which an individual belongs. But of course each of us is a member of overlapping sets of discourse communities. Not only do such communities have no strict boundaries, but each is in itself expandable; almost everyone is a member of several, and one can always enter a new one. Indeed, if one comes to think about it, while the term "discourse community" is meaningful, it describes an area of temporarily accepted usage, not a set of boundaries. The beliefs of a community to which one belongs are influential, but, since one belongs to a number of communities, never decisive. Two married prosperous middle-aged male Methodist republican farmers from the middle of Kansas may have a great deal in common, but if, for instance, one understands the theological bases of Methodism while the other merely attends church on Sundays, or one is an avid reader of *Science Today* while the other reads only the newspapers, or one is a member of the Veterans of Foreign Wars and the other is not, they cannot be said to belong to precisely the same discourse community. Moreover, it is not necessarily true that each will give the same importance to each of the sub-communities to which he belongs. Like social science categories generally, the idea of a discourse community is useful only as an aggregate. As F. A. Hayek notes, "the concrete knowledge which guides the action of any group of people never exists as a consistent and coherent body. It only exists in the dispersed, incomplete, and inconsistent form in which it appears in many individual minds . . . (29–30). The result of this is Bakhtin's "heteroglossia," which exists in a much greater degree than most readers of Bakhtin perhaps realize.

The point I am making here applies to Stanley Fish's explanation of how change occurs in what he calls "interpretive communities." (The terms discourse community and interpretive community are essentially interchangeable since the relevant beliefs of a discourse community are the grounds of their interpretation of either literature or extra-linguistic experience). Fish forcefully argues that an interpretive community is in itself an "instrument of change"; it is such an instrument "because its assumptions are not a mechanism for shutting out the world but organizing it, for seeing phenomena as already related to the interests and goals that make the community what it is" (Ch, 150). Each interpretive community is indeed constantly processing new information, but Fish's description makes it sound as though each of us belonged to a single or at least primary community. But in fact each community is made up of individuals with different hierarchies of goals acquired from other communities. Within the discourse community of an English department, or within the community of specialists on Victorian literature, or within that of the professors of literature generally, some persons will have a primary allegiance to the Marxist community, some to the feminist, some to a particular philosophical perspective, others to a rough and ready New Critical orientation. Some indeed will have primary allegiance to their profession while others may in fact identify themselves primarily as Catholics or Baptists or advocates of gay rights or parents or private entrepreneurs. Interpretive or discourse communities thus dissolve before our very eyes. Fish partially sees this when he speaks of each person holding nested beliefs which may alter each other (Ch, 146), but he does not, I think, consider that each individual's nested set is both unique and constantly shifting.

One of Fish's difficulties can be seen in his fondness for the argument that we can't compare our frames of reference with a world seen apart from some frame of reference. All description may be paradigm specific, but that does not mean that we cannot compare paradigms with our experience, which is made up in great part by sense reports of brute reality. Paradigms that prove less successful in fitting our total human experience tend either to disappear or be held by a very small minority. That what we define as evidence depends on what we are looking for, and what we are looking for depends on what we expect to find is true – but only partly so. Of course the more one knows about the thing one is looking at or investigating, whether a scientific phenomenon, a text, or a crime, the better idea one has about what it is important to look for in relation to a particular purpose. But to equate searching for and seeing is a particularly blatant equivocation: we see things not sought and fail to find things we seek.

Again, while understanding and interpretation always take place within a framework, competing frameworks jostle in every mind. For the individual, to concentrate on anything is to relegate a great many other things to the background – a framework necessarily changes whenever anything causes one to bring a particular question, problem, or issue forward and push others into the background. Frameworks are always provisional, and no framework is all-encompassing. Some frameworks contain others, all interact with others. To the extent that thought is enclosed by language, culture, and particular discourse communities, it is enclosed in something much more like a dynamic network than a static framework.

Which leads to the complementary perspective that no discourse community is an isolated, self-sufficient domain. Each is based on assumptions common to others: for instance, the knowledge and beliefs that underlie the "communities" of public accountants, protestants, Lacanians, physicians, New Critics and Rotarians all assume not only the existence of discrete human beings with certain physical attributes but a vast social apparatus that makes possible the activities peculiar to each. While the differences are enormous between whatever may be the human group least well furnished with material comforts and knowledge of other human cultures and the residents of Fifth Avenue or Belgravia, all members of each group share the minimal physical and emotional experiences and needs out of which the manifold cultural structures have emerged.

Another formulation of the framework argument is that we cannot get outside the system of beliefs that constitutes what we think is true. To some extent this is plausible enough, especially if we take belief to be that for which no empirical evidence can be given, to be equivalent to faith, "the substance of things hoped for, the evidence of things not seen" (Hebrews, 11, vs. 1). The Hindu growing up in India is going to have a difficult time believing Christian dogma, just as the Methodist growing up in Kansas is going to have a hard time accepting the Hindu faith. But such examples have little to do with the interpretation of discourse. *Knowing that* is not *believing that*. For purposes of interpreting what another is saying I need not believe what the other person believes; I need only know what that person believes and what that person probably believes I believe. I may not be able to understand how a friend can believe in Freudian psychoanalysis, and I may not fully be able to understand all his arguments even though I think I do, but I can understand that he is interpreting certain phenomena according to one framework of belief and I according to another. I may very likely be able to state his position in terms that he will accept as being accurate. It is always possible that one of us will discover an important inconsistency in our own position that will cause us to accept the other's framework – which change cannot consist simply of altering what we believe true of psychoanalysis but will cause modifications of other, perhaps larger frameworks.

Stanley Fish insists that one cannot get outside one's beliefs in order to evaluate them, but it seems reasonable to ask how it is possible for even the most powerful rhetoric to cause us to change our beliefs without at least a momentary balancing of what we have believed with what we will in a moment believe. The analogy we are asked to accept is actually a physical one, as the common phrasing that we can't get *outside* our belief structure suggests. It's quite true that we must physically always be in one place or another (though even so we can be half in and half out of somewhere). But it is not true that we cannot look at our beliefs from a point outside them. We can also compare two beliefs or two possibilities. Of course the position from which we look at them can also be described as a belief, but it is not the same as the two we are comparing. The new position to which we move probably always seems like a larger or more authoritative frame of reference, whether it is or not. But if we ever change our minds, it must be as the result of our ability to move outside an established framework into one that seems to us to provide the authority to make the decision.

A special version of this form of argument has it that we cannot get outside the interlocked set of scientific explanations to which we hold – at least until we are driven from one set to another by what Thomas Kuhn calls a new paradigm – I will give particular attention to this in Chapter 4. However, to anticipate slightly, Kuhn has said that when science rejects one major explanatory theory and moves to another, the successive paradigms are essentially incommensurable. That is, an older paradigm cannot really be subsumed into the subsequent one because the paradigm shift has changed the meaning of certain of the key terms. Belief in the incommensurability of successive paradigms has been very attractive to hermeticists because it seems to fit both psychological relativism (each individual responds somewhat differently as a result of biological and experiential differences) and cultural relativism (each culture has evolved different patterns of response and judgment as a result of its history, ecology, and language). What has to be remembered by theorists of literature (and of culture generally) is that the incommensurability of scientific paradigms is required by Kuhn's dedication to the belief that paradigm shifts represent radical leaps: what was inexplicable in the previous paradigm becomes explicable in the new one precisely because a central mode of explanation has been altered, yielding new formulas and definitions. What is *not* being said is that the scientist accepting a new paradigm cannot understand how things looked to a scientist (who may be himself) who held the old paradigm. After all, scientists moving from the old to the new model or paradigm presumably understand it, or come to understand it, as well as the former one. It is evidently nonsense to say that once they understand the new one, they can no longer understand the old one.

The confusion to be found both in Fish's position and among those who misunderstand or exaggerate Kuhn's view of science is between belief in and attitudes toward something on the one hand and knowledge of it on the other – a very common confusion among hermeticists. The difference between the two is even greater outside the realm of physical science. We must share a common background to understand what a sentence is intended to mean, but we do not have to agree in our *beliefs about* or *attitudes toward* the knowledge of which is part of that background. One can understand "witch" and "warlock" without believing that there have ever been human beings with supernatural powers; one understands the parent who says "I love my children" even if one regards those same children as the most obnoxious set of brats one has ever encountered; one understands the statement "Manet is the greatest of French impressionists" even if one personally believes that Manet would have profited greatly from more rigorous training in handling perspective and treating texture.

After a detailed examination of framework arguments, Paisley Livingston sums up:

> we have seen that framework relativism is either incoherent or trivial. It is incoherent when it asserts that truth always or necessarily comes in limited and incommensurable frameworks . . . for this very assertion is an unlimited thesis about what is necessarily the case about knowledge and reality. When framework relativism avoids this contradiction, it typically reverts to saying that if you happen to see the world from its perspective, then you see the world from that perspective – which is trivial. (59)

It is true that increasingly literary-critical discussions have tended to occur within fixed boundaries controlling what is discussable, or at least of possible interest, at that particular moment in the history of literary study. The result is like a game in which successive sets of rules are determined by a general acceptance among the players that only certain moves by certain pieces will now count. However, if it were not always possible to step outside any given game and point to its artificiality, to the value of changing the rules, it is hard to see how any change could occur. This is of course a version of the problem Saussure created for himself: the problem of the forces that could cause a system of language viewed as a synchronous totality on say, January 1, 1900 to have changed from the system of January 1, 1850 (or January 1, 1899 or indeed December 31, 1899) and to continue to change diachronically so that any synchronous slice will differ to some degree from all others.

Of course what is significant about the framework theory is its presumed ultimate entailments: (1) that everything is relative, and (2) that there is no possibility of fruitful discussion between those whose thought is based on different frameworks. Let me take the second of these first and state it more fully as what Karl Popper has called "the myth of the framework."

A rational and fruitful discussion is impossible unless the participants share a common framework of basic assumptions or, at least, unless they have agreed on such a framework for the purpose of discussion. (*MF*, 3)

Three points seem worth making about this myth. First, as Popper notes, if there is a total agreement on the framework, the discussion is likely to be pointless, having no function. Second, only in those cases in which a relatively narrow topic is being viewed from a rather restricted framework is such agreement possible – as suggested above, the diversity of overlapping frameworks which each individual will necessarily have acquired insures that. And third, the internal tensions that exist as a result of the almost certain incongruities among the frameworks provide openings for changes in the sets of beliefs that constitute those frameworks. This is pretty close to the explanation for the understanding of changes in belief that Fish offers, although I don't believe he sufficiently recognizes the necessity and functioning of such tensions. Indeed, new pragmatists generally – Richard Rorty seems exemplary – give insufficient attention to how the changes in belief that are presumably the fruit of the constant discussion they so earnestly recommend can possibly come about. Moreover, it is not enough recognized that there is one particular belief or framework that makes a special difference to all others: the belief that not all one's own beliefs are likely to be perfectly correct or adequate. So long as one holds that belief, other beliefs will be held less tenaciously. It is Stanley Fish's failure to allow for such a belief that produces his seemingly airtight system: "I may, in some sense, *know* that my present reading of *Paradise Lost* follows from assumptions that I did not always hold and may not hold in a year or so, but that 'knowledge' does not prevent me from knowing that my present reading of *Paradise Lost* is the correct one" (DvP, 359).

As for the relativity that the framework argument offers, one needs to distinguish between the arguments that all truth is relative and that all value is relative. No one really doubts truths of fact: sugar dissolves in water; all animals require food and water; Kant distinguished between noumena and phenomena; the United States declared war on Japan and Germany in 1941; Jimmy Carter did not receive a second term as president; the resistance of the British populace to the poll tax forced the government to abandon it; President Clinton promised to address the problem of medical costs. What is relative is judgments of value – indeed most of the "truths" that are questioned are really statements of value such as "a person's life should be preserved as long as possible regardless of the quality of that life," or "justice has nothing to do with retribution."

What has all this to do with literary criticism and theory? Two things. First, the existence of many and overlapping frameworks and interpretive communities makes possible – indeed guarantees – discussion, while the unavoidable testing of all concepts against experience sets limits to relativism. Second, the existence of overlapping frameworks invites the kind of distancing, rethinking, and hypothesis-framing which literature offers, while extra-linguistic reality provides for the testing of such hypotheses.

Notes

1. Among the most salient discussions of the confused views that have been attributed to Saussure are John Holloway's "Language, Realism, Subjectivity, Objectivity," Raymond Tallis's *Not Saussure*, Cedric Watts's "Bottom's Children" and A. D. Nuttall's *A New Mimesis*.

2. "It may appear unnecessary to insist that there is no direct connection between say 'dog,' the word, and certain common objects in our streets, and that the only connection which holds is that which consists in our using the word when we refer to the animal. We shall find, however, that the kind of simplification typified by this once universal theory of direct meaning relations between words and things is the source of almost all the difficulties which thought encounters" (12).

3. It is perhaps necessary to say that in such a use the lion designated may be real, artificial, figurative (a man of instance, or a cat). Only if no creature or object to which the world could be attached were anywhere in evidence would the word as used in such a sentence lack reference. If one found that it did lack reference, one would probably begin edging away from the speaker.

4. To avoid possible confusion, it may be well to say here that illustrations of Sherlock Holmes or paintings of unicorns can be referred to in the full meaning of reference, that is they may be denotata, but this does not affect that Sherlock Holmes and unicorns actually have no reference, no denotata. Obviously what one is dealing with are understood ellipses in which a sentence such as "that is a unicorn" is an understood abbreviation of "that is a painting of a unicorn." "That is a painting of a unicorn" has no different status from "That is a painting of a bear" although the source of the image that the painter drew upon is ultimately different.

5. Cedric Watts's comment on this passage is acidly incisive. "It is quite true that in grammar the 'I' which is the subject of the verb is the nominal subject and not a flesh-and-blood person; the grammatical fact does not prove that flesh-and-blood people do not exist. Barthes' reasoning is, again, on a par with that of a man who, on finding that the word 'food' does not satisfy hunger, concludes that real food does not exist" (26). Barthes may have had in mind some other argument, but since he gives none, there is no way of knowing what it might have been.

6. See Barthes' *Writing Degree Zero* (1953), "From Work to Text" (1971) as well as "The Death of the Author."

7. Barthes queried the passage in the same way in *S/Z* (172), published two years after "The Death of the Author."

3

The Fallacies of
Hermeticism

*But just as we say that the gardener mows the lawn when we know that
it is the lawn-mower which actually does the cutting, so, though we
know that the direct relation of symbols is with thought, we also say
that symbols record events and communicate facts.*

Ogden and Richards, p. 9.

The fact that every philosophy is by definition a dialectical game, a
Philosophie des Als Ob, *has caused them to multiply. There is an
abundance of incredible systems of pleasing design or sensational type.
The metaphysicians of Tlön do not seek for the truth or even verisimili-
tude, but rather for the astounding. They judge that metaphysics is a
branch of fantastic literature. They know that a system is nothing more
than the subordination of all aspects of the universe to any one such
aspect.*

J. L. Borges, "Tlön, Uqbar, Orbis Tertius," *Labyrinths*, p. 10.

Matthew Arnold, who thought criticism, literary and other, might
do something worthwhile for the world, wondered whether the
time would come when a member of parliament would be disturbed by social anomalies. Although I am an admirer of Arnold,
his naiveté shows strongly here: it is not just that elected government officials are primarily concerned only about positioning themselves for the next election, but, more striking from my point of
view as a denizen of an English department, is his touching faith
that well-read critics would be disturbed by intellectual anomalies.
We now find that not only anomalies but obvious fallacies of kinds
against which thinkers have been warned at least since Aristotle are
not only tolerated but celebrated. Has the penchant for fallacies and
strategies whose purpose appears to be to obscure rather than clarify
been with us since the beginning of the poststructuralist ethos?
And is it simply old-fashioned to object to modes of thought long
regarded as sources of error – have such fallacies as equivocation,

absolutism, and hypostatization been enfranchised, even ennobled, by a new access of wisdom, or have they simply been allowed to creep in? Is it an antique notion that error breeds error, or in an age that seems happily to accept the formula that all reading is misreading, is it absurd to speak of error at all?

My own position, obviously enough, is that fallacies disable rational discussion of any issue, and that if reason and the principles of logic, traditional logic, are abandoned, discussion becomes pointless. The arguments of the hermeticists depend upon the reader's accession to logical principles even when they seek to disable those principles. The very meaning of the aporias and contradictions adduced by deconstructive criticism depends upon traditionally accepted modes of reasoning. While it is necessary to question much in the histories of philosophy, linguistics, and rhetoric promulgated by the leaders of hermetic thought, to analyze the bases on which their arguments are constructed proves difficult because the fallacies which run through them make them remarkably slippery. It has therefore seemed better to concentrate primarily on the prevalent forms of fallacious argument than historical distortions or metaphysical improbabilities.

As all good historians know, there is no point in seeking an absolute point of origin, but one can often make a reasonable claim for the moment when something became identifiable in the form in which we now recognize it. Desiring to get back as close as possible to the moment when the most characteristic fallacies were introduced, I began by carefully rereading Saussure. Whether one agrees with Saussure or not, his painstaking development of all that is entailed by looking at language synchronically does not depend on untenable eristics. Nothing in the elements of Saussure's analysis of language inaugurated the weirdly improbable modes of thought that followed. Barthes, Lévi-Strauss, Lacan and others projected Saussures created in their own image, the master illusionist being of course the arch-rewriter of Saussure, Jacques Derrida, who more than any other begat the hermetic nature of thought. He is the best example of a handling of standard forms of fallacy so cunning that the results became rather like certain Escher lithographs and wood engravings – so cleverly contrived that it seems ungrateful to try to work out how the trick of perspective is performed. A distinction is necessary here. I am not questioning the whole of the skeptical conclusions about the possibility of ascertaining truth or discovering reality that have become so widely accepted. No doubt what we call true or real is mediated by the capacities of the human mind – as Kant, not to mention the Greeks of the third century BC, told us. On the other hand, none of us could get through a day without believing that language can state things that are true and real from the human perspective – which is a quite sufficient perspective given that we are neither gods nor grasshoppers. My concern here is whether certain modes of thought – equivocation, begging the question, false dichotomization, and the rest of what have for centuries been categorized as logical fallacies – are not as misleading as they have traditionally been thought to be.

There is no better exemplary catalog of the fallacies on which so much hermetic argument depends than Derrida's famous essay, "Signature Event Context" that led to the well-known exchange between Derrida and John Searle. It is an especially significant early essay because Derrida's comments on Austin and speech-act theory to which Searle took exception were not a chance example. Since speech-act theory is an especially visible part of the hermeneutic current of thought which seeks to explain how we go about determining meaning rather than why meaning is necessarily indeterminate, it constituted a target that Derrida could hardly afford to ignore.

Derrida's essay, a paper read at a conference on the theme of communication, appears in the first volume of the poststructuralist journal *Glyph* (1977). Primary deconstructive strategies appear from the opening paragraph.

Is it certain that the word *communication* corresponds to a concept that is unique, univocal, rigorously controllable, and transmittable: in a word communicable? Thus in accordance with a strange figure of discourse, one must first of all ask oneself whether or not the word or signifier "communication" communicates a definite content, an identifiable meaning, or a describable value. However, even to articulate and to propose this question I have had to anticipate the meaning of the word *communication*: I have been constrained to predetermine communication as a vehicle, a means of transport or transitional medium of a *meaning*, and moreover of a *unified* meaning. If *communication* possessed several meanings and if the plurality should prove to be irreducible, it would not be justifiable to define communication *a priori* as the transmission of a *meaning* even supposing that we could agree on what each of these words (transmission, meaning, etc.) involved. And yet, we have no prior authorization for neglecting *communication* as a word, or for impoverishing its polysemic aspects: indeed this word opens up a semantic domain that precisely does not limit itself to semantics, semiotics, and even less to linguistics. (SEC, 172–3)

ABSOLUTISM

Now the opening strategy is to assume that the determination of meaning, and therefore the possibility of communication, depends on a concept that can be shown to be "unique, univocal, rigorously controllable, and transmittable" – an excellent statement of the *absolutism* that haunts so much hermeticism. That a concept must be transmittable if it is to be transmitted is obvious, but that the concept must be so clearly defined and so wholly different from any other concept as to be unique, univocal, and rigorously controllable is in fact one of the points at issue. Absolutely univocal, apodictically certain statements are perhaps the goal of metaphysics – Derrida (like many before him) is right enough in therefore denying that traditional metaphysical speculation could ever reach its goal. But the understanding of ordinary human endeavor, including the use of language, has been regarded by most thinkers to be, though never certain, usually possible and definitely useful. One can hardly imagine the human condition if our attempts at communication were more often misunderstood than not, if an order for filet mignon would as likely result in one's being served spaghetti or fish and chips. On the other hand, the most straightforward expression can always be asserted to be ambiguous if enough ingenuity is applied; the requirement that a statement be proof against all challenges, however improbable, would produce a mute world.

The demand for a degree of perfection or accuracy that is both unattainable and unnecessary is a hoary eristic fallacy. The old sophists' demand to know the loss of which hair made a man bald demonstrated the vagueness of certain words but also demonstrated that their vagueness did not undermine this usefulness. It did not in the least prove the non-existence of baldness. Thus it is an evident simplification to say that a person must be either happy or unhappy – there is a considerable range between pure felicity and its polar opposite (assuming that it is possible to speak of either pole as an absolute). This fallacy is closely related to a confusion that is obvious when directly stated, though it is perhaps helpful to consider it in terms of the logician's traditional square of opposition. "All literary criticism is absurd" and "No literary criticism is absurd" are contraries: if one is true the other must be false, but *both* may be false; "Some literary criticism is absurd" obviously does not entail "All literary criticism is absurd"; it simply leaves the truth of "Some literary criticism is not absurd" undetermined. Fallacious bifurcation leading to an all-or-nothing absolutism in which the falsity of a proposition is taken to demonstrate the truth of its contrary lies behind a good many poststructuralist arguments, as I trust will become manifest.

EQUIVOCATION

As important as absolutism to the deconstructive mode of argument is *equivocation*, a play on two different senses of a word. Equivocation is the source of many jokes, quibbles, and bits of whimsy. One finds it in two of Thomas Hood's best known lines.

> They went and told the sexton,
> And the sexton toll'd the bell.

Equivocation is the foundation of many a simple joke:

> "Do you like Mozart?"
> "I don't know; I've never met him."

or

> The trouble with political jokes is that they so frequently get elected.

However, equivocation can be an argumentive ploy in which the conflation of the two senses is intended to reduce real difference to an apparent identity. When play on two senses is hidden, it is likely to obscure the differences between act and entailment, type and token, intention and actualization, and knowledge of and knowledge that. Thus, although Derrida first refers to communication as a "concept," he turns out to be questioning "the word or signifier." But signifiers can of course correspond to a number of concepts or signifieds; that is, "concept" is used in the beginning as though it means "signified," and later as though it means that which the signified designates, which allows Derrida to suggest that "the concept" is ambiguous although it is the word taken by itself that is ambiguous because of its several senses.

Equivocation is rife in Derrida, though its operation is not always easy to delineate briefly. To take another uncomplicated instance from the present essay, one which Searle pointed out in his reply to "Signature Event Context," in maintaining that "the green is either" has meaning because it "signifies *an example of agrammaticality*," Derrida shifts between the use of a word sequence and its mention (SEC, 185, 203). This could equally be cited as an example of confusing intended meaning with symptomatic significance as I have defined those terms, but the effect is still equivocation. Let me also take a relatively simple example from Derrida's reply to Searle in "Limited Inc abc . . ." as published in volume 2 of *Glyph*. Derrida finds an "infelicity" in Searle's having copyrighted his "Reiterating the Difference." "It resides in the fact that if Searle speaks the truth when he claims to be speaking the truth, the obviously true, then the copyright is irrelevant and devoid of interest: everyone will be able, will in advance *have been able*, to reproduce what he says" (LI, 164). The equivocation here is of course between "already known to everyone" and "that which thought or investigation will lead one to agree with." Thus it is true (that is, investigation will verify) that as of June 1993 the British Library catalogue did not include a copy of the Duke and Forstman translation of Schleiermacher's *Hermeneutics*; this however is hardly part of everyone's common stock of knowledge. Again, not everyone knows how heavily Derrida depends on equivocation, but investigation will prove that he does.

Much of what is described somewhat pretentiously as the polysemy of language amounts to no more than the ambiguities that make equivocation possible; these are discussed in every elementary logic text. Aristotle comments on this early in the *Sophistic Elenchi*.

> For, not being able to point to the things themselves that we reason about, we use names instead of the realities as their symbols, and then the consequences in the names appear to be consequences in the realities. . . . But it is not so. For names, whether simple or complex, are finite, realities infinite; so that a multiplicity of things is signified by the same simple or complex name. (3–4)

I should add that I am here using the word "equivocation" as a kind of umbrella. Linguistically based fallacies may be classified in a variety of ways. For instance, a commonly used example runs:

Buffaloes are a vanishing species; the ones in the zoo must therefore be in the process of vanishing.

One can see this as an example of the fallacy of division – as a confusion of what is true of the whole with what is true of the individual. But it can also be seen as an example of equivocation which plays on "vanishing" in the two senses of the dissolving of an individual buffalo before one's eyes and the dying off of the species. I will therefore simply stick to equivocation as the most useful term for a large class of fallacies.[1]

ARTIFICIAL ISOLATION, INDUCED OBSCURITY, IMPLIED PROFUNDITY, SMUGGLED ASSUMPTIONS, FALLACIOUS HYPOSTATIZATION AND REFLEXIVE ENTANGLEMENT

Since "communication" is the announced theme of the conference at which Derrida originally delivered his paper, it is reasonable for him to point to its various possible senses, its "polysemy" in fashionable critical parlance. However, concentration on a single word in a sentence so as to lift it out of context is a standard deconstructive practice. This is the strategy of *artificial isolation*, one which operates directly against universal human practice: when we actually meet with single words, we immediately try to put them into the most probable context. As Walker Percy succinctly puts it, "Single-word utterances are either understood as sentences are else they are not understood at all" (MB, 166); to lift a word out of the context in which it exists is to deny everything we know about language. Almost any individual word – for instance a word found written on a blackboard or sheet of paper – is ambiguous, or better, simply a bundle of potentialities. Words may be homonymous, having obviously different senses or related senses that nevertheless must be distinguished. They may be used figuratively or literally. Nevertheless, no heavy theorizing is required to make the point that in discourse we almost always know which sense of a word is required from the context given by the individual sentence or surrounding text (the "cotext") together with the situation (the pragmatic context), behind which stands knowledge of the language and culture.

A fourth strategy is the construction of *induced obscurities* presumably intended both to exemplify that indeterminacies are necessary and to keep the reader off balance. Thus, "in accordance with a strange figure of discourse" is wholly obscure: what figure, and how does it cause one to ask the question Derrida attributes to its motive force? The question itself – whether or not " 'communication' communicates a determinate content, an identifiable meaning, or a describable value" – is made equally ambiguous. One simply can't know whether the three members of the series are to be taken together as three necessary aspects of any meaning, or as three different alternatives, and, if the latter, what difference it makes to Derrida's argument. The effect is to keep the reader from bringing his or her analytical facilities to bear on the steps of the argument – there are too many lacunae. One should note however that these gaps are wholly created by the choice of phrasing; any one of the possible meanings between which one is forced to hesitate could have been expressed clearly enough. The effect could equally be called *implied profundity*: readers are presumably to charge whatever lack of clarity they encounter to their own inadequacies. As Bunthorne explains about his "idle chatter of a transcendental kind" in Gilbert and Sullivan's *Patience*:

And everyone will say,
As you walk your mystic way,
If this young man expresses himself in terms too deep for *me*,
Why, what a very singularly deep young man this deep young
   man must be!

Next, one notes the strange wording of "we have no prior authorization for neglecting *communication* as a word, or for impoverishing its polysemic aspects." "Authorization" is quite a weighted word here, for it implies that to do other than consider all possible senses of a word would violate some generally acknowledged principle, whereas the ordinary principle upon which use and interpretation are both based is the expectation that context will make possible determination of which of several senses is relevant. I am quite aware that Derrida denies the possibility of determining the relevant context, but this is simply one more exercise in absolutism: that one cannot list every element of a context that might be relevant does not deny the necessity of our seeking to construct the most likely context of almost everything said to us. This is an instance of what I will call the *smuggled assumption*, one form of begging the question. In passing, one also may note a version of the *fallacy of hypostatization*: "communication," we are told, "opens up a semantic domain," whereas it is obviously the user initially and the interpreter subsequently who decide what "semantic domains" are relevant in a particular use of language. The effect of using an abstraction or non-active noun with an active verb is, as Bernard Bergonzi remarks, "to remove or reduce human agency, making events seem the consequence of impersonal forces such as ideology, the unconscious, history, or language itself" (103).

A final strategy, the appeal to *reflexive entanglement* is nicely exemplified in the opening sentence of "Structure, Sign, and Play in the Discourse of the Human Sciences." "Perhaps something has occurred in the history of the concept of structure that could be called an 'event,' if this loaded word did not entail a meaning which it is precisely the function of structural – or structuralist – thought to reduce or to suspect" (SSP, 247). The production of this kind of reflexiveness – in which discussions of meaning become enmeshed in the problems of analyzing a word the consideration of which requires that word – is another common characteristic of hermetic discourse,[2] though it may be noted that such discourse implicitly denies another kind of reflexiveness: that in which the mind recognizes possible contradictions and circularities and by reflection finds ways to avoid being trapped in them. To adapt a comment by A. D. Nuttall, this argument is rather like saying that one cannot train a telescope on a lens factory (28). While one cannot get very far using a word to define that word itself, no metalanguage is needed to discuss language. (It is similarly possible for a painting to comment on the techniques of painting, or a cartoon to comment on the art of the cartoon.)

MORE ON EQUIVOCATION

The most important of the deconstructive strategies are equivocation, absolutism, and artificial isolation (the latter two are often combined: absolutism authorizes the practice of isolation, while, once isolated, the word or sentence can easily be shown to be contradictory or ambiguous). Equivocation is especially seen in the play on the word "writing" employed in the attack on J. L. Austin. Although the epigraph is taken from Austin – "Still confining ourselves for simplicity to *spoken* utterance" [Derrida's emphasis] – Austin is not specifically discussed until halfway through Derrida's essay, when his emphasis on intention, context, and the assumption that there are both normal and parasitic uses of language (the speeches made by characters in a play are parasitic in this sense) comes under attack. Derrida's antipathy to Austin's emphasis on speech as opposed to writing echoes (somewhat obscurely) the argument he initially mounted against Ferdinand de Saussure in *Of Grammatology*. Stripped of Baroque flourishes, the argument is simply that Saussure had assumed that speech was logically and chronologically prior to writing, whereas writing, which in Derrida's opaque definition amounts to the capacity for using language, was the real foundation. Writing for Derrida, it turns out, is not the system of notation by which sounds are transcribed into marks on a page (at least in Western languages), but is that which makes language possible. "By a hardly perceptible necessity, it seems as though the concept of writing – no longer indicating a particular, derivative, auxiliary form of language in general . . . no longer designating the exterior surface, the insubstantial double of a major signifier, *the signifier of a signifier* – is beginning to go beyond the extension of language. In all senses of the word, writing thus *comprehends* language" (7, and see 56–7). By choosing "writing" as his designation for the very possibility of the use of language – either spoken or written — Derrida is able to attack all who give spoken language any sort of priority over written language. He thus gains a polemic instrument of wide application through an equivocation made possible by the conflation of "writing" in its usual sense and writing in the quite new sense Derrida gives it.

"Signature Event Context" affords example after example of Derrida's typical strategies, but two, the play with the concepts of "absence" and "signatures," deserve particular mention in their combination of equivocation with absolutism. Nothing is more Derridean than the pair presence/absence. Since words are not only different from things but can stand in the place of things, their use evidently often implies the absence of what they stand for. One can thus argue that language assures us of the irremediable gap between absence and presence that language pretends to bridge. Moreover, "absence" can be conceived in such a way that it appears to deny not simply determinate meaning but non-linguistic reality:

if language not only can never refer to presence but is the source of
the illusion of presence, everything beyond language must be illusory. If one defines presence as "that which is immediately present,"
that is, present in the mind or word without any mediation, presence is obviously impossible. But such a sense of present goes beyond absolutism to absurdity. Here we again encounter the creation
of a special sense which can be played against the more usual senses.
The fact that words can and do function in the absence of that to
which they refer of course lends a specious plausibility to the suggestion that that which language makes present to the mind is always absent. The Derridean strategy is further made plausible by
the already noted difficulty philosophers have always found in
explaining reference – but the mystery of reference hardly cancels
the fact that it *is* possible for language to refer (there would otherwise be no reason for its existence). If language did not, Derrida
would hardly be able to refer to Austin or the text *How to Do Things
with Words*. Vincent Descombes nicely sums up a *non sequitur* at the
center of the deconstructive argument: "*Since* in fact signs are useful and even indispensable in all communication, whether their
subject is absent or present in the setting of the conversation, *therefore* things are never truly present" (66–7).
    Toward the end of the essay occurs Derrida's famous play with
the concept of the signature.

Effects of signatures are the most common thing in the world.
But the condition of possibility of those effects is simultaneously,
once again, the condition of their impossibility, of the impossibility of their rigorous purity. In order to function, that is, to be
readable, a signature must have a repeatable, iterable, imitable
form; it must be able to be detached from the present and singular intention of its production. It is its sameness which, by cor-
rupting its identity and its singularity, divides its seal [*sceau*].
(194)

The equivocation that allows the production of apparent contradiction is of course the conflation of "same" in the sense of "self-
same" or "self-identical" and in the sense of "the same in relevant
characteristics" (as in "the team won the game with the same play
with which they had scored previously"). Thus this second sense
refers to every person's having a characteristic way of writing his

or her signature. Further, a copy (as by photoduplication) is not identical with the original in the first sense, but may be in the second sense depending on what characteristics are relevant to the discussion. As Karl Popper points out in another context, even if we ignore the difference in time of occurrence, few of the repetitions we experience are precisely the same: in general, repetitions are repetitions only from the point of view that emphasizes their similarity and thus views them as repetitions. We can choose whether to give differences or similarities priority (*C&R*, 44–5). There is a further play with "same" as "self-identical through time" and the manifest contradiction of an object occupying the same point in time at different times.

Reading the whole of "Signature Event Context" followed by John Searle's reply published in the same issue and then Derrida's reply in *Glyph* 2, one cannot but feel how much Searle's careful answer is overshadowed by both of Derrida's pieces. Searle's error was strategic: he assumed that Derrida was serious in his argument and answered him with an excess of seriousness – he should have recognized that Derrida was serious only as a debater in a contest is serious: a debater wishes both to win and to impress by his or her cleverness in the process. But what imperative is there to be serious, to avoid fallacious argument? It is at this point that the connection between language and human non-linguistic experience becomes crucial. If language were merely a mechanism for our amusement, it would be of little importance. But no one really imagines language to have come into being for word play – and indeed the existence of word play depends on its serious use. The most trivial word play depends on our seeing that two contexts are in play, producing two senses that are simultaneous yet at odds,

Adriana: Say, is your tardy master now at hand?
Dromio of Ephesus: Nay, he's at two hands with me, and that my two ears can witness.
Adriana: Say, dids't thou speak with him. Knowest thou his mind?
Dromio: Ay, ay, he told his mind upon mine ear. Beshrew his hand, I scarce could understand it.
Luciana: Spake he so doubtfully, thou couldst not feel his meaning?
Dromio: Nay, he struck so plainly, I could well feel his blows, and withal so doubtfully, that I could scarce understand them.
Comedy of Errors, II, sc. 1.

Derrida is correct that Austin left out important aspects of language in use when he excepted jokes and non-serious uses from his analysis in *How To Do Things with Words*, though Searle's reply is eminently sensible:

> Austin's idea is simply this: if we want to know what it is to make a promise or make a statement we had better not *start* our investigation with promises made by actors on stage in the course of a play or statements made in a novel by novelists about characters in the novel, because in a fairly obvious way such utterances are not standard cases of promises or statements. (204)

Searle continues:

> Once [however] one has a general theory of speech acts – a theory which Austin did not live long enough to develop himself – it is one of the relatively simpler problems to analyze the status of parasitic discourse . . . (205)

In any case, H. P. Grice supplied what is necessary in his discussion of the mind's response to any violation of the "Cooperative Principle." The indirect route of expression, which goes by way of what Grice calls implicature, may be pursued through the figurative, allusive, humorous, or seemingly irrelevant, but the fact is that we assume that the choice of that route is intentional, the destination discoverable, and the reason for not taking the direct route meaningful.

Not to challenge fallacies such as equivocation is to allow the wells to be poisoned. Language is absolutely essential to the creation of the institutions that enable us to do all sorts of things impossible to bare unaccommodated man, whether beneficial or deleterious. Language is the single tool we have for building human institutions, for measuring them to see if they fit our needs, and for remodeling them or pulling them down when they do not. Karl Popper wrote in 1960:

> The belief of a liberal – the belief in the possibility of a rule of law, of equal justice, of fundamental rights, and a free society – can easily survive the recognition that judges are not omniscient and may make mistakes about facts and that, in practice, absolute justice is never fully realized in any particular legal case. But the

belief in the possibility of a rule of law, of justice, and of freedom, cannot well survive the acceptance of an epistemology which teaches that there are no objective facts; not merely in this particular case, but in any other case; and that the judge cannot have made a factual mistake because he can no more be wrong about the facts than he can be right. (*C&R*, 5)

To claim to be a liberal these days is to open oneself to the derision of the surprisingly large number of neo-Marxists inhabiting the academy, but few of us in practice would care to deny the values Popper associates with that word. If Popper is right, the legal system and a good many other institutions are in considerable danger at present; if he is wrong, nothing in the hermetic argument demonstrates that he is. Carelessness in language invites carelessness of thought. These days critics' and theorists' modes of presentation are frequently described as "moves": "Critic A's first move is to deny Y," or "At this point critic B makes the interesting move of affirming X." Often no support for the affirmation or denial is offered, either by the writer commenting on the move or, if one checks back, by the original writer – the move is simply a tactic in a verbal game presumably without consequences in extra-linguistic reality.

Before closing this chapter, I should distinguish fallacies in discourse from logical errors per se. Although all fallacies are sometimes referred to as logical fallacies, if we define logic quite strictly as the employment of the syllogism, or trains of syllogisms, the phrase "logical fallacies" ought to be restricted to invalidly derived syllogistic conclusions. Fallacies such as equivocation of course invalidate syllogisms in which they occur, but their occurrence is not confined to syllogistic premises. I make this point because it has become a commonplace that pure logic is relevant to a very small part of life's experiences. As Aristotle knew, apodictically certain premises from which one can suspend a chain of syllogisms are few. Moreover, the influences on much human experience are too complicated to be crammed into syllogistic form. But non-syllogistic fallacies produced by careless use of words or illegitimate dichotomies undercut exact thought wherever they occur. They are effective in the service of humor, or satire, or as ways of stimulating thought, but they become pernicious where they seem to explain human thought and action. No bets were placed on the tortoise just because Zeno presented a plausible argument that the hare could never overtake it.

Notes

1. Ogden and Richards, employing the term "Utraquistic subterfuge"
    for equivocal use of words, comment that it "has probably made more
    bad argument plausible than any other controversial device which
    can be practised upon trustful humanity. It has long been recognized
    that the term 'perception' may have either a physical or a mental
    referent. Does it refer to what is perceived, or to the perceiving of
    this? Similarly, 'knowledge' may refer to what is known or to the
    knowing of it." (134).
2. This strategy of course becomes formalized in Derrida's use of terms
    "under erasure."

4

Hermeticism and Science

There are good grounds both in epistemological arguments and in their greater fruitfulness for opting for hermeneutical sciences of man. . . . We cannot measure such sciences against the requirements of a science of verification: we cannot judge them by their predictive capacity.
Charles Taylor, "Interpretation and the Sciences of Man," 51.

THE APPEAL OF HERMETICISM

Why has a mode of thought which is so reductive in its treatment of literature, which makes literature so marginal, which is so sterile in its conclusions been so influential in literary studies? The wave of hermetic criticism appears to have crested, but the terminology and modes of thought it provided linger. How is it that these have so thoroughly infiltrated the language and structures of argument in literary study, and why has hermeticism had so much greater an effect on literary commentary than elsewhere?

The last decade, and especially the last five years, has seen a phalanx of cogent protests against the poststructuralist or hermetic orthodoxy. These include André Lefevere's *Literary Knowledge* (1977), Richard Levin's *New Readings vs. Old Plays* (1979), A. D. Nuttall's *A New Mimesis* (1983), the essays collected in Laurence Lerner's *Reconstructing Literature* (1983), Geoffrey Thurley's *Counter-Modernism* (1983), Frederick Crews's *Skeptical Engagements* (1986), Patrick Parrinder's *The Failure of Theory* (1987), Raymond Tallis's *Not Saussure* (1988), Paisley Livingston's *Literary Knowledge* (1988), M. H. Abrams's essays as collected in *Doing Things with Texts* (1989), James Battersby's *Paradigms Regained* (1991), and a considerable number of essays, among which I will cite here only Robert Pattison's "Trollope Among the Textuaries" (1983) and Quentin Kraft's "Toward a Critical Renewal" (1992). The focus in these varies, but each author is hostile to patent and what seem at times wilful confusions found in hermetic theory and practice.

The challengers have dissected deconstruction and the hermetic poststructuralism of which it forms the core in varied ways, but there is considerable agreement about the constituent errors and fallacies, most of which I have touched on above. The hermeticists have virtually rewritten Saussure and necessary distinctions have been dissolved in a headlong rush to absolutism. Deconstruction excepts only itself from the principle that propositions can never be true and indeed their meaning never determined; the principle that there is nothing outside the text condemns the hermetic critics to remain in the realm of *langue* even though they pretend to be discussing *parole*; the practice of lifting out a small portion of a text and discussing it as though it can be understood in isolation and yet somehow represents the whole similarly violates the basic conditions of how language is used. Poststructuralist readings in general are remarkable primarily for the carelessness of their presumably "close" reading; that the prevailing tendency of hermeticists to regard their denial of determinate meaning as a form of political protest is distinctly odd; and the obsession with puns, playful associations, and unsupported suggestions of arcane relationships is, in Frederick Crews's phrase, just "verbal doodling" (130). On the other hand, the number of critics who have felt it necessary to counter poststructuralism in itself testifies to the disturbing power of that which they attack, while the fact that little that they have written has the kind of reputation gained by the wielders of hermetic theory suggests the influence hermeticism still carries. The relative tardiness of these replies (deconstruction was having a distinct influence on literary studies by the mid-1970s) says something about how difficult it was to counter the first surge. The question of hermeticism's power still requires investigation.

A number of answers carry plausibility. The simplest is that deconstruction in particular gave a new source of commentary to a field that seemed to have pretty well exhausted what there was to say about literature from the prevailing perspectives while at the same time authorizing much looser canons of valid argument. The New Critical approach having done what it could to display the unity of the literary texts it found interesting, deconstruction opened a wholly new field by concentrating on their contradictions. Moreover, the goal of commentary could be shifted from demonstration of a thesis to the exhibition of intellectual play. The benefits of deconstruction could hardly be better summed up than by Frederick Crews. "In the first place, the deconstructionist denial that there are standards of evidence by which one critical judgment might be found more adequate than another effectively turns criticism into a mystery controlled by high priests" (118). "Secondly, the deconstructionist position frees the critic himself from an obligation to make reasonable inferences" (118–19). "Thirdly, the inquisitive sociologist cannot avoid noticing that the deconstructionist program promises to allay one of the besetting self-doubts of academic critics, a fear that the things worth saying about the finite number of authors in one's field have already been said" (119).

Second, the old assumption of the ethical power of literature had begun to fail. As George Steiner comments, "The study of literature was assumed to carry an almost necessary implication of moral force. It was thought self-evident that the teaching and reading of the great poets and prose writers would enrich not only taste or style but moral feeling; that it would cultivate moral judgment and act against barbarism" (TCG, 77–8). The positive delight in cruelty exhibited over many years by a large number of "cultivated" Germans and the at least tacit acceptance of genocide by almost the entire German nation was the most potent force in toppling such a belief, but it had already begun to dissolve. Hermeticism's denial of traditional humanist beliefs seems a recognition that the arts have no relation to the world outside themselves and especially that texts necessarily undercut their own values. Third, in partial contradiction to the preceding view, hermeticism gave to those who felt that large-scale cultural changes were necessary what seemed a timely weapon. If one wished to assault certain of the prevailing values of the culture, what better weapon than a form of thought that undercut such values by showing them to have no solid meaning, to be self-contradictory? That the argument itself allowed for no alternative positive values was a matter to be dealt with later.

However, I think more of the power of the hermetic view of the world than has been realized was a direct reaction to the failure of the structuralist dream of founding a true science of literature. Saussure had forecast a science of signs, of language; if language could be approached scientifically, so could literature. Roman Jakobson's influential "Linguistics and Poetics" (1958) was an elaborate exemplification of his statement "Since linguistics is the global science of verbal structure, poetics may be regarded as an integral part of linguistics" (L&P, 350). Structuralism, which based itself so largely on linguistics, saw itself as the new, the scientific, form of poetics. Thus in 1967 Barthes argued that "structuralism, itself developed from a linguistic model, finds in literature, which is the work of language, an object that has much more than affinity with it; the two are homogeneous." "We can understand then why structuralism should want to found a science of literature, or, to be more exact, a linguistic of discourse" (SvL, 897). That structuralism was to be a science in the full sense was essential since science was the source of whatever could seriously be called knowledge. Barthes' view was not uncommon: structuralism was quite widely seen as endeavoring to become a science. Robert Scholes could write in 1975: "By moving from the study of language to the study of literature, and seeking to define the principle of structuralism that operates not only in individual works but through the relationship among works over the whole field of literature, structuralism has tried – and is trying – to establish for literary study a basis that is as scientific as possible" (FCF, 10).

THE RELATIONS OF SCIENCE AND LITERATURE

In suggesting that the failure of structuralism to become a science produced a negative absolutism as a reaction, I have opened the question of the relationships between literature and science. Scientists have rarely felt the need to define what they do in relation to the arts, but the arts, and especially literature, have frequently thought it necessary to define themselves in terms of their differences from science, especially physical science. The implicit assumption of those speaking for the arts would seem to be that while the value of science need not be argued, the value of the arts requires periodic explanation. On the whole, those who love or have a vested interest in literature seem much less sure of themselves than the practitioners and advocates of science. The value of science has been assumed; what has seemed to require defense is the value of literature. Even the recent insistence by literary theorists on the inconclusive nature of science can be seen as essentially a different kind of defensive maneuver.

However, arguments about the relationship between literature and science have frequently failed to recognize a fundamental asymmetry. Scientists use language in a particular way to talk about physical phenomena while literary critics use language in another way to talk about the literary use of language. Physical phenomena are a kind of bedrock while literature is a form of language beneath which lie our ordinary concepts about the world beneath which lie the experiences made possible by the nature of the physical world. It is true that our grasp of the physical world is partly constituted by the human senses and the concepts embodied in language, but our senses and conceptual schemes are responding to something that is what it is even if we cannot wholly know what it is. Literary commentary is discourse about a discourse while scientific commentary is discourse about something that is ultimately non-discursive.

Thus if we compare scientists and literary critics, scientists never have to defend the importance of the physical world – if it did not exist, neither would the scientists – nor the rest of us. (If the assertion of the existence of a physical world seems naive – it's a curious world in which it could seem so – I will attempt to make what I mean more precise as I go along.) On the other hand the value of literature, like that of all the arts, can always be questioned. The history of that question is not of primary concern here, but it is worth noting that, although his phrasing seems quite outmoded, the values of science and of literature that Ruskin asserted in 1853 in *The Stones of Venice* were repeated in various vocabularies for the next 100 years. "Science deals exclusively with things in themselves; and art exclusively with things as they affect the human soul" (para 8, chap. 2, vol. 3). Ruskin was a bit ahead of his time in distinguishing between the works of art and science (the primary sense of "art" was still simply "skill"); however, the important point is that he was contrasting the work of the scientist with that of the artist, *not* with that of the commentator on literature.

The same sort of odd alignment lurks beneath the surface of the well-known debate between Matthew Arnold and T. H. Huxley in the early 1880s. In effect Arnold argued that a knowledge of science was a very good thing but of itself insufficient to meet human needs while Huxley argued that a knowledge of literature was quite desirable but not to be purchased at the expense of a knowledge of science. Thus there was tacit agreement that the study of literature and science were very different things, and that literature's appeal was to what Arnold called the instincts for conduct and beauty and Huxley was content to call the desire for pleasures that do not degrade. However, while Huxley was primarily interested in increasing the number of scientists, that is, creators of science, Arnold was interested, not in encouraging creators of literature, but rather in the effect of literature on those whose careers would lie outside a literary or critical vocation. And one notes that even though Arnold was speaking for the old-established human tradition, he seems more on the defensive than the confident Huxley.

When I. A. Richards came to the defense of the value of literature in *Principles of Literary Criticism* (1925) he was essentially championing the views of Ruskin and Arnold against the rising influence of logical positivism. Since I will be paralleling structuralism with logical positivism, it will be worthwhile to say something more about the positivist movement here. The remarkable group of scientists and philosophers who gathered in the 1920s around Moritz Schlick to form the Vienna Circle quickly became enormously influential – they were, and have remained in certain ways – much more influential than is acknowledged by the dismissive way in which humanists tend to refer to them today. Taking aim at the attempts by metaphysicians to define truth and reality by abstract reasoning, the logical positivists substituted the question of what was meaningful. The answer was essentially a refinement of one of Auguste Comte's basic principles: "any proposition which does not admit of being reduced to a single enunciation of fact, special or general, can have no real or intelligible sense" (171; *Cours*, VI: 600).[1] The more direct way of saying this is simply A. J. Ayer's: "the meaning of a proposition is its method of verification" (LP, 13). Verification might well involve a long chain of deductions, but at the end was observation, sense-perception. Statements for which no mode of verification could be suggested were meaningless metaphysical mystifications. Clearing away language that had no verifiable meaning and tightening up the meaning of scientific terminology would contribute to the logical positivist dream of the unification of all science.

Positivism's ultimate goal was to reduce all phenomena – physical, psychological, or social – to explanation in terms of a single set of principles probably to be located in physics. An interesting artifact of this program is the essay written by Rudolf Carnap in the early 1930s, "Psychology in Physical Language," which asserts that "every sentence of psychology may be formulated in physical language" or, that is, "all sentences of psychology describe physical occurrences, namely, the physical behavior of humans and other animals" (PPL, 165). Thus, "psychology is a branch of physics" (197). The developing theoretical network was to produce hypotheses of higher and higher levels of generality; those that are verified will overarch more and more fields, leading finally to a unified field theory. The pursuit of a single unified science was identified successively with the journals *Annalen der Philosophie, Erkenntnis, Journal of Unified Science,* and finally the *International Encyclopedia of Unified Science.*

A strong tradition lies behind the hope of reducing manifold phenomena to a single principle, model, or system, a tradition clearly bound up with scientific thought. Some such dream had lain behind the ancient Greeks' search for a single substance or principle underlying all things – water for Thales, air for Anaximenes, fire for Heraclitus, harmony for Pythagoras. The key post-Renaissance formulation may be that of Laplace. "A mind that in a given instance knew all the forces by which nature is animated and the position of all the bodies of which it is composed, if it were vast enough to include all these data within his analysis, could embrace in one single formula the movement of the largest bodies of the Universe and of the smallest atoms; nothing would be uncertain for him; the future and the past would be equally before his eyes." (3) A more direct line is from Saint-Simon, who for a time thought the basic explanatory principle lay in the law of gravitation, to Auguste Comte, the first to claim the name "positivism." Comte, while giving up the idea of a single all-explanatory principle, proclaimed that "the fundamental character of all positive philosophy is to regard all phenomena as subject to invariable natural *laws*, whose precise discovery and reduction to the smallest number possible is the aim of all our effort" (171; *Cours* I, 16).

Now the status of literature was in fact not directly threatened by the logical positivists. They were indeed concerned with a more accurate use of language, but their definition of what was meaningful had reference only to assertions about what they regarded as the objective world. Their attitude toward art in general was somewhat condescending, but, rather like Huxley, the Logical Positivists were perfectly willing to differentiate between the metaphysics they abhorred and works of art, to which they allowed a certain value. Rudolf Carnap thus accepted the realm of aesthetics as valid for the "expression of the general attitude of a person towards life" (EMLA, 78). More directly, "art is an adequate, metapysics an inadequate means for the expression of the basic attitude" (79), which formula allowed him to go on to dismiss metaphysicians as neither scientific nor artistic: "Metaphysicians are musicians without musical ability" (80).

Nevertheless, the positivist's definition of meaning rankled humanists who, ignoring Ogden and Richards's ground-breaking *The*

Meaning of Meaning (1923) took "meaning" univocally: something either had meaning or it did not. Richards's distinction between the language of science, which is referential, and the language of literature, which has the purpose of evoking attitudes and emotions, served an important defensive function for a generation of critics even though it was not so much a challenge to the logical positivists as a reassuring affirmation of the value of a kind of meaning with which the positivists were not concerned. "A statement may be used for the sake of the *reference*, true or false, which it causes. This is the *scientific* use of language. But it may also be used for the sake of effects in emotion and attitude produced by the reference it occasions. This is the *emotive* use of language" (*PLC*, 267).

What is equally important in Richards is his recognition that literature is one thing and its study another. In distinguishing between the use of language in scientific discourse and its use in literary texts, he was *not* distinguishing between the activity of scientists and that of literary critics. Indeed, he seems to have been the first Anglo-American critic to seek to support his approach to literature by drawing on another, presumably more scientific, field. The latest work in psychology was invoked in his *Principles of Literary Criticism*: "a theory of feeling, of emotion, of attitudes and desires, of the affective-volitional aspect of mental activity is required at all points of our analysis" (*PLC*, 91). Richards's diagram of the mental processes that accompany reading a poem – which schematically traces the response from the "auditory verbal image" through the "articulary verbal image," "free imagery," "references," and "emotions" to "attitudes" – reflects his need for a kind of scientific support.

In a way, Richards's use of the science of psychology as a grounding for the study of literature was an answer to a question which first clearly emerged in the argument over the introduction of the study of literature in English into the formal curricula of Oxford and Cambridge. "Is there an adequately rigorous method of considering, commenting on, or analyzing a literary work?" It is easy to become confused about the central issues in this debate. First, the question was not the value of English literature (American literature was given little or no consideration in this discussion), but the value of *teaching* English literature. Those who were opposed did not deny that literature other than that of the Greeks and Romans could improve human conduct and encourage the proper emotions; rather, they questioned if literature in one's native tongue need be taught, and, if so, how one would go about teaching it. While no one questioned the value of scholarly study of literature in English, or critics' valuation and revaluation of it, whether commentary on literature was a full-fledged field of study with a methodology of its own was moot. Literature was something one knew when one had read it, and upon which – and this was of course the point of Arnold's "The Function of Criticism at the Present Time" – one could draw for reference points and perspectives for thinking about non-literary issues. No methodology, certainly no theory, was necessary for understanding it. There was not only nothing substantial to *teach*, but little to study except its history, a respectable enough activity but hardly a vineyard which required or could support many workers.

Richards's example was of great importance in changing all that. While the New Critics followed Richards in contrasting literature and science, their concern for close analysis of the poem's meaning was in part authorized by his doctrine that art and literature worked by harmonizing psychological tensions. Thus the emphasis on irony and paradox. Psychology was the obvious science of choice, and while the New Critics as a whole avoided direct importation of psychological theories, Freudian and Jungian psychology began to have their influence. Even Kenneth Burke, whose approach was largely guided by his concept of rhetoric, strove to construct in *A Grammar of Motives* and *A Grammar of Rhetoric* a kind of rhetorically based psychology that would explain human thought, expression, and action. On the other hand, it would be hard to argue that the New Critics were concerned with meeting the canons of scientific analysis. Their goal was the best meaning of the text (that is, the most comprehensive and illuminating); that the goal might never be totally achieved or definitively validated did not much worry them.

Enter structuralism. If one of the distinguishing marks of a true science is a distinct delineation of its field of investigation, Saussure fully achieved that. His division of the linguistic sign into the signifier and the signified together with his insistence that the two were only arbitrarily linked, which seemed to many to break the connection between language and the presumably external objects to which language refers, allowed a tidy boundary to be drawn around language and literature. Most important, Saussure's description of a language viewed at any point in time as a total system in which each signifier and each signified received its value from its difference from all other signifiers or signifieds seemed to suggest the possibility that all uses of language were underlain by universal systems. Hence the potential for the new science of structuralism which would extend well beyond literary phenomena but was likely to be especially useful in explaining such phenomena.

Although not all structuralists shared the same methods and goals, it is well to remember that none of their programs was modest. What they thought Saussure had shown – that language was in some sense or other a system in and of itself only arbitrarily related to reality – could be interpreted in various ways. It could mean that language corresponded to the structure of the human mind, or that the development of each language imposed a particular structure on the thoughts of speakers of that language, or that the most basic structure of language – semantic units organized according to syntactic rules – was the most basic form of the organization of human thought, and, as a corollary, of the organization of human culture. At the very least the structure of language could be taken as the model for the structure of literature. Thus what might be called maximalist structuralism could hold that, as Terence Hawkes put it in 1976, "the ultimate quarry of structuralist thinking will be the permanent structures into which individual human acts, perceptions, stances fit, and from which they derive their final nature" (18). Minimalist structuralism held that the way meaning is conveyed in language, and especially in literary texts, can be understood by likening the whole of a text or discourse to a sentence. Thus Roland Barthes: "If a working hypothesis is needed for an analysis whose task is immense and whose materials are infinite, then the most reasonable thing is to posit a homological relation between sentence and discourse insofar as it is likely that a similar formal organization orders all semantic systems" (ISA, 83).

At the same time, while Marxists have always regarded their economic and political analyses as scientific, Althusser saw structuralism as a way of making Marxism more truly a science. In Steven Smith's summary, "what Althusser and the structuralists contend is that man, who was previously considered to be the author of his own actions, can, when submitted to scientific analysis, be shown to be subject to the same causal laws as everything else in nature" (194). Others have felt that by incorporating both Saussurian linguistics and Lacanian psychoanalytic theory, they could buttress their scientific claims while coopting those tendencies of post-structuralism that might seem to undermine their own certainties.

Literary criticism became the site on which the result could best be demonstrated. Thus Catherine Belsey, who devotes a number of pages to weaving together the structuralist Barthes, the deconstructionist Derrida, the psychoanalyst theorist Lacan, and the varieties of Marxist thought found in Althusser and Macherey, is able to proclaim "Criticism is the science which offers a knowledge of this mode of production [the production of the text by determinate conditions] and so, finally, a knowledge of history" (138). Belsey is too canny not to be aware that her argument makes it necessary to speak of knowledge as "produced" rather than found. "In producing knowledge of the text criticism actively transforms what is given. As a scientific practice it is not a process of recognition but work to produce meaning" (138). Nevertheless, the word "knowledge" is evidently intended to be read as distinguishable from and superior to the non-knowledge produced by other modes of thought, and the word "science" equally evidently intended to announce that the only adequate approach has now been discovered.

Given the centrality of language to almost everything that seems distinctive in the human animal and the culture it has created, the foundation of the structuralist enterprise in linguistics suggested the especially exciting possibility of a union of the humanities and the social sciences. The famous conference held at Johns Hopkins University in 1966 was called "The Languages of Criticism and the Sciences of Man." Where earlier twentieth-century attempts to apply psychoanalytic, anthropological, and sociological approaches to literature had come to seem overly reductive, it now seemed possible to link the social sciences with literature (and perhaps all arts), history, and philosophy through their dependence on the system(s) of language use.

What structuralism proposed, then, is strongly reminiscent of the logical positivists' dream of unification of the sciences although, while logical positivism sought primarily to unite the social with the physical sciences, structuralism sought to unite the social sciences with the humanities. If the logical positivists' desire to unify the physical and social sciences had pointed toward physics as the ultimate ground of explanation, the structuralist program for the unification of the social sciences and humanities pointed toward language. Or, stated another way, even though logical positivism strove to stay within sense experience while structuralists strove to stay within the system of language, what the structuralists hoped to discover would have exemplified the kind of absolutism assumed by the early logical positivists. Certain forms of human thought would have been demonstrated to be necessary, either because they lay behind a universal structure of language which makes thought possible or because the structure of a particular language controlled them.

INVERTED ABSOLUTISM

The failure of the structuralist program is pretty much a matter of history. Attempts to treat literature as if it had the structure of a language (characters being regarded as nouns, actions as verbs, etc.), or to see literary structures as the result of basic structures of human thought, or to causally link differences in languages with incommensurable differences in modes of conceptualizing the world either failed to be convincing or proved trivial. More specifically, although it is possible to analyze a literary text as though its elements correspond to the syntactical units of a language, nothing much seems to be gained by the process, while the assertion that texts are structured in accordance with inescapable patterns of human thought proved to be impossible either to prove or disprove. On the other hand, the proposition that language sets the limits of conceptualization proved impossible to maintain: since even where direct translation is not possible, the view of the world presumably implied by one language can be stated in another, thought can comprehend concepts developed in other ways than those specified by the lexicon and syntax of a given language. In short, there proved to be a considerable chasm between a theory of language and a scientific treatment of literature.

Although the promise of structuralism was exaggerated, the intellectual investment of quite a few critics was too heavy for it to be abandoned without a struggle. The claims of structuralism therefore underwent a process of increasing moderation. Jonathan Culler's *Structuralist Poetics* (1975) can be seen as largely an attempt to domesticate the structuralist program into a study of poetics understood as the study of conventions defining literature and producing readers' interpretations. Another interesting document bearing on the attempt to save structuralism by moderating its claims is Tzvetan Todorov's 1981 *Introduction to Poetics*. In the introductory chapter Todorov seeks to substitute "poetics" for "structuralism" as the proper name for a science of literature, at the same time softening the use of the term "science" to avoid any suggestion that it seeks absolutes. Similar strategies were employed by others, but such maneuvers did not prove to have sufficient appeal. The very modifications of structuralism revealed the depth of the problem. To discuss what structures cause a text to be regarded as literary, or produce certain effects, or lead to certain interpretations requires agreement about what is literary, what effects are actually produced, and what interpretations are reasonable. One is inevitably led back to the question of meaning: what is literary meaning? And is such meaning anything that can be definitively determined?

Roger Scruton has made this point nicely in comparing the overall effects (the illocutionary force and perlocutionary effects) of a literary work on the reader to the tertiary qualities of a physical object.

> There comes a point [beyond primary and secondary qualities], we feel, when it is only a manner of speaking to refer to a property of an object. The real fact of the matter is the response of the observer. If we speak of a property of the object this is only a way of saying that the response may be justified (as when we describe a landscape as "fearful"). If we think of meaning in literature on the analogy with "tertiary" qualities we see why there is both a pressure towards objectivity and also a pressure in other directions. Meaning [the meaning of a text as a whole] in literature would be (at its most objective) something like the aspect in a picture, observable to a being with the requisite intellectual and emotional capacities, but irreducible to any structural properties of the work itself. ("Structuralism" could then be seen as the (vain) attempt to describe meaning as a *primary* quality of the thing that possesses it.) (54–5)

Structuralism had set out in its own way to define what was *necessarily* meaningful, and failed: If so seemingly well-grounded a method of explaining meaning was unsuccessful, perhaps meaning was a chimera. Thus occurred the great reversal: if it was not possible to construct a system that would yield absolute interpretations, it could be argued that the interpretation of meaning was an impossibility – an absolute impossibility. Adopting the principle that only if it were possible to achieve the structuralist goal of a totally valid explanatory system could language and the issues language tries to treat be non-contradictory and truly meaningful, hermeticists construed the failure of their endeavor as evidence of the illusoriness of the absolute truths traditionally sought by metaphysics. The necessity of indeterminacy could be explained by pointing out that the meaning of the individual word could not be guaranteed by establishing a one-to-one correspondence with a knowable reality. Therefore, the meaning of any text was open to multiple interpretations, none of which was the "true" one – which did not matter since we are unable to know any "true" reality. When Derrida, who had moved beyond structuralism, writes in 1967, "The concept of writing should define the field of a science," he is of course speaking of what may better be called an antiscience, that is, Grammatology (*OG*, 27). (I am not attempting to trace or explain the process of thought of Derrida or any other specific thinker – I am trying to elucidate the general intellectual movement that made deconstruction and the poststructuralist ethos so congenial to so many).

The structuralists' discovery that the chains of reasoning are dependent on language that is not wholly univocal has, then, led to the dismissal of the possibility of even relatively determinable meaning. On the other hand, although the logical positivist's ambitions for a unified science and the accumulation of a body of irrefragable knowledge have been drastically curtailed, yet physical science, incorporating yet modifying the impetus given by the positivists, has proceeded on its accustomed path merrily enough. Although one may wish to avoid speaking of new knowledge, Science can be said to have discovered how to do a world of new things. The more one looks at figures like Derrida, de Man, or Lacan, the more they come to look like Lucifers who, having chosen to expel themselves from the realm of certainty in which they no longer believe, must go about the earth denying the human ability to make valid judgments about anything. Hermeticism is replete with paradoxes, but one of the central ones is that poststructuralist thinkers have clung to an absolute relativism, a negative absolutism, while invoking what they understand as the relativism of science as support for that absolutism. Camouflaging despair as discovery, most of those swimming with the current of hermeticism have found themselves denying not only the possibility of transforming literary criticism into a science, but finally the possibility literary criticism, although not, again curiously, of the possibility of endless criticism of criticism. And in a final turn of paradox, despite all the Derridean talk of the illusions of metaphysics, the reasoning that has supported hermeticism is of just that kind that the logical positivists, and Comte before them, set out to eliminate. Since there is no way to seek to verify hermetic theorizing, there is nothing in the realm they seek to investigate that can answer back as does "brute reality" or what some scientists simply call "space-time." Not being testable, their position is wholly metaphysical.

THE NON-FALSIFIABILITY OF LITERARY COMMENTARY

The envy of literary critics and their desire to emulate the sciences is of long standing. "In its philological and historical methods the field of literary study reflects a large hope, a great positivism, an ideal of being something like a science, and we find this all the way from Auguste Comte to I. A. Richards," wrote George Steiner in 1965 (TCG, 77)[2] just before the literary structuralist movement got under way. The structuralist attempt to assimilate criticism to science was just somewhat more direct – and arrogant – than previous instances. Now that the failure of the structuralist enterprise has led to a negative absolutism quite different from the attitude with which scientists pursue their calling, a goodly number of literary critics and theorists seek to identify themselves with a scientific worldview in a new way: reversing earlier arguments, they now look to the philosophy of science to support their arguments for the indeterminability and relativity of all human understanding and the futility of any talk of truth or reality. They point with evident delight to the developing consensus among philosophers and historians of science that scientific theories are never "true," never give us the truth about the way physical reality "really" is. The problem here is the ease with which the mind moves from "we cannot know the truth about reality" to the fallacious conclusion "it must be true that there is no reality." But few of the representatives of the more extreme hermetic positions seem to have read with sufficient care the sources they delight to cite in this regard, for instance Karl Popper and Thomas Kuhn.

Popper has successfully maintained that no number of verifying experiments is sufficient to establish a theory as true; it is always possible that a predicted phenomenon that has legitimately been derived from the theory may not be experimentally verified – in other words, it is always possible that it may be falsified.[3] Even the most well established natural science theory is forever on probation: that is, neither the possibilities of error in experimentation nor the possibility that a phenomenon it predicts may fail to occur can ever be ruled out. It has become generally accepted that a theory is *not* conclusively established by the successful production of the phenomena it predicts, no matter how often it does this. Nevertheless, the concept of verification has not lost meaning. If no hypothesis can be proved to be certainly true, even by repeated verifications, hypotheses can nevertheless be shown to be false by the failure of adequately conducted attempts at verification. Rather than what is true being that which has been verified, the more accurate statement is that what is meaningful must be falsifiable (capable of being tested) and that a statement that satisfies this criterion of meaningfulness and is not inconsistent with other statements held by scientists to be provisionally true is itself provisionally true if it has not been falsified by any experiment. Scientists may best be described as holding not to relativism but to what C. S. Peirce called "fallibilism." That is, a meaningful, tested, unfalsified theory is to be treated as provisionally correct. Moreover science as an institution – with exceptions that are so few as to be quite anomalous, a fact that accounts for their notoriousness – holds to no more than one explanatory theory at a time. It is true that there are at times competing theories in new areas of explanation, but the expectation is ever that only one will eventually remain unfalsified, and that expectation is almost always fulfilled. In short, the physical scientist operates on the assumption that one and only one theory explains a particular set of phenomena even while knowing that any theory, however long it has been held and however often it has been tested, may be proved false. To use terms that have become common in discussions of physical science but are perhaps employed most clearly and carefully by Mary Hesse, while scientists are willing to accept that their theories are always underdetermined, what is important is that they be "instrumentally progressive." "There is instrumental progress in the sense that we now have vastly increasing pragmatic possibilities of predicting and controlling empirical events by means of experimentation and theory construction" (RR, xi). Or again, "the claim of science to yield objective knowledge comes to be identified with the cumulative possibilities of instrumental control rather than with theoretical discovery" (RR, 174–5). The second presumed support for the indeterminability of everything is Thomas Kuhn's now famous argument that science proceeds not by a continuous step-by-step approach to a more and more accurate description of physical reality, but through a process marked by major "paradigm shifts." Such shifts occur when "normal science," which has been proceeding with the investigation of phenomena understood in terms of an accepted constellation of theories, discovers so many anomalies that a new explanatory theory becomes necessary, a theory so radically different as to shift the way other theories are understood. The occurrence of such paradigm shifts makes it difficult to regard science as engaged in an orderly progress toward fuller and fuller knowledge of "reality" or greater and greater "truth."

Totally overlooking the implications of the working assumption that competing theories will eventually be reduced to a single theory, hermeticists have with evident enthusiasm exaggerated Kuhn's position into an absolute relativism that regards "reality" as a wholly human construct. Although many scientists and philosophers of science take issue with various aspects of Kuhn's thesis, the details of the debate between Kuhn and those who disagree have been sufficiently recondite to repel close analysis by literary critics. However, those scientists who are not made uncomfortable by the notion that science does not inexorably approach nearer and nearer to a knowledge of reality nevertheless accept that there is a non-linguistic reality that answers back, says yes or no to every experiment. If this were not so, the principle of falsifiability and the agreement that falsification can occur would have to be given up – and if they were, there would be no reason to develop new theories to explain discovered anomalies – indeed, no anomalies. Clearly something "out there" produces the sense reports that produce the anomalies that drive paradigm changes as well as support the consistencies that make normal science possible. That all evidence for scientific propositions has been derived ultimately from sense reports was one of the earliest principles of logical positivism, and one which science has never relinquished, however long the path from sense reports to theory.

The use of Kuhn to deny extra-linguistic reality ought finally to be put to rest by his own statement on the matter. Kuhn writes "... no part of the argument here or in my book [*The Structure of Scientific Revolutions*] implies that scientists may choose any theory they like so long as they agree in their choice and thereafter enforce it. Most of the puzzles of normal science are directly presented by nature, and all involve nature indirectly" (RMC, 263). (If "reality" has become too pretentious a word, one can always go back to speaking of "nature.") Perhaps the simplest statement of the minimal foundation essential to physical science is that of W. V. Quine, one of the philosophers most chary of any reference to reality or truth. "Our overall scientific theory demands of the world only that it be so structured as to assure the sequences of stimulation that our theory gives us to expect" (22). But that is no trivial demand. Similarly, one finds in Popper, "Nature very often resists quite successfully, forcing us to discard our laws as refuted; but if we live we may try again" (*C&R*, 48).

In relation to the exaggeration and inaccuracies in the understanding of Kuhn among so many literary theorists, it is worthwhile to take note of statements such as the following made by one of the contributors to *Critical Terms for Literary Study*: "Thomas Kuhn showed that the history of the physical sciences is a story not of the pragmatic discovery of a truth lying in wait to be found but of the gradual shift from one explanatory paradigm to another under the pressure of a wide range of *social forces* (257, italics mine). The words "social forces" are quite misleading, especially since there is nothing to modify them in the context surrounding the sentence I have just quoted. Kuhn was not speaking of social forces in the sense of theories, beliefs, or cultural currents operating from outside the scientific community, but simply of the theories shared within that community.

The possibility and means of distinguishing between the propositions and procedures that properly belong to science and all those that do not is generally referred to as the "demarcation" question. There are of course ongoing debates over the relationship of scientific theories to reality (which word can of course be defined in a variety of ways), over how to define scientific method, even over whether there is such a thing as scientific method. Nevertheless basic to the procedures of the natural sciences is the verification of hypotheses through the production of as yet unobserved phenomena predicted by deduction from those hypotheses. In short, theories are verified by testing that which they predict.

Literary discourse stands quite clearly on the far side of the demarcation boundary in that it lacks at least four principles of the structure of the procedures of research in physical science. First, the demand that theories be mutually supporting is absent; the fact is that only in matters of historical fact has even moderate agreement characterized discourse about literature. Second, although new paradigms (or at least theories) are generated all too frequently, and many of these are taken up at least for a time by significant numbers of critics, there is no imperative that the field of literary study as a whole move to a new paradigm. Even were a particular theory to be judged superior by the great majority of scholars and critics, those who contest it can never be ruled out of court. While by 1960 most literary critics were converted to a more or less New Critical perspective, some of the most prestigious critics and scholars were not. Moreover, editors and journal referees who, for instance, do not believe in Freudian theory, are nevertheless likely to accept an interestingly argued Freudian analysis.

Third, the requirement that experimental tests be replicable makes no sense in matters literary; such procedures as checking birth and death dates in parish records or examining manuscripts for evidence of author's revisions or printer's errors are replicable, but no one expects one reader's responses to a text to replicate another's. Literary research involves no true experiments – the closest approximations are social-science-like studies of responses yielding statistical averages. Fourth, and most important, literary discourse is incapable of generating predictions of a kind that might be tested. Regarded in reverse order, these points imply each other. *Because* the verification of theories through the testing of deduced implications is impossible, it makes no sense to speak of replicating test results, no sense to speak of a particular theory as being verified, and no sense to be concerned about whether theories about different aspects of the experience of literature support each other.

One needs to be clear about this matter of verification. If verification meant simply the making of a plausible argument through the citing of evidence drawn from one or more texts or an author's life or historical contexts, it would be more accurate to say that any theory can be verified, and, indeed, that none can be falsified. As R. S. Crane argued with a mixture of high good humor and serious concern in *The Languages of Criticism and the Structure of Poetry*, theories of poetic meaning always turn out to be able to explain what they set out to explain.[4] Richard Levin similarly notes that "the [critic's] reading is a self-confirming demonstration" (*NRvOP*, 4).[5] Thus while the critic may seem to be engaging in an activity similar to a scientific experiment, "there is a crucial difference between them: the experiment can produce negative results, but no reading on record has ever failed to prove the critic's thesis." Explanatory theories must necessarily be applied retrospectively, allowing the reader who applies them to pick out the evidence that will support the theory. And given the richness of an interesting text and the sheer mass and complexity of possibly relevant evidence surrounding the author, situation, and presumably intended audience, who is to say that the evidence chosen is less relevant than that which is passed over? I don't intend this as a (wholly) cynical point: it is not that each critic picks out just that evidence and concentrates on just that argument that will support the chosen theoretical approach: rather, the theory in a sense generates the relevancy of the evidence. What critics are likely to notice is what their theories commend to their notice (that this does not mean that critics, or readers generally are imprisoned in rigid frameworks has been discussed in Chapter 2).

This phenomenon is of course equally operative in the physical sciences: it is what allows distinct observations to be grouped in such a way as to produce a hypothesis in the first place. As Comte noted long ago, although theories are generated by the observation of facts, "facts are observed only through the guidance of some theory" (*Cours*, I: 12). The difference is that nothing warns the literary critic that his/her theory is disregarding a relevant aspect of the text under investigation – indeed there exist no criteria by which to judge what is relevant. In the physical sciences it is possible to confirm by experiment whether a particular fact is relevant or not: if a chemical reaction is found to occur only at temperatures above 150° Centigrade, temperature becomes a relevant factor in any explanation of the reaction. As a specific area of science develops, the existing network of accepted theories will help guide the development of new hypotheses, each of which is a candidate for testing to the extent predictions can be deduced from it. Moreover, in science what counts as true is cumulative in that theory B may be substituted for theory A only if theory B not only accounts for things that could not be accounted for by theory A but accounts for everything that theory A did account for. Thus if what seems a core theory in physical science is falsified (as happened for instance in atomic theory through the discovery of the existence of additional atomic particles), the core does not simply drop away – it is replaced by a new or modified theory that retains what has been verified, explains what had seemed anomalous, and predicts new phenomena. That is not the case in literary commentary. As André Lefevere writes,

> Present theories of literature are not, I submit, really progressive in nature in the sense described above. They do not build upon

each other because they have no core to build on. We do not have a theoretical evolution in the history of literary theory that will allow us to predict . . . some novel, hitherto unexpected fact. Instead we invent some new theory, most often designed to contradict and discredit its predecessors, not to supplement them, *after* the fact. (27)

All the above principles rest upon the recognition that the efforts of physical scientists are guided, constrained, and validated by a physical reality that they may never be able adequately to understand, envision, explain, or model, but which nevertheless acts to confirm or deny their beliefs about it. Science can advance because it constantly receives feedback from what some scientists, wishing to avoid the word "reality," simply refer to as "space-time." "Observation language and even perceptions are theory laden, yet they are rich enough to contain feedback that contradicts the theory" (*CR*, 8), write Michael Arbib and Mary Hesse. Or again Hesse describes what she calls the "pragmatic criterion" that drives science: the "overriding requirement for empirical science is to exhibit increasingly successful prediction and hence the possibility of instrumental control of the external world" (*RR*, xviii–xix). A. F. Chalmers advocates describing science as pursuing an "unrepresentative realism" in which it is recognized that the physical world "is the way it is independently of our knowledge of it" and that while physical theories cannot be thought to describe the world exactly, they prove to be as applicable outside the lab as in it (163).

LITERARY COMMENTARY AND THE SOCIAL SCIENCES

Since I have been contrasting literary commentary with the physical sciences, it is reasonable to object that if we are to consider the possibility of literary theory being scientific, it is the social sciences to which it should be compared – after all, those are the sciences with which structuralism primarily linked itself. However, although verifiability may be much more difficult in the social sciences, it remains the goal there as much as in the physical sciences. Thus the opening sentence of the article on "Theory" in the *Encyclopedic Dictionary of Semiotics*: "A theory is a general system of abstract propositions which accounts for a set of observations by means of a set of laws and uses these laws to construct descriptions of future events" (2:1092). Moreover, it is interesting, if not downright suspicious, that when literary theorists turn to the social sciences for explanatory theories, they are attracted primarily to those areas where competing theories are still in active contest, that is, where none of the theories has been accepted as the provisionally true one by the bulk of the researchers in the field. In psychoanalytical theory the competition goes on, *inter alia*, between Freud, Jung, Lacan, Rogers, and Horney. Not only are the majority of political scientists and economists not Marxist, but within Marxism one can choose a whole spectrum of positions; the literary Marxist can choose, for starters, between Lukács, Goldmann, Althusser, Macherey, Eagleton, Jameson, and Ryan. Anthropologists may have become much more wary of making ethnocentric judgments and much more concerned about ways in which their methods of study may influence their observations, but there are still historicist, structuralist, evolutionist, functionalist, and materialist theories to choose among.

Moreover, within the competing theories, the most popular have been those that are, in André Lefevere's words, "self-immunizing" (25). Freud's concepts of sublimation, displacement, and resistance make it possible to ignore any charge of lack of evidence just as the Marxists are always able to answer any criticism by saying that their critics are blinded by their ideologies. Macherey's argument that the absences in a text are evidence of what is being repressed adds a wonderfully self-protective weapon to Marxism – whatever one wishes to find in a text will be there either *in presentia* or *in absentia* – one has found what one has found either way.[6] Such theories, unfortunately for their advocates, are not however wholly unfalsifiable in that they do make predictions. The possibility of curing psychological ills is a prediction of sorts – few now care to make claims for the therapeutic power of Freudian psychoanalysis. And even before the sudden collapse of the USSR, it was apparent that Marx's predictions about the course of history were hardly on target. Events since 1990 have only made it more obvious that however correct Marx may have been about the degree of human exploitation in society, he was wrong about history, economics, and human desire.

A REITERATION AND A CLARIFICATION

The fields of study traditionally constituting the humanities are not able to describe replicable procedures, make falsifiable predictions, or construct general laws. No validity tests are possible, much less replicable. Chaim Perelman reminds us, "Let us not forget that the categories developed in the humanities do not have the fixity and stability of objects and are not guaranteed by biological relationships as in the animal species; rather, they are constructions of the mind" (*RR*, 100). The same is true of a considerable portion of the social sciences. As William Dray argues in the case of history, explanations of a phenomenon produced by intentional acts of humans cannot subsume these under general covering laws. The historian's answers must necessarily be of the "how possibly" rather than the "why necessarily" kind, and in fact this is the kind of explanation frequently produced by the social sciences. But whereas even in a portion of the social sciences as well as throughout the physical sciences the "space-time" realm gives one feedback that is independent of the surrounding culture, there is no such feedback mechanism in literary commentary; no possibility of constructing a predictive experiment. If it is true that semiconductors have such and such properties, then the transistor and ultimately the computer chip are possible; if it is asserted as true that George Eliot actually reflected a masculine view of the world, or that Dickens was really an apologist for capitalism, or that Samuel Johnson's view of the world was spectacularly sane, or that Shakespeare strove with might and main to undermine the throne (or the opposites of these), the only feedback possible is the agreement or disagreement of other readers. One can of course say to oneself, "If Dickens was continually ambivalent about the concept of the gentleman, I ought to be able to find evidence of this throughout his works." The problem is that one can almost certainly find evidence for almost any assertion about symptomatic meanings in a literary work; what one cannot do is perform any experiment to determine whether the assertion is correct, whether one has misinterpreted what seems to be evidence or overlooked contradictory evidence or given undue prominence to certain aspects of the text.

I have argued that literary theorists have been wrong in seeking to link the interpretation and criticism of literature to the methods and results of science, whether science is regarded as pursuing an absolutely correct knowledge of reality or as a human construction that is incapable of reflecting the nature of reality. So persistent have been both kinds of error that it seemed necessary to review those errors at some length. While it is essential to recognize that literary interpretation and criticism can never achieve certainty, it is equally essential to recognize that they can never achieve the kind of verification possible in the sciences. On the other hand, it is no more impossible to say things that are probably correct – that are adequate for most human purposes – about literary texts than about the phenomena on which the sciences focus.

"Pickwickian" is perhaps the most courteous description of the habitual hermeticists' dependence on a combination of equivocation, illegitimate extrapolation and simple misunderstanding of the very methods of science they employ for both contrast and comparison. Of course the overwhelming *non sequitur* in hermeticism generally is the very use of words to express the belief that it is impossible for words to have a non-infinitely-deferred, determinable meaning. If all utterances are indeterminate, the meaning of literary commentary is as impossible to interpret as the literature itself; if literature is, as some argue, especially indeterminate, the literary commentary that prides itself on being like literature must necessarily be most without meaning. Those who point this out are often regarded as taking refuge in an especially commonplace, not to say vulgar, argument, especially since Derrida has anticipated it by insisting that it is impossible to achieve the dismissal of metaphysical illusions without using words that carry metaphysical meanings. Nevertheless, the logical inconsistency of expecting to be understood through the use of language that by one's own definition necessarily contradicts itself remains. There are names for this sort of problem: one is autophagia, which Chaim Perelman defines as a situation in which "a rule is incompatible with the condition or the consequences of its assertion or application" (*RR*, 57). Raymond Tallis uses "pragmatic self-refutation" to refer to the kind of contradiction "where the very act of asserting something provides the best possible counter-example to what is being asserted." This seems to be, he says, "an occupational hazard of post-Saussurean thinkers" (*NS*, 59).

Notes

1. Where I use F. A. Hayek's translation of Comte as incorporated in *The Counter-Revolution of Science*, the first number in the citation gives the page in Hayek's volume from which the translation is taken; the second gives the volume and page number in the 1864 edition of *Cours de philosophie positive* from which the passage is taken.
2. See in this connection Quentin G. Kraft's "Science and Poetics, Old and New."

3. See *Conjectures and Refutations*, 228ff and 238ff.
4. For instance, Crane notes how largely New Critics employed dialectical "reduction terms" or contraries ("good and evil," "reality and appearance," "emotion and reason," "nature and art"). "Of such universal contraries, not restricted in their applicability to any kind of work . . . it will be easy enough for us to acquire an adequate supply, and once we have them, or some selection of them, in our minds as principles of interpretation, it will seldom be hard to discover their presence in poems as organizing principles of symbolic content" (*LCSP*, 123–4). Of myth criticism: "The patterns we are concerned with are actually *in* the poems (on the assumptions of our method) if they can be seen there; and they will be seen, and thought important indices of latent meanings, by all such readers, at least, as have been conditioned by temperament or the contagion of current literary thought to look upon poetry as necessarily an imitation or reflection, in its greatest moments, of those deeper human realities that have been disclosed to us most clearly, after long neglect, by the psychologists and cultural anthropologists of the early twentieth century" (*LCSP*, 139).
5. Levin amusingly describes this tendency as "Fluellenism" in allusion to the form of Fluellen's proof that Henry V is a second Alexander the Great (*NRvOP*, 209–29).
6. For a similar reason, philosophy has been a more fertile source of theory even than the social sciences. Ayer is pretty much on target in saying that "so long as it is free from inner contradiction it is hard to see how any philosophical thesis can be refuted: and equally hard to see how it can be proved" (*P&L*, 27).

5

Hermeneutics

*[H]ermeneutics depends neither on uncritical analysis of our language
. . . , nor on the incommensurable activity of language and forms of life,
but on the assumption that cross-cultural understanding and self-
reflexive critique are both possible and illuminating.*
Mary Hesse, *Revolutions and Reconstructions in the Philosophy of
Science*, 58.

Hermeneutics – as I use the term – assumes that texts result from
an author's intention to communicate, and that the intended communication is almost always largely interpretable with reasonable
accuracy.[1] At this time in history any discussion of hermeneutics
had best begin by addressing the extraordinary confusions over the
concept of authorial intention that have darkened literary commentary for almost forty years.

Fortunately, the great wall isolating a text from its author's intention appears to be collapsing – actually silently dissolving – and
explicit recognition of intention is creeping into literary commentary once more. Indeed it was always in hiding inside the walls: one
fond of fashionable phrases could say that it was "always already"
there: every contemptuous dismissal of the unenlightened who still
thought in terms of intention was an intentionally constructed attack on the intended meaning of those attacked. Now there seems
a growing recognition that, in the words of Frederick Crews,
"the refusal to acknowledge authorial intention rarely yields more
than trifling results," leading, "in one manifestation, to a program
of reducing criticism to a sandbox amusement for the ultra-
sophisticated" (128). Stanley Fish's reiterated view that argument
always depends on persuasion rather than demonstration is in itself
a granting of the place of intention in discourse. To say that all use
of language includes at least a tacit element of persuasion is to
grant the intentional use of language, for what is really being said
is that all uses of language intend to persuade – if only to persuade
the hearer/reader that the speaker/writer is joking, or desiring the
answer to a question, or, perhaps, not really desiring an answer.

It is not by chance that the rehabilitation of the principle of authorial intention has proceeded alongside discourse analysts' insistence on the pressure of context in guiding interpretation of meaning: interpretation presupposes a contextual structure surrounding each instance of language-in-use. Not yet so fully recognized is the necessary role of a third concept: that of the assumed unity of the text that guides the reader in selecting what of all the possible elements of context are likely to be relevant.

INTENTION

Nothing is more basic to the mind's activities than the formulation of our intentions and the attribution of intentions to others. As soon as one awakes in the morning the question comes, what do I intend to do today? The immediate answer on some a blessedly inexigent day may be, "I'm not sure," but that will be promptly followed by: "What do I intend to do until I decide what I intend to do?" We are made curious by the actions of another person which seem to have no intention. If I see a person repeatedly walking up and down in front of my house, I become interested if not suspicious. If it becomes plain that the person is looking for a lost dog, I'm satisfied, but if I ask the individual and am told "Oh, nothing," I will watch all the closer and perhaps be sure the door is locked when I go inside.

One cannot *not* intend; to not intend is to have intended something else. Not to have intended to knock over and break one of my hostess's crystal wine glasses is to have intended to pick up the salt or pass the roast beef. Only in moments of abstraction, as when, intending to go to the hardware store, one finds that one has turned the opposite way and is heading toward the office, do our acts seem to occur without intention, and then, of course, our falling prey to habit is the result of a kind of internalized intention. Now it may be that we are all simply bits of fluff blown hither and thither by cultural conventions. It may be that when I go to buy a new CD player, I am simply responding to the internalized imperatives of a capitalist culture just as certain Marxists tell me, but I nevertheless get to the right store and succeed in purchasing the piece of equipment I had in mind because I intended to do so.

The point of the rehearsal of these truisms is simply that the assumption that when a person speaks or writes something, that the utterance or thing written is intended to accomplish something is part of a larger set of ineradicable human expectations. Further, it is evident that the accomplishment of whatever one intends to accomplish through the use of language depends on the addressee's adequately interpreting what one says. Persons speaking or writing must be able to convey what they intend to convey in such a way that those addressed are able to grasp that which was intended. (I must ask pardon for the wordy and convoluted form in which I express this, but the question of intention has become so vexed that one must speak by the book to be sure of conveying exactly what one intends to convey.) Adopting the parlance but not the conclusions of the reigning mode of hermetic philosophizing, so much of the individual person as is represented by his or her intentions is "present" in the utterance. As Raymond Tallis insists,

> If we are not present in our speech acts then, surely, we cannot be present in any other acts; indeed we must be non-present in our entire lives. For deliberate speech acts . . . seem to be intentional to a degree exceeding all else that we do; for the primary purpose of such an act is the production of meaning whereas other acts serve non-signifying intentions and only secondarily or incidentally convey meaning. (*NS*, 215)

How then can even the most confused literary critic deny the importance of authorial intention? Not the least of the oddities surrounding the matter is that the whole question was opened – at least for the Anglo-Saxon literary world – by a carefully developed attempt to clarify the relationship between interpretation and intention. In any event the effort made in the 1946 essay on "The Intentional Fallacy" by W. K. Wimsatt and Monroe Beardsley created a confusion lasting for several decades. The authors of the essay were confronting the long tradition of relating what an author has written to the author's life. The temptation to do so is enormous – we feel we know an author from the texts he or she has produced – we want to put that voice back in the context from which it emerged. The fear that the academic study of literature would fix upon the details of the author's life at least as much as on the text was one of the causes of the resistance to a School of English Literature at Oxford. Alexander Bain spoke for many:

> But when a man gets into literary criticism at large, the temptation to deviate into matters that have no value for the predominating

end of a teacher of English, is far beyond the lure of alcohol, tobacco, or any sensual stimulation. He runs into digressions on the life, the character, the likings and dislikings, the quarrels and friendships of his authors; and even gets involved in their doctrines and controversies. (213–14)

As has been pointed out by a number of commentators, including Wimsatt and Beardsley themselves,[2] the explicit argument of their essay is not that there is no relationship between a literary text and its author's intentions in writing that text, but simply that one cannot argue from an author's announced intentions to the meaning or value of a text. The two critics were concerned to cast doubt on both prospective and retrospective statements of intention. Prospective intentions frequently shift a good deal as the act intended is approached. I may have the general intention of buying tea at the supermarket but decide only when standing in front of the tea shelves whether I want loose tea or tea bags, how large a package I want, which brand to get, and what price seems reasonable. These four decisions may have an ideal order, but in actuality the order will almost certainly vary from occasion to occasion. I may have decided I want a large package of Brooke Bond tea bags and then find only loose tea of that brand on the shelves and therefore decide to get Typhoo but find that only smaller packages of Typhoo are available and so end up buying Twining's. Similarly, an author may find that what was intended to be a short story seems to demand greater length, or that an intended scene won't fit. Clearly the more complicated the process of actualization, the longer the process takes, and the more one has to take into account others' responses, the greater the gap between the initial intention and final realization. And of course one may fail to actualize what seemed one's final intention. Just as I may reach for the Twining's tea bags and find when I'm home that I somehow took a package of loose tea by mistake, authors may think they have conveyed all sorts of meanings which readers never recognize because ineffective means were chosen for their conveyance.

Retrospective statements are equally likely to be wide of the mark. Neither before nor after actualization need my own description of my intentions be accurate. Looking ahead, one can never be sure what factors, including newly conceived intentions, may alter one's prospective intentions; looking back, one can never be sure that one's reconstruction of the interplay between one or more intentions, practical considerations, situated chances, and later realizations produced a particular act. To quote Raymond Tallis again, "There is a darkness at the heart of intention and there is an inescapable indeterminacy in the relation even to the actions that seem most precisely to realize them" (234). The situation is even more complicated when one's intention is to communicate something – for then enter the possibilities of failure to choose the proper means of communication.

For all these commonsensical reasons, authors' statements of their intentions, whether made before or after they have sent their final revisions to the printer, are inadmissable as evidence of the meaning of what they have written. Thus the "intention" in a literary work is precisely limited to what is presented in the work, directly or indirectly – an author's intentions as reported outside the text are irrelevant (they may of course give clues about what to look for, but there is no guarantee that the presumed intention has been effectively expressed). That is the argument Wimsatt and Beardsley later said they had made. But their essay has proved a prime exemplification of the argument against the extra-textually announced intentions that it sets forth. Although some readers have evidently understood quite clearly the point Wimsatt and Beardsley have said they intended to make (and which ordinarily careful reading will find there), the essay is not so explicit as it might have been. Many readers have taken the essay as a dismissal of the relevance or possibility of discovering authorially intended meaning. The tendency to so read the essay was no doubt reinforced by other New Critics' statements dismissing biographical and other "extrinsic" modes of approaching a text. Nevertheless, the New Critics tacitly took the general context into consideration. Donne's sonnets were understood against the background of the science of the time, Wordsworth's poems were seen against that of increasing urbanization, George Eliot's novels were read against that of the growing debate over the degree of human control of life's choices. Although something of the kind is often said, it is simply not true that New Critics "produced a cultural artifact, the 'autotelic' or 'autonomous' literary text that they defined as utterly separate from the surrounding environment."[3] In any case, once the phrase "intentional fallacy" had got into circulation, the capaciousness of the general notion of intention almost inevitably led to misunderstanding. The result was that the majority of an entire generation of academically trained readers, many of them having taken assiduous notes in graduate school on "The Intentional Fallacy" without ever having carefully read the essay itself, tried as hard as possible to avoid all reference to authorial intention.

Once this curious mode of thinking about literature was widely accepted, it is not surprising that the structuralist statement that language speaks, not the individual human, seemed less absurd than it would otherwise have done. The author banished, the text could be spoken of as an active agency, as in "The poem juxtaposes two major images . . ." or "The text's reflexive structure leads us to confront the basic question it poses . . ." Actually such phrasing proves more cosmetic than substantive: one suspects that everyone except the most ideologically committed hermeticist silently translates "poem" into the name of the poet (Wordsworth, or Tennyson, or Eliot) and "structure of the text" into authorial design (Sterne's or Melville's or Graham Greene's).

E. D. Hirsch's *Validity in Interpretation*, originally written as a challenge to confused New Critical ideas about authorial intention, was published just in time to become a challenge to structuralist anti-intentionalism as well. His distinction between meaning and significance and his careful definition of intention served well as a clarification of the Wimsatt-Beardsley argument and a challenge to the structuralists, but it was almost immediately opposed by the rising interest in the role of the reader, which was (somewhat oddly) considered to be reinforced by deconstructive arguments[4] and politically oriented theories that regard the idea of authorially intended meaning as an imposition on readers' freedom. These are transparently captious objections. First, the reader can obviously be said to make the text's meaning in that the meaning must be constructed, a process that depends on the reader's knowledge of the possible senses of the words encountered, the syntactical rules of the language, and the total context that makes it possible to decide upon the senses of individual words (signifiers are often linked to more than one signified), the relation of each sentence to those preceding it, and whatever general information and cultural attitudes the author assumed the reader could supply. But an author necessarily takes the intended reader's knowledge into account (as far as it can be known or assumed) in order to guide the reader in reconstructing the intended meaning.[5] The deconstructionists' challenge is once again based on the confusion of words regarded as lexical items and words employed in discourse. The author does not send forth naked words but words clothed in contexts. The reader can of course choose to ignore the internal context, disregard the external background, dismiss syntactical conventions, and give private senses to the individual words. But no reader does this in a wholesale way – in practice a reader who consciously or unconsciously ignores authorial meaning does so with high selectivity: a small group of words, a small portion of the background, a small portion of the cotext is explored or metamorphosed. Second, the sufficient answer to those who deny intentional meaning in the name of freedom of individual response is that it is the intended meaning – or what we believe to be the intended meaning, to which the individual responds. Such meaning is not imposed; we construct it in order to respond, whether by challenge, acceptance, or modification. It is in fact doubtful that anyone has ever in practice abandoned the belief that Richard Levin nevertheless felt forced to repeat as a fundamental principle in his 1979 *New Readings vs. Old Plays*: "that the dramatist [one may interpolate, poet, novelist, or essayist] wanted to be understood" (*NRvOP*, 202). Hermeticists often seem to presume that the reconstruction of an author's meaning is so pervasive (even if often covert) in literary commentary because readers are still the dupes of a pernicious metaphysics, or humanistic pieties, or capitalist-sponsored illusions of the autonomy of the individual. Certainly interpretation of authorial intention has continued heavily to influence, if not dominate, criticism of individual texts in the teeth of hermeticist principles. Every reader of contemporary books and essays on literature recognizes that a majority of these, dressed up as they may be in the trappings of current theories and plentifully garnished with trendy terms, are at core old-fashioned New Critical interpretations of authorially intended meanings. It can hardly be otherwise so long as no one doubts that, in practice, speech and writing result from individual experienced intentions.

Interestingly, in his 1992 essays in *Interpretation and Overinterpretation*, Umberto Eco develops – in the learned historical manner one expects from him – almost precisely the New Critical position Wimsatt and Beardsley had attempted to state in "The Intentional Fallacy" and that E. D. Hirsch set forth in *Validity in Interpretation*. Only the phrasing is different as Eco seeks to define the limits of reasonable interpretation; regarding "the intention of author" as referring to the unknown intentions with which the author sat down to write, Eco chooses to speak of "the intention of the text."

LIMITS OF THE INTERPRETATION OF A TEXT

Two clarifications of the limits of interpretation of authorial intention are necessary. First, one of the real oddities of contemporary literary commentary is that critics and theorists have focused on the difficulties their version of Saussurian linguistics creates in the interpretation of individual words (primarily) or single sentences (sometimes) rather than the difficulties of interpreting the meaning of the text as a whole. Now it might seem that this is reasonable enough; after all one can't be said to understand the whole if one can't understand the units making it up. However, where the hermeticist's difficulties with the meaning of individual words and sentences are almost wholly artificial, the difficulty of grasping the meaning of a text as a whole is undeniable. Indeed, when we speak of the meaning of a text, even though we still have authorially intended meaning in mind, we are using the word rather differently than when we speak of the meaning of a word or sentence. The narrative action of a novel or a play is for the most part so easily understood that we don't think of the process of understanding the story of, say, Fielding's *Tom Jones*, Austen's *Pride and Prejudice*, Wilde's *The Importance of Being Earnest*, Hemingway's *For Whom the Bell Tolls*, or Arthur Miller's *The Death of a Salesman* as interpreting, though the process is, in each case, an extremely complicated one. However, the next step, from understanding the dialogue and narrated actions to adequately grasping and stating the perlocutionary intention of the total work, is a large one. It is more difficult to be confident of or adequately express the perlocutionary intention even of an individual sentence than its proposition or illocutionary force, and much more difficult to express the intended effect of an extended text. As applied to a total work, a better term than intended or perlocutionary effect may be "theme," so long as the word is taken in the particular sense that is sometimes expressed as "central idea," "informative vision," or "summative meaning," (the latter seems to me especially apt).

Different as they are, once one is beyond the generic descriptions of Wilde's play as a witty comedy and Miller's as a contemporary form of tragedy, their themes or summative meanings are not so easy to state. The difference in the effect of Hemingway's novel and Miller's play, both of which fall into the broad category of tragedy, is even more difficult. The greater number of contentions over meanings have in fact to do with the specification of intended effects of the text as a whole, of themes. The difficulty of course varies enormously: *The Comedy of Errors* lies toward one end of the scale, *Measure for Measure* the other. Plays are perhaps the most difficult to interpret summatively because the dialogue and stage directions are less definitive than the narration of a novel or the argument of a lyric. Thus in performance *Measure for Measure* can vary from light to dark comedy.

What happens as one reads, of course, is that every sentence becomes part of the context of each later sentence just as each preceding sentence was part of the context in which that sentence must be understood. Every statement of the lyric poet, every narrated action or event together with every bit of dialogue in the novel, every action that occurs as well as every speech uttered on the stage becomes part of the context for everything that follows. That may well seem so obvious that one need not say it, but it is the reason that the reading of each sentence has both a temporal and a spatial dimension: each sentence is interpreted in terms of the contextual pattern produced to that point while it alters that pattern if only in the slightest degree. But since each sentence (for "sentence" one can also read image, figure, event, action, narrator's statement, bit of dialogue) is only part of the total pattern, summing up the meaning of the whole without being reductive is difficult – or more accurately, impossible. To take a typical example, Gaskell's *North and South* ends with what, out of its context, is simply a slightly understated romantic ending. Mr. Thornton has taken some withered roses from his pocketbook and shown them to the novel's heroine, Margaret.

"They are from Helstone, are they not? I know the deep indentations round the leaves. Oh, have you been there? When were you there?"

"I wanted to see the place where Margaret grew to what she is, even at the worst time of all, when I had no hope of ever calling her mine. I went there on my return from Havre."

"You must give them to me," she said, trying to take them out of his hand with gentle violence.

"Very well. Only you must pay me for them!"

"How shall I ever tell Aunt Shaw?" she whispered, after some time of delicious silence.

"Let me speak to her."

"Oh, no! I owe to her – but what will she say?"

"I can guess. Her first exclamation will be, 'That man!'"

"Hush!" said Margaret, "or I shall try and show you your mother's indignant tones as she says, 'That woman!'"

But of course the scene is freighted with the hundreds of pages preceding it so that the reader is aware that Margaret now recognizes the positive values of the industrial north and Thornton the values of a larger human sympathy, of the less driving South. The class snobbery that denies the manufacturer a place among gentlemen has been anatomized. The possibility that a balance can be struck between justice and kindness, energy and thoughtfulness, the rights of the master and the rights of the workers is at least suggested. The danger of too quickly judging others has been shown and, in this instance, the error has been overcome. The meaning of the novel encompasses all this and more – the total pattern is so rich that to adequately develop one of these points is almost certainly to slight others.

Richard Levin's chapter "Thematic Reading" in *New Readings vs. Old Plays* saliently and wittily states the danger of the search for a single master theme of a literary work. One of his most cogent arguments is that in seeking as inclusive a statement of *the* theme as possible, "it is not at all clear where or why we should stop. If 'folly' is more central to *Volpone* than 'avarice' because it includes 'avarice' ... then the theme of 'mankind' should be even more central because it includes 'folly,' and so on up the ladder, or the Platonic divided line, to something like 'Being' ..." (*NRvOP*, 37).

The terminology of speech-act theory can be applied to the whole of a text, then, only by loose analogy and with careful realization that the interpretation of a complete text, whether sonnet or long novel, has different limits than the interpretation of a sentence. The action of a narrative and the structure of an argument are, like the proposition of a sentence, usually accessible. Hamlet does die from a poisoned rapier, James's Isabel Archer does return to Gilbert Osmond, and Wilde's Gwendolyn and Jack do marry. What the speaker means in Shakespeare's sonnet 55 ("Not marble nor the gilded monuments") is hardly in doubt: he is saying that his poetry in praise of the person to whom it is addressed will outlast all material monuments. What more or less corresponds to the illocutionary force of a text, a specification of its kind (its genre in the loose sense of that term), is more difficult, but we generally feel that we understand it. Just as speech-act theory categorizes one sentence as a protest, another as a description, another as a plea, we may understand a particular poem as a political satire, a particular play as a domestic tragedy, a particular novel as a historical romance. Sonnet 55 is an example of the species of love poem in which the lover specifically identifies himself as a poet. But what corresponds to the recognition of perlocutionary intent, the total effect that the author presumed the work would produce in the reader, is, as I have tried to suggest, made up of so many currents that no definitive interpretation can be given. Is the emphasis on the power of poetry or the especial desirability of the poet as a lover, or the qualities in the individual praised that have inspired the poet to create so lasting a monument, or this particular poet's celebration of his own powers?

On the other hand, the effects that can validly be attributed to authorial intention are bounded by each text. A Marxist can find much in *North and South* with which to support the argument that even the best-intentioned capitalist brutalizes the workers; a feminist can fault Margaret for tacitly subordinating herself to Mr. Thornton; the relations between Thornton and his mother, and between the mother and the daughter who is her only other child offer a good deal to the Freudian or Lacanian. Yet all such readings are produced by imposed schemes of analysis; they produce symptomatic meanings, not intentional ones. More directly, although almost any kind of critical argument is conceivable, we know that Hamlet's death is not intended to inspire laughter, that Isabel Archer's decision is meant to be controversial, that we are not to mourn the union of Wilde's Jack and Gwendolyn.

Another fertile source of confusion arises out of the ambiguity in the term intention that results from failure to discriminate between intention to communicate and intention to accomplish something by the communication – one may or may not (often not) wish to communicate the latter. An obvious corollary of the principles of interpretation set forth above is that since a text can communicate only what its structure of sentences as interpreted in the light of the principle of contextual assumptions makes possible, a reader cannot penetrate behind the meaning thus expressed to determine why the author chose to express that meaning for some more ultimate purpose. The purpose of Shakespeare's sonnet 55 is debatable: was the poet merely playing a variation on a convention to show how well he could do it? Was the sonnet part of a series meant to call forth the love of a particular person? Was it using the convention of the love sonnet to state something the poet really believed about the nature of poetry? We cannot know, for all such questions ask not meanings but more distant purposes. Was Florence Dombey's character created as one more tribute by Dickens to his lost sister-in-law Mary Hogarth, or simply as the most effective foil to Mr. Dombey, or as the kind of young woman he thought sentimental readers would like (thus increasing his sales)? We cannot know from the text.

Of course authors frequently take advantage of the impossibility of one character's being sure of the purpose of another's utterance to produce dramatic irony as in the well-known scene from Rostand's *Cyrano de Bergerac* in which Cyrano, hidden in the darkness under Roxane's balcony, pretends to be Christian and woos her in words beyond what the unfortunate Christian can command. Roxane, Christian, and the audience all understand the illocutionary force of Cyrano's words; Roxane thinks she understands the perlocutionary intent of Cyrano's words and is right insofar as she thinks the intention is to make her fall in love with Christian but partly wrong (and partly right) to the extent that she thinks the intention is to make her fall in love with the person who actually utters the words; and as for Cyrano's ultimate purpose, the audience assumes that Cyrano does what he does both for the pleasure of saying to Roxane what he wishes he could say *in propria persona* and because of his quixotic loyalty to Christian, but that the exact mixture of motives cannot be explained adds piquancy. As for Rostand's purpose in creating the scene, the perlocutionary effect, and with high probability, the perlocutionary intent is a sentimental irony, but his purpose in creating that effect must be wholly conjectural – and would of course remain so even if Rostand had given a sworn statement of his purpose.

There are several converging ways to regard the difference between authorial intention and the ultimate purpose. The concept of the "implied author" was developed partly to draw this distinction: the "personality" or general attitude of the implied author is of course a product of the text behind which stands the real author whose purposes may not be at all part of the intended meaning. If, let us say, a novel was written with the ultimate purpose of earning money, or of expressing a strongly held vision of the world, or of attempting to exorcise a psychological problem, such a purpose may well not be expressed in the text itself. It is not part of the reader's construction of the implied author, not part of the text's *meaning*, even at the outer limit of the theme. If, on the basis of one's own way of regarding the world or through private knowledge (that is, knowledge of details of the author's life which the author would not have assumed his or her anticipated readers would have), one wishes to argue that one of these was the ultimate purpose (conscious or unconscious) of writing the text, one has entered the realm of significances. That the author may have more than one purpose, and that these purposes may be clear, vague, or largely unconscious complicates the matter further. The purpose(s) even of a sentence with what seems obvious perlocutionary intent may not be apparent. "Get off the grass" has the illocutionary force of a demand or command (depending on the authority of the utterer) and can be presumed to be intended to get someone to move off the grass. But it could be that the utterer's purpose is to pick a fight in which he can show off his physical prowess to a woman he wants to impress in order to get her to marry him in order to gain access to her money. Similarly a book could be written with the purpose of gaining a reputation that would be useful in running for political office in order to champion a cause that has nothing to do with the book. Even if an author specifically includes in the text a statement of what he or she wishes to accomplish through the text, there may well be a reason for not wishing to communicate the reason for wishing to express what the text expresses.

Nevertheless, although the processes of interpretation by which the meaning of a text is interpreted cannot discover the ultimate purpose that motivated the author to write the text, to argue that the meaning of texts is indeterminate because one cannot know the author's ultimate purpose or motivation is, I repeat, to confound intention and purpose.

CONTEXTUALITY AND THE POSSIBILITY OF INTERPRETATION

"BUT," one hears the hermeticist cry, "your out-dated common-sensicality takes no heed of all that has been discovered in the last twenty-five years: the polysemy of individual words, the figural possibilities lurking in every expression, the manifold chances of indirection, the intertexuality that inhabits every utterance. Language is not like money. If you wish to pay someone $17.36, you simply count out the correct denominations of bills and coins. That is not the way language works."

Indeed it is not. Nevertheless, although the calculation required by the recipient of the utterance is a good deal more complicated, it is hardly impossible or we would have no language with which to talk about language. If when Ik thought he had conveyed something like "Look out for the sabre-toothed tiger!" the Uk or Ok to whom he spoke thought he intended something like "Aren't sabre-toothed tigers handsome?" or "There are no such things as sabre-toothed tigers," the language project would never have got off the ground.

Perhaps the best way to approach the question of how the interpretation of meaning is possible is by translating "polysemy" and "figurality" into operational questions. How do we know which sense of a word with several distinct senses is intended? Is a particular instance of the word "root" to be understood as botanical, metaphorical, or mathematical? How are we to interpret the tone, the illocutionary force of a given sentence or sequence of sentences? How does the freshman who has never read Shakespeare before know that Antony's "For Brutus is an honorable man?" is ironic? How do we interpret allusions – either literary/cultural ("Jim tricked Bill as easily as Iago misled Othello") or contemporary ("Fred had the same regard for Steve as Bush for Perot")? How is it that to describe a person as a political candidate immediately associates that person with an immense number of necessary, likely, and possible past, present, and future actions? In each case the answer requires no abstruse linguistic theorizing: it is "by context," the immediate context, the situational context, the cultural context, and the overall context of general background knowledge.

As vital as is the context in the interpretation of language-in-use, few dictionaries of literary terms have included an entry on the word, and perhaps few who might wish to query its meaning would think of going to a specifically literary rather than a conventional dictionary. Indeed, the word is so common, and its most general sense seems so easy to grasp, that comparatively few readers have ever felt the need to look it up. Although context has figured in hermeneutic theory in an abstract way from the time of Schleiermacher, the problem seemed for a long time to be essentially that of the recovery of meanings obscured by the passage of time (the difficulties of which were increasingly foregrounded from Dilthey to Gadamer). The sheer question of how one mind responds to discourse formulated by another – that is, how a mind limits multiple possible lexical meanings and recognizes implications through the construction of context – was not directly considered. Nor does the question really figure among the problems addressed by the founders of modern semiotic theory. It is not one of Saussure's topics in the *Cours* despite his explicit differentiation between *langue* and *parole*. Although almost anything can be found somewhere in the writings of C. S. Peirce, I don't remember encountering it there, and the editors of the 8-volume Harvard edition of his work have not entered it into the index. (However, its necessity for the understanding of any use of signs is evident from Peirce's brief discussion of "collateral observations," 8.179). The primary quarry of both Saussure and Peirce is the individual sign, not the sign-in-action. Even Ogden and Richards, who give considerable attention to how language is used, have little directly to say about the relation of context to the interpretation of *parole*, although it enters through the back door in the famous supplement by Bronislaw Malinowski, "The Problem of Meaning in Primitive Language."[6]

Where linguists long tried to equate meaning with semantics and syntactics alone, Charles Morris's distinction between semantics, syntactics, and pragmatics (*Foundations of the Theory of Signs*, 1938) was already looking a bit more fully into the no-man's-land of discourse that had been shunned. Wittgenstein's concept of language-games as it is presented in the 1953 *Philosophical Investigations* can be understood as an argument for the essentiality of context: each instance of language use participates in a particular language-game, the game, which depends on and produces the context, does not merely add or modify a core meaning: it produces meaning. (However, although Wittgenstein's example of the family relationship between games lends intelligibility to his concept of the language-game, the phrase itself misleads if "game" is taken trivially.) Close analysis of the pragmatics of language began at something like that point – that is, by asking how single spoken sentences are understood. By 1961 in the essay "The Symbolic Structure of Interpersonal Process," Walker Percy was beginning to argue that Peirce was right in giving attention not merely to the sign, concept, and object represented in the sign, but to the user of the sign. He went on to regard the "intersubjective relationship" between the person initiating the utterance and the person interpreting it (the "contextual assumption" in my terms) as having the capacity to create a relationship of "quasi-identity" between the sign and the object.

J. L. Austin's 1955 lectures *How to Do Things with Words*, which not only founded speech-act theory but fully recognized the importance of context, saw print in 1962. As late as 1975, Walker Percy was still able to point out how rarely the mystery of discourse had been addressed, how rarely the innocent-sounding question had been asked: "What happens when people talk, when one person names something or says a sentence about something and another person understands him?" (DF, 14) In that same year, almost a decade after Jacques Derrida set out to render meaning meaningless, H. P. Grice more or less sidled into giving additional emphasis to the role of context in addressing the question of how indirectly expressed meanings are understood. Only in the 1980s does the analysis of discourse get strongly under way; by 1983 Robert Longacre can write as the first sentence of the Introduction to *The Grammar of Discourse*, "As a book on discourse, this volume is dedicated to the thesis that language is language only in context" (xv).

Thus the answer to the question hardly anyone had thought it worthwhile to ask directly until the second half of this century began to be spelled out just about the same time that the impossibility of determining meaning began to be asserted. A full understanding of what is necessary beyond syntactical and lexical knowledge has come only with the efforts of speech-act theorists, discourse analysts, semioticians, and sociolinguists. All have contributed to the investigation of how it is possible for a meaning to be transmitted across the ever-expanding plains of *différance*, around the moats of aporia, and through the barbed wire of indeterminacy postulated by the poststructuralists. Determinable meaning is possible because the author assumes that the reader has certain information, beliefs, and attitudes; the reader assumes that the author has constructed his or her text in accordance with this assumption; and the author assumes that the reader will assume that such is the basis of the construction of the text.

Every time we say or write a sentence, we take into consideration our previous sentence (if any), as far as we can the entire sequence of the sentences making up the particular utterance or text, what we assume to be general knowledge, and what we assume the particular individuals addressed know or don't know, believe or don't believe, feel or don't feel. Each sentence we hear or read is interpreted in terms of the text, dialogue, or many-sided conversation that preceded it and our assumptions about what the author assumed the anticipated audience would know, believe, and feel together with the assumption that the author assumed the audience would assume that the author had made such an assumption. These are the two sides of the communicative contract.

One recalls that in 1941 Kenneth Burke opened *The Philosophy of Literary Form* with the following paragraph:

> Let us suppose that I ask you: "What did the man say?" And that you answer: "He said 'yes.'" You still do not know what the man said. You would not know unless you knew more about the situation, and about the remarks that preceded his answer. (1)

The role of context can be stated more exactly in speech-act terms. In the absence of any context even the proposition resulting from a particular locution may be in doubt. "In 1945, Franklin D. Roosevelt was president of the United States" is a proposition in which the reference is so clear that no context is needed, whereas "The lions are red" has only a broad range of possible propositional meanings (one would probably guess that heraldic or decorative lions are being referred to, but one couldn't be sure). The propositional meaning of Burke's "yes" is even more context-dependent since it implies an unstated proposition which could be, among many other possibilities, "Yes, it is true," or "Yes, I will go," or "Yes, she did it." The illocutionary force of a contextless utterance will in most cases be more difficult, often impossible, to conjecture and there is no point in speaking of the perlocutionary intent of that which is without context.

G. K. Chesterton has his hero Father Brown make a version of this point in the story "The Invisible Man."

> "Have you ever noticed this – that people never answer what you say? They answer what you mean – or what they think you mean. Suppose one lady says to another in a country house, 'Is anybody staying with you?' the lady doesn't answer 'yes; the butler, the three footmen, the parlour-maid, and so on,' though the parlour-maid may be in the room, or the butler behind her chair. She says: 'There is *nobody* staying with us,' meaning nobody of the sort you mean. But suppose a doctor inquiring into an epidemic asks, 'Who is staying in the house?' then the lady will remember the butler, the parlour-maid, and the rest. All language is used like that; you never get a question answered literally, even when you get it answered truly." (92)

Umberto Eco provides a recent version:

> [w]hen a text is produced not for a single addressee but for a
> community of readers – the author knows that he or she will be
> interpreted not according to his or her intentions but according to
> a complex strategy of interaction which also involves the readers,
> along with their competence in language as a social treasury. I
> mean by social treasury . . . the cultural conventions that language
> has produced . . . (67–8)

I think that felicitously said, so long as one keeps in mind that the
author's intentions rejected by Eco are not those actually operative
ones in the text that have been produced by anticipating readers'
strategies and thus guiding them as far as possible.

The basic practical principle for finding the intended meaning,
then, is obvious: one must know as much as possible of the expectations, beliefs, assumptions, prejudices, knowledge, and current
interests the author could have assumed he/she either shared with
or could attribute to the intended reader.[7] Since the interpretation
of meaning depends on the reconstruction of presumed background,
it can never be certain. All that one can definitely rule out are
suggested meanings that are dependent on contextual assumptions
that the author could not have made.[8] Thus, to return for a moment to the author's life, only that portion of his or her life that the
author could assume readers would have known about at the time
of publication are part of the context that governs interpretation. If
one accepts the currently prevalent view that our concepts are the
products of our language and our culture, all one need recognize is
that in communicating a particular meaning, we explicitly organize
only certain of the relevant concepts and rely on shared concepts
and attitudes to fill in the rest. "The world looks a lot better to me
today" can mean "I just got a good job," or "Clinton was elected
president," or "The stock market rose steeply," or "I won't have to
have surgery after all," or "It has finally stopped raining." No one
would have difficulty stating the circumstances under which each
of the meanings would be conveyed by the same nine words. Of
course there are misunderstandings, but these comparatively rare
occurrences (and they *are* rare in comparison to the number of times
that we feel we have been adequately understood and others indicate in one way or another that we seem to have adequately understood them) are almost always caused by a miscalculation of the

relevant local context. Usually they are noticed in the course of the discourse itself as a participant finds it impossible to fit one or more utterances into what he or she has presumed to be the relevant set of contexts. In clearing up such confusions, "I meant that . . . " usually amounts to "I assumed that the context was . . . "

It is primarily the context that determines whether a word is to be interpreted literally or figuratively. The assertion that there is no literal use of language, is, like many another such assertion dear to the hermeticists, true in one sense and false in another. (J. Hillis Miller's version of the deconstructive argument – which largely chimes with that of Paul de Man – is built primarily around the repeated assertion that meaning oscillates between literal and figurative possibilities.)[9] That language is heavily figurative is true in two ways: many present senses of words were originally figurative, and perhaps most have the potential for figurative use. On the other hand, most discourse can be said to be literal in the sense that what is grasped is a single intended meaning constructed employing words used in their generally understood sense, or, to use speech-act terms, a proposition with a single, direct, specific illocutionary force. (One could not speak of a word as having figurative uses if it did not have at least one literal sense.) Although words can be used either literally (in senses no longer recognized as figurative however they may have been derived) or figuratively (where the deviation from usual senses is noticeable), the existence of divergent possibilities does not produce an undecidable ambiguity. That a word that might be used figuratively is not so used in a specific instance no more interferes with the interpretation of intended meaning, given the appropriate background assumptions, than the unexpectedly figurative use of a word.

This is the case even though some of the senses that are understood as a result of the context have been figuratively derived over time. "I'm going to a concert this evening" will, in most contexts (certainly in those which first come to mind) be interpreted as "I am planning to go to a place where music will be played this evening – and will go unless something unforeseen happens." "Concert" as applied to musical performance is derived from "agreement," a sense still recognized in phrases like "acting in concert." However, except in such special formulas, a speaker cannot expect it to function in that now largely disused sense unless the person(s) addressed are alert to that possibility. If, as is just possible, a man were to say "I am going to a concert this evening" with the intended meaning that he was attending the signing of a contract, he would either be addressing someone who was familiar with the possibility of that particular play on words (an in-house lawyer's joke, perhaps) or intending to mystify, intending to be misunderstood. Again, the sentence might be used to mean, "I am going for a walk on which I expect to hear birds singing and crickets chirping." If and only if used *in the proper context* such an interpretation of the intended meaning would be quite possible.

The communicative success of a text then depends on the author's or utterer's strategic use of what he or she assumes to be the knowledge, beliefs, attitudes, and expectations of the anticipated readers. Whatever an author wishes to communicate that lies outside that territory must be translated into that which lies within. Key words evoke much of the background against which all reading proceeds: the reader holds in readiness one cluster of information if a fictional character sets off to go to a circus, a different cluster if he or she sets off for the opera house. Other background information may be evoked by allusion – thus the reference to Saint Theresa in the page and a half Prelude to *Middlemarch* summons up and reinforces the reader's assumed knowledge of the rarity of historically significant achievement. The reader's background knowledge can also of course be directly supplemented – although Eliot's brief comments on Saint Theresa are framed as though she and the reader share considerable knowledge of the Saint, they contrive to give the reader pretty well all the information needed for Eliot's purposes. If unfamiliar information is to be presented to the reader, it can be worked in so smoothly as to be unnoticed. A simple example of the provision of a bit of inessential but helpful information occurs in Helen Forrester's 1981 autobiographical account of the life of an impoverished family in Liverpool in the 1930s. At one point the mother makes the discovery that sometimes money has been left in a public telephone. Until some time in the 1970s a person using an English public telephone had to push a button marked 'B' to get the coins back if the call was not completed, an action easy to forget. Many older English readers would perfectly understand a quick reference to punching button 'B,' but younger readers would not. Forrester's solution is simple: she quotes the instructions that the mother reads on the telephone. "Insert two pennies. When the telephone is answered press button A. If no reply, press button B for the return of the twopence." Or again, in *Barchester Towers*, during the discussion of Mr. Slope's insulting sermon, the dean would certainly not need Dr. Grantly to tell him that he has the power to refuse the pulpit of Mr. Slope; Grantly's doing so is at least as much for the reader who may not know much about the governance of a cathedral as it is a contribution to discussion with the dean. A more complicated example is Dickens's handling of the Doctors' Commons he wishes to satirize in *David Copperfield*; Steerforth's description of the Commons in Chapter 23 followed by the narrator's summation of Mr. Spenlow's observations in Chapter 26 contrive to give a tolerable explanation of the nature of the business conducted there even to the reader who has never heard of that branch of the English legal system. If yet more extensive background information seems necessary, this can be quite explicitly supplied – John Fowles indeed makes a virtue of the narrator's explanation of Victorian culture in *The French Lieutenant's Woman*.

An author can even convey an orienting perspective which, if it seems plausible enough, will be at least tentatively adopted by the reader as though it came from his or her own background of experience. Kipling relied a great deal on this technique, as in the opening to "Thrown Away."

> To rear a boy under what parents call the "sheltered life system" is, if the boy must go into the world and fend for himself, not wise. Unless he be one in a thousand he has certainly to pass through many unnecessary troubles; and may, possibly, come to extreme grief simply from ignorance of the proper proportions of things.

As already noted, none of the oddities of the history of literary commentary is more curious than the almost simultaneous development of hermetic modes of analyzing texts on the one hand and the renewed hermeneutic emphasis on pragmatics, the analysis of the interaction of text and context on the other. It is hardly possible to argue that either one was a reaction to the other, although both grew out of linguistics. The anomalies, ambiguities, and confusions in which hermeticists find delight are from the point of view of students of the pragmatic dimension of language just those which result from the failure to include the context in one's interpretive model. This, as I have already had several occasions to note, is the same as remaining within the realm of *langue* in order to deny intentional, or what A. D. Nuttall calls "operative," meaning. "When semantic meaning and syntax (*langue*) are actually used in a concrete situation (*parole*) a further kind of *meaning* emerges, and this is the kind I will call 'operative.' Operative meaning is governed not only by the conventions employed but also by the objective context in which it occurs" (48).

HOW MUCH CONTEXT?

None of Jacques Derrida's pronouncements has been more widely cited, and apparently accepted, than his denial of the possibility of determining what context is relevant. Derrida has been willing enough to admit that the interpretation of meaning depends on context – his point, echoed by Jonathan Culler, Miller and many others, is that context is "never absolutely determinable, or rather . . . its determination can never be entirely certain or saturated" (SEC, 174). Culler's way of putting this is that "Context is just more text, just as much in need of interpretation and in fact constituted by the same sort of inimical forces that produce the possible ambiguities it is being called on to resolve." Moreover, "while meaning is context-bound, context is boundless" (*FS*, 147–8; see also *OD*, 123). So it is, but the contexts that an author could possibly have assumed have definite bounds, and the contexts that an author was most likely to have assumed are hardly beyond reasonable conjecture. ("Assumed" is here meant to include both consciously calculated and almost automatic assumptions – we do not run through a mental inventory of all the knowledge and beliefs of each person to whom we speak or write even though we adjust what we say or write to each individual we address.)

J. Hillis Miller seems simply to misunderstand the whole issue of context. Replying to M. H. Abrams' criticism of his "On Edge," he writes as follows.

On the question of context: Abrams assumes that there is a solid context for the reading of detached texts, such as a short lyric poem like "A Slumber Did My Spirit Seal," in the grammatical competence of any reader or speaker of the language in which it was written. Derrida knows French, therefore he can read Rousseau, just as any other Frenchman can. I know English, so what's my problem with "A Slumber Did My Spirit Seal"? If Derrida and I are right, and we are, the enigma introduced into even the most apparently simple passage by its permeation or perversion by figurative language, one of the effects of this is to make each piece of language idiosyncratic, idiomatic, the generator of an idolect [*sic*] of its own. (OE, 190)

It is hard in such cases to know whether someone is deliberately misunderstanding in order to make a debater's point or so committed to a certain point of view that nothing foreign to that view permeates, but to assume that knowledge of the language constitutes the whole of the context of an instance of the use of that language – ignoring background information, the immediate situation of use, and the cotext – seems a willful obfuscation. To assume that the meaning of *parole*, language-in-use-in-a-context, is necessarily at the mercy of the figurative readings that could be assigned to the words that constitute it if they were considered in isolation is one more egregious confusion of language and utterance. Figurative senses exist only by virtue of context ("John is a fox" is not a metaphor if John is the name of a fox).

If I say "Miller pulls off these tricks with string and sealing wax, false bottoms and sleight of hand," the statement will not be taken as figurative if I'm referring to an amateur magician, though it will be if the context makes it clear that I am referring to J. H. Miller the critical theorist. Once again, *of course* one can choose to give a figurative or contextually alien sense to any word. In themselves, the words "A slumber did my spirit seal" could mean that a god of sleep poured wax over the cork in the whiskey bottle, or to take a less exaggerated example, it could mean that the persona in the poem, speaking from beyond the grave, has himself succumbed to death, which has sealed his spirit from participation in life – a reading that fits quite well with the poem's second line. However, the poem as a whole, the cotext in which the line appears, forbids such an interpretation – at least, fortunately, forbids it to most of us.

The central problem that most critics have felt in interpreting this poem, which has become a standard example of critical controversy, arises from the apparent inconsistency between Wordsworth's usual views and the last two lines of the poem:

> Rolled round in earth's diurnal course,
> With rocks, and stones, and trees.

However, if the poem is considered in terms of its propositional structure and the knowledge of the language and cultural background appropriate to the reader in 1788 or 1789 when the poem was written, no difficulty of interpretation arises. It is only if the poem is read against the background of Wordsworth's reputation as the proclaimer of the healing forces of nature that the question arises. Now one is of course perfectly free to read the poem symptomatically, either as casting light on aspects of Wordsworth's life or as something to be explained by his life and total oeuvre, but such a reading abandons the principles governing the pursuit of authorial meaning.

One may well suspect that Derrida dismisses intention because its interpretation requires the appropriate context, and dismisses the possibility of reconstructing the appropriate context because to do so would allow the interpretation of intentional meaning. But how *does* one define how much of the context is relevant? The succinct answer is, "all and only that which is necessary to satisfy the reader as to the intended meaning." An impossibly vague answer for a philosopher of language, but a quite practically exact answer nevertheless. What lies behind it, again, is the constant assumption that the speaker or writer intends to be understood and, in the process of formulating the bit of discourse in question, will have taken reasonable precautions to insure that it will be understood.

Perhaps the first reaction by an experienced reader to a puzzling passage is to guess that the author expected something to be in the reader's background knowledge and beliefs that just isn't there. Explicit but unfamiliar allusions obviously alert one. Where there is no specific guide to what one needs to know to solve the puzzle, the problem can be difficult, and obviously the older and more alien the text, the greater becomes the task of conscientious reading and the more welcome become editorial glosses. Of course one may fail to be puzzled where one should be, or fail to recognize that a violation of the Cooperative Principle or shared background is intended to express meaning indirectly. Hans-Georg Gadamer's argument that the past context or "horizon" cannot be fully known, and that therefore what is achieved can never be more than a fusion of present and past horizons, is pretty much self-evident: one can never know what differences in the cultural context are going unrecognized – if one knew, they would not be unrecognized. The only defense is to know as much as possible about the total external context in which the text is produced. Such knowledge of what authors and their audiences shared is precisely what is to be gained from historical scholarship. Oddly, certain theorists write as though historical scholarship has to do only with extra-textual documents produced by the author – "letters, diaries, manuscripts" are the examples Knapp and Michaels cite in their well-known "Against Theory" (10) – rather than the background or "default" knowledge without awareness of which almost nothing can be communicated.

In "Is There a Text in This Class?" Stanley Fish, in his usual eloquent manner, has made the hermetic argument that there are no truly determinate meanings because all interpretation depends on context. This argument, which any speech-act theorist would endorse, then takes an odd turn. Because his eye is wholly on the reader, with conscious paradox Fish assures those who fear total indeterminacy and relativism that, although meaning varies with context, no one can be a relativist because everyone necessarily interprets within his or her own total context. In short, general indeterminacy and relativism are inescapable, but "since everyone is situated somewhere, there is no one for whom the absence of an asituational norm would be of any practical consequence" (ITTC, 319). But in terms of the interpretation of utterances, the situation is wholly altered if we recognize the basic communicative assumption that what we need to know to interpret intended meaning is the author/speaker's assumption of the context in which the utterance will be interpreted – and in the example around which Fish builds the essay "Is There a Text in This Class?" it is precisely by recovering the speaker's assumed context that his student's meaning is correctly interpreted. There could actually be no better illustration of the operation of the communicative assumption than Fish's example – it is just that in his delight in confounding those who insist on a *determinate* meaning in *all* circumstances (I doubt that any of those to whom he attributes this position actually do so), he forgets that he himself has established the means by which an intended meaning becomes *determinable*. Moreover, it is quite possible for us to believe that we have achieved the correct interpretation (that is, to think no other interpretation that may be proposed to us or that we may formulate is as likely as the one at which we have arrived), and at the same time to recognize that we cannot be totally certain of that interpretation.

Fish's argument is perhaps given an initial plausibility by another confusion, that between being able to determine the truth of what is said and being able to determine the intended meaning of what is said. Even if we assume that what is true, or beautiful, or good varies with the cultural context and therefore cannot be absolute, intended meaning does not so vary precisely because it is a function of the assumed context. There is a difference between recognizing the problems of reconstructing the context assumed by a speaker or writer and recognizing that judgments about what was expressed by what was uttered in that context will vary with the situation of the hearer or reader. The difference is once again between that of interpretation and judgments of significance.

Which leads one back to the problem of bridging disparate contexts, either across cultures or across historical periods. However much authors may wish to write for posterity, they can hardly have the prescience to forecast either who their readers will be or what those readers will know and believe. Obviously there was no way in which Addison, Pope, or Johnson could have taken account of twentieth-century cultural manners, beliefs and attitudes, nor twentieth-century readers know with anything like the certainty of readers of the time what contexts were assumed by an author writing in, say, 1750. Equally obviously, Chinese or German or Nigerian or English authors write primarily for – that is assume an audience sharing the cultural contexts peculiar to as well as more universal than – readers of their own linguistic and cultural background. In most cases a combination of cultural and historical difference exacerbates the problem. Nevertheless, the only assumption necessary to a reader is that the author in question did assume that readers of his or her time and culture would assume that the author assumed shared contexts. The conjectural reconstruction of contexts has always been one of the primary tasks of hermeneutics. The distinction between "alien" assumptions that call attention to themselves and those that do not is like that between marked and unmarked allusions. The impossibility of being certain that one has not overlooked important contextual knowledge does not imply the impossibility of reasonable reconstruction, which is all we ever have even in the interpretation of contemporary literature – or of ordinary conversation. As several times noted earlier, only if we demand absolutely full reconstruction of all contexts the writer assumed can we deny the likelihood of interpretation and only if we demand absolute certainty that our reconstruction is accurate can we deny the possibility of interpretation.

Those that deny that earlier contexts can be recovered often cite changes not in what is known but in what is generally believed in a culture. A classic example is *Paradise Lost*: Agnostics will never feel the same way about the poem as those holding something like the beliefs Milton assumed believing Christians would hold. However, they can understand that those beliefs were held. We can know what others believe without holding their beliefs. When Stanley Fish writes "Beliefs are not what you think *about* but what you think *with*," (C, 326)[10] he is right in that we are not always conscious of alternatives to what we believe, but wrong in the implication that we don't distinguish what we *believe* to be true from what we *know* to be true. The argument can easily become confused here, for while it is perfectly possible to argue that knowledge is nothing but belief, that what we think we know is only what we believe, we all make the belief/knowledge distinction in our own minds, and it is the possibility of making such distinctions that allows us to know that others believe things that we don't believe, and further allows us to distinguish between differences in knowledge and differences in belief. Fish is also in error in implying that we are not conscious of degrees of belief. That there is no difference between knowledge and belief is a position that can be maintained only under a certain absolutist definition of knowledge. But even those who believe that there is no ultimate difference between what we think is knowledge and what we think is belief will still distinguish between others' beliefs and their own beliefs, and that distinction allows us to employ beliefs that we do not share in interpretation. Obviously, reconstruction of probable knowledge, beliefs, and attitudes the author could have assumed will not recreate the emotional responses of those who had the knowledge or held beliefs or attitudes no longer current, but it can yield highly probable interpretations of authors' meanings.

Stanley Fish never tires of writing of the importance of cultural and situational context: "Linguistic knowledge is contextual rather than abstract, local rather than general, dynamic rather than invariant; every rule is a rule of thumb; every competence grammar is a performance grammar in disguise" (Con, 321). But it is always the present reader's set of beliefs that Fish makes operative, as though one could not know that the existence of four humours was widely believed in Elizabethan days (or that a poet couldn't have drawn upon the current knowledge that such a belief was widely held – and have done so even if the poet did not believe in the four humours and knew that many others of his time did not believe in them either). Once again we meet the same fallacy of the confusion between what we believe we know and what we believe we know others believe (or believed) but we know that we do not believe.

One of the peculiarities of human discourse that has led theorists so deeply into unilluminating labyrinths of theory is the at least superficial paradox that, for the most part, speakers and their hearers or writers and their readers understand each other so easily. No sophisticated theory of language is required for anyone who gives thought to the matter to recognize that most words have more than one sense, many things have more than one name, language can be used either in established senses such as may be found in a dictionary or figuratively and thus perhaps uniquely, many words can serve more than one syntactical function, much communication is indirect, and, above all, utterances and their interpretation depend on multi-element calculations. It is hardly surprising that so complex a process would elicit complex, perhaps even mystical explanatory theories, including hermetic denials of its very possibility. The fact that the processes of formulating and interpreting utterances cannot be precisely modelled or satisfactorily duplicated by the most sophisticated computer is, however, irrelevant to their successful functioning.

Suppose I say to my wife something as simple as "That fellow reminded me of Septimus" – a remark which I in fact recently made. In doing so I made a number of assumptions about what she would know and believe and thus assume I meant, including assumptions about what I was assuming. Put as simply as possible, I assumed:

(1) that she would recognize that since we don't know any actual person named Septimus, the remark was an allusion to some sort of representation of a person named Septimus that I was assuming she would remember;

(2) that since we had a few months before seen Tom Stoppard's *Arcadia*, in which one of the major characters is named Septimus, she would remember that an important character in the play had that name and would assume that I remembered the name as well;

(3) that since we seemed to have had similar responses to the play, our impressions of the character Septimus would not differ greatly; and therefore since Septimus seemed to her a likeable character, she would assume that I was not suggesting an adverse judgment (and would qualify my comment if I were).

(4) that she would recognize that the similarity might lie in the

appearance of the character, or the personality portrayed, or in certain actions.

(5) that since I hadn't named the similarity, I was assuming that it was reasonably obvious but thought it would be more interesting for her to work it out than for me to be explicit.

(6) that she would consider possible similarities and would be likely, though not certain, to fix on the one I had in mind.

And of course, prior to all this, I had assumed that we share the ordinary lexical and syntactical knowledge necessary for the communication of the proposition, that the immediate situation or conversation made it possible to identify the antecedent of "that fellow," and, indeed, that such a remark would have a minimal degree of interest. There are probably other assumptions of shared knowledge and belief behind such a remark, and the order in which the necessary assumptions would come to either my mind or hers, the degree to which she and I might be conscious of some of these, the almost instantaneous corrections I might have made in the process of uttering the sentence or she in interpreting it are incalculable – no algorithm could be constructed to describe how the mind processes even such a simple sentence. For one thing, there seems no reason that any particular sequence might be pursued. Nevertheless, such processes occur as each sentence is spoken, written, or interpreted, and the possibility of the communicative efficacy of language under such conditions is only a little less certain than that, despite Zeno, the hare can overtake the tortoise.

The point has been made that because one can never be certain that one has not overlooked relevant knowledge or beliefs that the author presumed would be part of the background against which the text would be read, interpretation can never reach further than probability. But the impossibility of being certain one is correct does not deny the possibility of being correct, nor does the difficulty of being absolutely correct deny that there can be degrees of correctness and that one can be so close to full correctness as makes no difference. Here again absolutism must be rejected. It is one of the curious characteristics of the hermeneutic approach that although it is always conjectural, always looking to probabilities, interpretation would be of little interest if there were not the possibility of being correct. It is impossible to imagine discourse of any kind occurring without intention; as soon as one assumes intention one seeks it; we would not seek it if we thought it impossible at least to approximate it; as soon as we reflect on what is necessary to approximate it we recognize that we cannot be sure we have fully apprehended it; but that recognition is important only because we assumed authorial intention in the first place.

UNITY AS ENABLING ASSUMPTION

Intentions are interpretable only in context, but the extent of the context the interpreter brings to bear is determined by the requirement of unity. Or, to state the situation at full if tedious length: we not only expect utterances to convey an intended meaning and expect that the utterer will have taken into consideration the shared background needed to interpret the utterance, but at the same time we expect that we will be alerted to the lack of any elements of context of which we are not aware by a perceived lack of unity. When we say that something doesn't make sense, or we don't understand the point of an utterance, we are saying that we can neither find unity in the text regarded in relation to what we take to be its context nor account for the lack of unity.

Umberto Eco's recent injunction that in order to attempt to confirm one's interpretation of the intention of a text, one must "check it upon the text as a coherent whole" (65) probably came as a shock to many lay followers of the hermetic priesthood, whether or not they recognized it as a rephrasing of a central New Critical principle (Eco himself points out that the principle is to be found in Augustine). However, speech-act theory and discourse analysis have gone sufficiently beyond orthodox New Criticism so that a more accurate piece of advice is to "check it upon the text as a coherent whole as it rests upon the total context, internal and external, evoked and supplementarily supplied."

On the other hand, those not interested in authorial intention, and even more those who continue to regard the author's mind as simply the place where bits of language and antecedent discourse happen to fall together, have no reason to expect unity – and therefore no reason to be concerned about disunity or inconsistencies or contradictions. No one speaks of the unity or lack of unity in a patch of wild flowers, or a pile of rocks washed down from a mountain side, or the refuse blown into an odd corner by the wind even though these may display interesting patterns. There is something distinctly curious about those who deny that a text can possibly be a unified expression of an intention and yet speak of aporias and contradictions.

What linguists call coherence is another name for unity – for the fitting together which we take as the signal that we are interpreting rightly. For a basic example, take the old joke: "They say 'time flies.' But you can't; they're too irregular." The joke depends on our being so familiar with the expression "time flies" that it takes a moment for us to recognize that in order to fit the second sentence these words must represent not the statement that minutes, hours, and days pass quickly but an injunction that one should keep track of how often a certain flying insect circles, or lands, or buzzes by. But then take this string of sentences:

> The sound of the siren was loud. But loud colors look good on me. The opposite of loud is muted. Muting the sirens might have saved many a Greek sailor. But sailors are often loud anyway.

One can "recuperate" such a text only by assuming that it is intended not to express but to exemplify: it may be intended to represent the musings of a mind out of control or be an example of the fact that sentences can be cohesive without being coherent (which is its function here). In so recognizing it, we give up intended meaning in the usual sense; what we are looking for is symptomatic meaning.

The seeking of unity, whether in a sentence or two or a long novel, was not an arbitrary assumption of the New Critics, but part of the recognition of an essential portion of the communicative contract. Of course it is always possible to look at a text in a way that denies its unity, always possible to impose disunity. Contradictions may be produced by several of the strategies we have already found to be essential to the hermetic armory: (1) by insisting that the meaning of each word is a function of other words, thus producing a never-ending chain (an argument that depends on a denial of reference); or (2) through pursuing the range of meanings, both figurative and literal, that key words regarded in isolation might convey; or (3) through emphasizing that all discourse pushes certain aspects of experience into the background in order to foreground others. Since what could be included in a literary work, whether a love sonnet or the lengthiest of novels, is evidently a selection from among those thoughts, images, patterns, and beliefs that could have been included, it is always possible to point to a great deal that has been left out. A novel as broad in its sweep as *Middlemarch* does not include the full range either of existing evils or instances of change for the better. It does not treat the life of the really poor, though it passingly acknowledges their existence, nor bring into sharp focus the injustice of the distribution of wealth that has given Casaubon, Sir James Chettam, and Mr. Brooke so much and others so little, but neither does it recognize the gradual nineteenth-century improvements in sanitation, in laws governing the employment of children, or the curtailing of the worst abuses of Anglican clergymen lavishly paid for duties done by their curates.

In almost every case the hermeticists' strategies require a denial of the context the author assumed the reader would assume: a denial produced through artificial isolation and absolutism. Such a process is more self-contradictory than the text to which it is applied. Consider J. Hillis Miller's well-known deconstruction (in "The Critic as Host") of Wayne Booth's statement that deconstructive tactics are parasitical on the literal meaning of the text.[11] Miller accomplishes this by tracing the etymology of the word "parasite" to demonstrate that the parasite, regarded as the guest, is necessary to the concept of a host. However, Miller's nine pages of cleverly phrased argument would make a valid point only if the direction of the relationship were reversible – but it is not. A tree cannot be called a host without the presence of a parasite, but the tree can exist quite well without the parasite while the parasite cannot exist without the tree. That a tree is a host is a contingent circumstance. Moreover, even where we find concepts the definitions of which imply each other (as the definition of a tree does not imply the existence of a parasite) our valuations of the two will depend on our purposes. That cleanliness and dirtiness imply each other does not deny that there may be reasons for a preference for the first over the second. But the most obvious fallacy is that Miller's entire apparatus, mounted to deny the meaning of Wayne Booth's observation about the parasitical nature of deconstruction occurs because Miller has grasped the intended meaning of the statement; his deconstructive argument is thus evidently parasitic on that meaning.

Regarded as a criticism of exaggerated claims for the unity of a text, the hermetic denial of the possibility of absolute unity is salutary. The New Critical recognition of the regulating function of our expectation of unity can, and in too many cases did, become an obsession with demonstrating, by means of whatever degree of ingenuity, that every element of a text functions in a totally coherent way. However, hermetic writers fall into a more egregious absolutist error than the most uncompromising New Critic. It is not the case that a text either has a seamless unity or none. There can be degrees of unity just as there can be degrees of accuracy: no one would really wish to argue that a text of any length contains no unnecessary words, events, or images, no points at which the meaning might not have been expressed more clearly, nothing that seems at all incongruent. Moreover, incongruity is hardly contradiction. That in *Heart of Darkness* the Marlowe who announces his detestation of dishonesty fails to tell the truth to Kurtz's intended is not a contradiction, but a demonstration of the complexity of the contingent events amidst which human decisions must be made. One of the themes of *Oliver Twist*, that the young can hardly avoid being corrupted by the combination of poverty, an unfeeling society, and a criminal environment, is undercut by Oliver's ability to maintain his honesty and innocence, but it would be hard to deny that such a theme is nevertheless present in the novel. Again, to argue that because characters speak from different perspectives (that there is heteroglossia in Bakhtin's terms) imperils unity only if one construes "different" as irreconcilable. Richard Levin cogently points out that the clashes, tensions, and oppositions within a work not only give it much of its interest but are in fact contributions to its artistic unity. Those who find such oppositions to be sources of contradiction are, he notes, seekers of "ideological unity" (CMA).

The New Critics may also have been too occupied with the idea of the tension to be found in a successful work of literature and ill advised to so often refer to such tension as paradox or irony. Nevertheless, they understood that inconsistencies between characters' statements and actions, or between two perspectives – whether expressed by a single narrator, character, or lyric voice or by a narrator and a character, or by two characters – need not finally be explicitly or even implicitly resolved for the reader to have a sense of unity. After all, conflicts of perspective run through our own experience – a person can believe that charity and forgiveness are important virtues and yet desire revenge, or believe the destitute to be unfortunate victims while yet attributing his or her own comfortable circumstances to personal virtues.

Where we are puzzled not by the sense of a word, an apparent but untraceable allusion, or an inconsistency, but simply by the relevance of a portion of the text, we set it aside as inconsequential to summative meaning. Despite various attempts to justify them,

"The Man of the Hill" chapters in *Tom Jones* seem irrelevant to most readers. If it is important to Fielding's operative intent, the rest of the text should provide the appropriate context for understanding its relationship; alternatively, the episode ought to provide the appropriate context for understanding something elsewhere in the text. If neither seems to be the case, we assume it to be adventitious, unnecessary to the meaning of the work. It may be a flaw, but it does not interfere with interpretation.

Again, an allusion may be integral, that is, it may refer to persons, places, events knowledge of which is essential to the interpretation of meaning, or it may be extrinsic, that is, recognition of the reference may not be essential to interpretation but just a kind of bonus to the reader who understands it. Two examples of the latter from Dorothy Sayers' detective novels are convenient. In *Strong Poison* Lord Peter Wimsey tells Harriet Vane that he had once taken a course in logic because he was in love with a girl named Barbara. He took the course, "For the pleasure of repeating 'Barbara celarent darii ferio baralipton.' There was a kind of mysterious romantic lilt about the thing which was somehow expressive of passion" (83). Now Sayers' readers are perhaps a cut above average in their education, but nevertheless there must be a good many not familiar with the medieval mnemonics for the valid form of syllogisms ("Barbara" stands for the AAA form in which all three terms are universals, etc.). Those for whom the allusion is meaningful would recognize that Sayers was suggesting that Wimsey's anticipation of his one-woman audience was correct, since Vane is depicted as a well-educated woman. On the other hand, those who are not familiar with the allusion can well dismiss it, since nothing more seems to come from it. The reference to logic could send a very inquisitive reader off to a relevant reference book, but I very much doubt that many who have not understood the allusion have been much concerned, especially since Wimsey is talking more or less at random to divert Harriet Vane's mind. A much more obvious allusion appears at the end of that novel, when it seems that Wimsey has, after a long night in his library, solved the murder. He says, obscurely enough, to his butler, " '*Mithridates he died old*,' says the poet. But I doubt it, Bunter. In this case I very much doubt it" (159). A good many English readers would probably recognize this allusion, and there is a reference to *The Shropshire Lad* a few pages earlier to help. In any case, it becomes clear within a few pages that the murderer, like Housman's Mithridates, had built up a tolerance for arsenic that allowed him to eat from the same poisoned dish as his victim. Thus the plot is clear enough to a reader who has never read "Terence, this is stupid stuff." Both these allusions are in the nature of flattering bonuses to the reader who recognizes them; one who does not will not be troubled.

On the other hand, the reader of "Ivy Day in the Committee Room" who does not know something of Ireland's history will make little out of the story. The attentive reader can figure out that Ivy Day commemorates Parnell, but without a lively sense of the enthusiasm Parnell once inspired, the dreary half-heartedness of the political hacks gathered in the committee room is lost. Without an awareness of the general tolerance with which the English public accepted the numerous amours of Edward VII both before and after he occupied the throne, and of the Irish denunciation of Parnell for his affair with Kitty O'Shea, an important part of the story's depiction of the melancholy state of Irish politics is lost.

To "make sense" of a text is to feel that one has grasped a viewpoint that adequately relates the various portions of the text to each other and to the context. Interpretation is dependent on the expectation of such unity. As Grice so ably pointed out, when a text or utterance fails to fit the external context, our immediate assumption is that the Cooperative Principle is being flouted and we immediately look for an ironic, figurative, or otherwise indirect meaning. "What a lovely day" said by one's companion in the midst of a cold, driving downpour is understood to be ironic just as "He's a viper" said of a man is understood as a metaphor. Only if we cannot find such an indirect meaning do we begin to seek other explanations – usually by seeking an explanation in the external context. Grice's Cooperative Principle, regarded in a more comprehensive frame of reference, is what I have called the communicative contract. On those who wish to argue that the assumption of Cooperative Principle is merely a cultural response falls the burden of finding a culture in which such a response is not the normal one. Again, the other half of the communicative structure in which the author assumes he knows the background on which his or her readers will be able to draw is the readers' assumption that the author assumed such a background. Not until our minds have canvassed the possible relationships with the text and between the text and possible elements of external context do we give up our attempt to discover the authorial intention.

As authorial intention is once again being explicitly admitted to criticism, not only an understanding of the role of context, but an acceptance of the goal of a unified reading must reenter. The three concepts are inextricably linked. It is not that a reader can be presumed to recognize an explicit function for every word choice, every event, every nuance of the narrator's voice. We are satisfied when nothing more puzzles us, a principle that may be called that of sufficient harmony. Instead of saying that the reader is to find the context satisfying, it may be more accurate to adopt the social science neologism and say that the unity found must be "satisficing." Where "to satisfy" may have the sense of completely meeting some set of requirements as well as that of being "all that could reasonably be expected," "to satisfice" is specifically opposed to the first of these senses. The unity sought is sufficient when we are no longer conscious of being confused or puzzled or where our puzzlement seems so local that we are not bothered by our lack of understanding of a particular passage.

Notes

1. It is of course possible for an author intentionally to construct a text that is uninterpretable, or undecidably ambiguous, but these are the exceptional cases.
2. Wimsatt wrote in 1968: "What we meant in 1945, and what in effect I think we managed to say, was that the closest one could ever get to the artist's intending or meaning mind, outside his work, would be still short of his *effective* intention or *operative* mind as it appears in the work itself and can be read from the work . . . The intention outside the poem is always subject to the corroboration of the poem itself" (36). See also the section entitled "The Artist's Intention" (pp. 17–29) in Beardsley's *Aesthetics: Problems in the Philosophy of Criticism*.
3. The statement appears on p. 111 of *Critical Terms for Literary Study*.
4. Thus Derrida: "For a writing to be a writing it must continue to 'act' and to be readable even when what is called the author no longer answers for what he has written, for what he seems to have signed, be it because of a temporary absence, because he is dead or, more generally, because he has not employed his absolutely actual and present intention or attention, the plenitude of his desire to say what he means, in order to sustain what seems to be written in 'in his name'" (SEC, 181). Or again, "But the sign possesses the characteristic of being readable even if the moment of its production is irrevocably lost and even if I do not know what its alleged author-scriptor consciously intended to say at the moment he wrote it, i.e. abandoned it to its essential drift" (SEC, 182).

5. Perhaps the best single statement of the reader's activity in reading is that of Louise Rosenblatt's *The Reader, the Text, the Poem: The Transactional Theory of the Literary Work*. "The transactional phrasing of the reading process underlines the essential importance of both elements, reader and text, in any reading event. A person becomes a reader by virtue of his activity in relationship to a text. . . . A physical text, a set of marks on a page, becomes the text of a poem or of a scientific formula by virtue of its relationship with a reader who can thus interpret it and reach through it to the world of the work" (18–19).

6. Ogden and Richards consider the context in which words have occurred as the source of their lexical meanings while largely ignoring the way in which the context of use circumscribes limits to the range of possible meanings. However, Malinowski in effect reinterprets their concept of the "sign-situation" so that it becomes his "context of situation."

7. An argument for this theory is developed in my *Interpretive Acts*.

8. Citing his general argument in *The Role of the Reader*, Eco notes in "Between Author and Text": "I can certainly use Wordsworth's text for parody, for showing how a text can be read in relation to different cultural frameworks, or for strictly personal ends (I can read a text to get inspiration for my own musing); but if I want to *interpret* Wordsworth's text I must respect his cultural and linguistic background" (68–9).

9. For instance: "The impossibility of distinguishing for certain between literal and figurative language in the text, that is to say, the interference of rhetoric in grammar and logic, does not mean that no text is truthfully referential but that neither reader, nor teacher, nor student . . . can ever be certain whether or not the text is truthfully referential" (IT, 307).

10. In developing his point that different critical languages (often resulting from different senses of what is apparently the same word) presuppose different frameworks, R. S. Crane anticipated Fish on this point.

> For the diversities of [critical and theoretical] language we are here concerned with are matters of assumed principle, definition, and method, such as are not likely to show themselves, save indirectly, on the surface of a critic's discourse, and hence not likely, even in controversy, to force themselves on his attention. They pertain rather to what he thinks *with* than to what he thinks *about* – to the implicit structure and rationale of his argument as a whole than to the explicit doctrines he is attempting to state. (*LCSP*, 13)

11. Booth's essay is "Preserving the Exemplar": or, How Not to Dig Our Own Graves," *Critical Inquiry* 3 (Spring, 1977), 407–23.

A Note on the New Pragmatism

While the failure of structuralism led to the poststructuralist reaction, the sterile predictability of the resulting hermeticism has fueled several further reactions, one of which is a return to a version of pragmatism. A. O. Lovejoy distinguished 13 kinds of pragmatism in 1908, the disagreements between which centered in as many as four major issues. A census of philosophical positions having some claim to the term which extended to the present day would present an even more complicated picture. But within literary criticism the term has been captured by a set of arguments represented most directly by Richard Rorty, one of whose descriptions of pragmatism reads, "it is simply anti-essentialism applied to notions like 'truth,' 'knowledge,' 'language,' 'morality,' and similar objects of philosophical theorizing" (CP, 162). He continues, "let me illustrate this by [William] James's definition of 'the true' as 'what is good in the way of belief'" (this is in fact Rorty's favored formulation).

One may well ask what such a philosophical viewpoint has to do with the study of literature. Rorty's anti-essentialism and anti-foundationalism (as argued in *Philosophy and the Mirror of Nature*) has for a number of years given aid and comfort to hermeticists, but the term pragmatism more or less formally entered the vocabulary of literary commentary in the early 1980s after Knapp and Michaels claimed their position in "Against Theory" was a kind of pragmatism. Stanley Fish, who was drawn into the ensuing debate, is also now generally regarded one of the new pragmatists. Rorty's reiterated denials that there is any way to *ground* the concepts of truth or goodness, that there are any criteria beyond human practices, sounds very much like the anti-foundationalist argument that all belief is a function of the discourse community to which one belongs – a perspective specifically applied to (in fact it was developed through a critique of) theories of literary criticism. Moreover, Fish's view that beliefs are not produced and changed through demonstration because any demonstration is a function of the beliefs of a discourse community, and Rorty's insistence that all reality is always under a particular description because "language goes all the way down" appear quite close, especially since Fish believes change occurs only as the result of rhetorical persuasion and Rorty that whatever human beings believe can only be the result of an ever-on-going conversation. Thus Rorty characterizes the pragmatist as thinking "that in the process of playing vocabularies and cultures off against each other, we produce new and better ways of talking and acting – not better by reference to a previously known standard, but just better in the sense that they come to *seem* clearly better than their predecessors" (*CP*, xxxvii).

Now the obvious but essential first point to be made is that the question of the interpretation of meaning is actually quite separate from that of the possibility of grounding truth. However, it is also important to recognize that Rorty both undermines his own argument and continues to exhibit the central weakness of the pragmatism of William James and John Dewey that he admires. A very brief history will be useful at this point. The term pragmatism itself began its career as the denomination of a philosophical method with C. S. Peirce but underwent a significant swerve as it moved from the thought of Peirce to that of his friend William James. Peirce's most concise summation of pragmatism is probably this maxim: "Consider what effects, that might conceivably have practical bearings, we conceive the object of our conception to have. Then, our conception of these effects is the whole of our conception of the object" (5.401). His purpose in thus defining the conception of an object was very close to that of the logical positivists: to rid concepts of all qualities that could not be empirically observed. Finding the emphasis on the effects experienceable by humans in Peirce's pragmatism convenient for his purposes, James adopted it as a name for a view very different from that of Peirce. One of his succinct summations runs "ideas (which themselves are but part of our experience) become true just in so far as they help us to get into satisfactory relation with other parts of our experience" (58). Thus where Peirce's concern was in clarifying the *meaning* of concepts, James's was in defining "truth" in such a way as to align it with human satisfaction. The Jamesian use was so distant from his own that Peirce felt forced to make a formal distinction: "So then, the writer, finding his bantling 'pragmatism' so promoted, feels that it is time to kiss his child good-by and relinquish it to a higher destiny; while to serve the precise purpose of expressing the original definition, he begs to announce the birth of the word 'pragmaticism,' which is ugly enough to be safe from kidnappers" (5.414).

From the point of view of the reader of literature, whether critic, scholar, or common reader, nothing in Peirce, James, or Dewey denies the possibility of the intelligible communication of intentional meaning. Peirce's point was that persons might very well misunderstand each other, but such misunderstanding could be cleared up by defining problematic terms in the manner he suggested. That the meaning of signs arises from communal agreement and that to ask the "interpretant" of a sign (Peirce's interpretant is roughly Saussure's signified) led from interpretant to interpretant were part of Peirce's own views. Nevertheless, the communal basis made communication of meaning possible; moreover, Peirce recognized that signs always interact with the context of their use. What Peirce's definition of pragmatism was intended to accomplish was simply the denial of meaning to any characteristic of a concept that had no effect on human experience. This equally disposes of such questions as "Is God one or three persons?" and "Can computers think?" (the latter question gains meaning only if "think" is defined in terms of specific computer-generated responses).

James and Dewey, on the other hand, were interested in defining what was true in terms of human needs; they never doubted that language could encompass and allow communication about those needs and the experiences that satisfy them. Rorty's denial of any test for truth would not seem to affect the possibility of successful communication of what we intend to communicate about our experiences. His own insistence that language is socially based guarantees the possibility of communicating our different responses to the same stimulus or different attitudes toward the "same" concept. If A finds a particular dessert "delightfully rich" while B finds it "sickeningly sweet and heavy" they are able to communicate these responses to each other because "delightful," "sickening," "rich," etc. have communally agreed senses which are disambiguated by the context of tasting a dessert.

From the point of view of hermeneutics, whether it is useful to talk about truth is irrelevant: since meaning is a function of shared language, cultural background, and situation, its communication is always possible (though never certain since either speaker/author or hearer/reader may be in error about what is shared). That is, it *would* have seemed irrelevant before Rorty published "The Pragmatist's Progress," which directly challenges Umberto Eco's distinction between interpreting texts and using them. "This, of course, is a distinction we pragmatists do not wish to make," writes Rorty. "On our view, all anybody ever does with anything is use it" (PP, 93). Now the quick answer is simply that interpreting the text *is* using it – for the purpose of discovering as nearly as possible the author's intention. What makes this use special, special enough to justify the distinction between interpretation and all other uses – between meaning and significance or intended and symptomatic meanings – is that the text's existence and structure, which make it available for the other uses, are the result of the author's intention.

It is perhaps worth adding that hermeneutics can be roughly defined in terms of the notion of the "operational definition" that can be extrapolated from Peirce's pragmatism. That is, the ultimate way to define peach pie is to describe how to make one. If one follows the directions, the result will be a peach pie. A true interpretive pragmatism would say, "If one says X in this set of contexts, the meaning that will be presumed to have been intended will be Y." Or, considered from the point of view of the reader, "X said within the following contexts probably means Y."

There is, however, another way of illuminating Rorty's error, one revealed quite clearly in the following passage.

> I was dismayed to find him [Eco] insisting on a distinction similar to E. D. Hirsch's distinction between meaning and significance – a distinction between getting inside the text itself and relating the text to something else. This is exactly the sort of distinction anti-essentialists like me deplore – a distinction between inside and outside, between the non-relational and the relational features of something. For, on our view, there is no such thing as an intrinsic, non-relational property. (PP, 93–4)

But of course intended meaning can hardly be said to be non-relational – the communicative contract guarantees that the words making up the text have been chosen in relation to the senses of the words and the cultural and situational context presumed available to the reader at the time as well as the internal contextual relations.

Rorty seems to believe that if there is no criterion for truth there can be none for meaning. If that were true, of course, the "conversation" which Rorty wishes philosophy to be understood to be – the "study of the comparative advantages and disadvantages of the various ways of talking which our race has invented" (CP, xi) would become quite pointless – if our understandings of what others said about the variousness of human talk were as various as the ways of talking, there could hardly be a conversation, much less a study. Moreover, the value which Rorty accords literature would disappear. For him that value lies in the possibility of "an encounter with

an author, character, plot, stanza, line . . . which has made a difference to the critic's conception of who she is, what she is good for,
what she wants to do with herself: an encounter which has rear-
ranged her priorities and purposes" (PP, 107) is hardly possible
unless the reader (why Rorty writes "critic" I don't know) encounters a meaning that is other than he or she was already in pos-
session of. Of course the major problem of pragmatism in the
James-Dewey-Rorty tradition is brought into relief by the evangeli-
cal ring one hears echoing in the passage I have just quoted. What
is the point of rearranging one's "priorities and purposes" unless
the new arrangement is a better one? And how would one know
that it is better? How can a Rortian pragmatist even speak of
"better"?

Rorty remains in the same difficulty that left James so open to
criticism. The difficulty with James's pragmatism evidently lies in
the word "satisfactory" – how is one to judge what is a satisfactory
relationship? Could the word mean anything more than "I like the
results of holding this belief; it does good things for me?" The same
objection evidently applies to the Jamesian phrase "what is good
in the way of belief." Although James tried to meet this objection
by insisting that beliefs were not to be held against evidence, what
would count as evidence remains a question. John Dewey attempted
to meet these objections by a version generally know as "instrumen-
talism" which emphasizes that all human inquiry is evaluative in
that it seeks to satisfy human needs. However, the basis for judging
between competing needs (desires) and competing modes of satisfying them remains unclear, which is why pragmatism as a movement was for a time largely dissolved into the process of clarifying
problems through logic. By 1967 H. S. Thayer, the author of the
article on pragmatism in the *Encyclopedia of Philosophy*, could write,
"While there continues to be an interest in the philosophies of Peirce,
James, Dewey, and Schiller, pragmatism as a movement, in the
form outlined in these pages, cannot be said to be alive today"
(6:435). That was of course before Rorty took advantage of the general
intellectual receptiveness toward indeterminacy to revive James and
Dewey, but he has not succeeded in filling the vacancy that haunted
them. The lack of criteria for truth or value is immaterial to
hermeneutic practice, but not, I shall suggest in Chapter 9, to considerations of the value of literature.

6

The Pretensions of Theory, the Necessity of Pluralism, and Terminological Promiscuity

To insist on the priority of theory over literature is bad enough. It is as though no one were allowed to go to church without first taking a degree in theology.
John Gross, *The Decline and Fall of the Man of Letters*, 328.

The history of literary criticism is largely the history of a vain struggle to find a terminology which will define something. The triumph of literary criticism is that certain of its terms – chiefly those defined by Aristotle – still retain some shreds of meaning.
Ezra Pound, *The Spirit of Romance*, 13.

It is perpetually tempting to the critic to make his style and method so imposing to everyone that nobody will notice or care when he is wrong.
Randall Jarrell, "The Age of Criticism" in *Poetry and the Age*, 85.

THEORIES AND PRINCIPLES

Given the polemic atmosphere, not to mention pretentiousness, now surrounding the very phrase "literary theory," some clarification is in order. As far back as 1918, H. L. Mencken found it intriguing when literary criticism went beyond the criticism of literature and began to criticize the modes of criticism themselves. He would presumably have found it even more intriguing that the field has in recent years been heavily occupied with theories of literary theory itself, although, having noticed that "a professor must have a theory, as a dog must have fleas" (5), he would not have been surprised. On the other hand, as Mencken employed it, "theory" was very loose; and indeed it is tightened only marginally when it appears in the title of René Wellek and Austin Warren's highly influential *Theory of Literature* (1949). The Preface announces: "The naming of this book has been more than ordinarily difficult" for "Even a proper short title, 'Theory of Literature and Methodology of Literary Study' would be too cumbersome" (7). The authors do not mention how nice a calculation is reflected in the absence of either a definite or an indefinite article in the title chosen. "*The* Theory" would have sounded somewhat too pretentious, even for scholars of the eminence of Wellek and Warren, while "*A* Theory" would have suggested that there were a number of already extant theories with which their volume competed. The actual title seemed simply to announce "this is what you need to know about ways of approaching literature" – and a full generation of graduate students was grateful for the distillation. That the volume was not entitled "Theory of Literary *Criticism*" is equally significant; even though Wellek and Warren were concerned with both, in many minds in 1949 criticism was still opposed to scholarship in many minds. Moreover, they were thinking of the many modes of studying literature and surveying the range of questions that had historically been raised and the range of answers that had been given. Interestingly none of the senses of "theory" in the OED exactly corresponds to what they were about, although sense 4b comes reasonably close: "That department of an art or technical subject which consists in the knowledge or statement of the facts on which it depends, or of its principles or methods, as distinguished from the *practice* of it."

In the late 1960s, after discovering that it was useful to speak of "thematizing," practitioners moved on to "theorize" certain aspects of literature and its study. The age of what J. G. Merquior calls "theorrea" had arrived. Nevertheless it is often hard to know exactly what is meant by the word "theory" in recent writing about literature. Of course it is possible to use "theory" in the weak sense of "unproved hypothesis" as in sense 6 in the OED: "In loose or general sense: A hypothesis proposed as an explanation; hence, a mere hypothesis, speculation, conjecture; or an idea or set of ideas about something; an individual view or notion." Something like that is the only sense Samuel Johnson gave to the word: "Speculation; not practice; scheme; plan or system yet subsisting only in the mind." However, while many an essay in the social sciences reports the result of an experiment testing what is explicitly stated to be a hypothesis, very few essays of literature proceed in this way. The

three major patterns are easily described: observations about a text
followed by a generalization drawn from these observations, or the
statement of a generalization which is then shown to apply to one
or more texts, or the citation of a generalization formulated by
someone else followed by a demonstration that the generalization
is incorrect. Clearly the producers of these three kinds of essays do
not think of their comments on a text as hypotheses to be tested,
but rather as explanations the applicability of which is demonstrated
in the course of their essays.

Gerald Graff has sensibly proposed that "literary theory" ought
to be regarded, not as a foundational system seeking to govern or
control meanings but "simply an inquiry into assumptions, premises,
and legitimating principles and concepts" (*PL*, 252). However, this
is not the prevailing usage. For Jonathan Culler, theory "today has
come to designate works that succeed in challenging and reorienting
thinking in fields other than those to which they ostensibly belong
because their analyses of language, or mind, or history, or culture
offer novel and persuasive accounts of signification" (*FS*, 15). Culler
is here thinking of "theory" not as reflection on the practices of a
field such as literary commentary, but as a means of disrupting,
shaking up, challenging conventional or established views. The
examination of literature in terms of psychoanalytical or anthropological or political/economic theory which exemplifies such practice has undoubtedly shaken up the field and produced a much
wider range of symptomatic meanings. On the other hand, while
one would not wish to argue that fields of study cannot or should
not illuminate each other, it is important to recognize that the
working principles and even vocabulary of each field have been
developed to answer specific questions regarded as especially important to that field; these can be applied to another field only with
considerable care and tact (a point to which I will return below).

Almost certainly influencing Culler's view of the function of theory
is the Marxist use of the terms as the generic name for weapons to
be used against particular ideologies and capitalism generally. This
sense of the meaning and function of theory, which has developed
most directly from Althusser, is expressed quite directly by Terry
Eagleton who explains the contemporary "outburst of theory" as
the result of "the role of the 'humanities' in late capitalist society'
(*ST*, 28). Since "the humanities are not . . . a mere hypocrisy, icing
on the cake of capitalism; [but] on the contrary, they still have
an enormously significant role to play in the construction and
reproduction of forms of subjectivity which that society finds

ideologically indispensable," the role of theory must be to undercut capitalist ideology. " 'Theory' was born as a political intervention, whatever academic respectability it may since have achieved" (30) and "[t]he question of the uses of theory, then, is in the first place a political rather than an intellectual one" (34). Now it seems rather an exaggeration to see the major lines of poststructuralist theory as originating as political weapons, although they were early adapted to such uses, particularly by Barthes. John Gross's more guarded statement is perhaps closer to the mark: "In many respects modern theory might have been invented (and in some respects perhaps it was) in order to fill the gap left by the decline of classical Marxism" (328). It is, however, hardly debatable that much of the interest in theory has been in its political uses. Symptomatic readings which point to the capitalist (or patriarchal, or ethnic) assumptions to be found in a text are of course as legitimate in principle as any other explorations of symptomatic meaning and are to be evaluated in terms of the convincingness of the reading. However, as more than one observer has noted, there is something very curious about the belief apparently held by many eager young Marxists that practicing an anti-capitalist form of literary commentary will have a significant effect on a world torn by religious, ethnic, and nationalist strife as well as competition for a larger share of the material goals prized by a market economy. Moreover, Marxist use of the hermetic arguments in support of a critique of non-Marxist ideology must necessarily be cosmetic. If language is autonomous and primarily reflexive, if its use in discourse is undecidable, if authors and readers are indissolubly bound to their ideologies, there seems little reason to devote Marxist energies to the analysis of literature or, in fact, to try to use either literary texts or critical arguments to oppose the present means of material production. Indeed, full hermeticism would seem to deny the possibility of any relationship between the material base and cultural superstructure however sophisticatedly described.

For the most part those who offer literary theories appear to want "theory" to carry the strong positive sense it has in the physical sciences, an explanation of why something is as it is. As I have indicated, when it became evident to literary theorists that confirmations and therefore strictly scientific explanations are not possible in their field, the result was not necessarily, as might have been expected, the abandonment of the search for explanatory theories; rather, undaunted and incorrigible, theorists began to subsume the activity of theorizing under itself, to theorize theorizing. One result has been the development of theoretical statements of the impossibility of theories for the understanding of literary (or any other) texts.

The best-known argument against theory – that is, against the possibility of a theory of literature which could have any practical relevance, is the essay "Against Theory" by Steven Knapp and Walter Benn Michaels. The argument developed by Knapp is appealingly simple: "The mistake made by theorists has been to imagine the possibility or desirability of moving from one term (the author's intended meaning) to a second term (the text's meaning) when actually the two terms are the same" (12). As I hope the previous chapters have made evident, I agree that to seek the meaning of a text *is* to seek the author's intended meaning. But a complex process necessarily intervenes between an author's intention to convey something through a selected set of works and a reader's reconstruction of as much as possible of the author's intention. The fallacy can also be described, as it was in William Dowling's response to the Knapp & Michaels essay, as a confusion between an entailment and an identity.[1] Or again, the fallacy may be seen as the confusion of logical with chronological priority that K & M enter in saying that "Hirsch is imagining a moment of interpretation before intention is present" (14).[2] In any case, since the set of syntactically arranged words that make up the text before one is not self-identical with the intended meaning of the author, one or more principles of interpretation is required to mediate between the two. It was the need for some such principle that gave rise to the long tradition of hermeneutics, the existence of which could never be guessed from Knapp and Michaels's essay. The explanation of the essay's effect probably lies in the trendy speciousness of much of what is taken to be the most sophisticated form of literary theorizing. Although arguments for the total disjunction of author from text, for the subservience of the speaker to the language of his or her utterance, and for the indeterminacy of textual meaning have never been either wholly discredited nor wholly accepted (they remain more like weapons that may be used at need than controlling beliefs), critical discourse was already tiring of them by the time of the Knapp and Michael's essay.

PRACTICES WITHOUT THEORETICAL CASTLE-BUILDING

It is another absolutist error to argue that where large-scale theories are not to be had, practice is without any sort of guidance. Most human activity is in fact guided by principle, where "principle" designates a general guide derived from experience. It thus rests on a kind of knowledge, but not on an explanatory theory. For example, Sir Marc Brunel is supposed to have gotten the idea for the construction of his tunnel under the Thames by watching ship worms. What he acquired was a principle, not a theory (though, since it pertains to physical phenomena, presumably it can be theorized). By principle I mean the sort of advice (received from someone else or given to oneself) that if one wishes to achieve A, the most likely path is by doing B. If one has lost an umbrella while shopping, one tries to retrace one's steps rather than beginning by asking for the umbrella at shops one did not visit. Such a principle may not succeed (the umbrella may have been stolen, it may have fallen where it can't be seen, it may even, by some odd chance, have ended up in a shop one had not entered), but the principle is self-evident. The hermeneutic principle stated in Chapter 5 is equally self-evident: anything an author could reasonably have assumed his anticipated readers would know is potentially relevant to the understanding of authorial meaning while nothing that an author could not have assumed anticipated readers would know can be relevant to that meaning.

EXPLANATION AND UNDERSTANDING

The word understanding as used here requires a gloss. It was Johann Droysen who initiated the distinction between *explanation*, the goal of scientific theories, and *understanding*, the goal of historical investigation of human actions and expression. Wilhelm Dilthey further developed the distinction, assigning explanation to the natural sciences and understanding to the whole of human sciences. In this use explanation results in a scientific model or theory that gives the structure and conditions under which a phenomenon occurs and makes possible predictions about the production of other phenomena. The humanities, thought Dilthey, can achieve understanding of human intentions, but not explanations. Understanding may be said to occur when one has a grasp of how a thing works, or what a person intends to communicate by a certain utterance, or what is likely to follow from a certain act or event.[3] The basic process of understanding is that of relating something new to something already familiar. We understand a new word when given a synonym or example; we understand a bank statement when we have related the entries to transactions of which we are aware (depositing money, cashing checks); we understand certain simple things about the invisible "flow" of electricity by relating it to the visible flow of water; we understand an utterance by relating it simultaneously to our knowledge of the language, the specific situation, and aspects of the cultural background. Geoffrey Thurley has used the interpretation of the map of the London Underground as an example of the understanding of meaning (18–19). Such a map does not produce predictions of things not previously known; although it can give news to someone unacquainted with the system and even allow the prediction that if one takes the Piccadilly line west from Russell Square one will eventually arrive at Hammersmith, it is not a theory but a diagram of what is known about the layout of the Underground system.

The example suggests a further mark of understanding as opposed to explanation as these terms are here being used: understanding is essentially existential as opposed to theoretical. It is related to human problems more closely than to questions generated as theoretical ramifications. Whereas understanding a map of the Underground may give a definitive solution to a finite problem, getting from point A to point B, such understanding is a "making familiar with." Similarly a play about rebellious children does not – at least not if it is to be successful – present a theory of child–parent relations; rather the play and the experience of those in the audience interact. Certain aspects of the play are better understood because familiar – certain aspects of life's experience are better understood because "familiarized" in the play. To understand *Middlemarch* is to know the events of the story, to recognize the major motivations of the characters, and construct as well as possible the general attitude toward life the novel as a whole appears to convey. There is no element of prediction about the matter. Although I cannot agree with Paisley Livingston's view that literary research *ought* to offer explanations in the strict (scientific) sense, he is clearly correct in saying that literary-critical explanations "are not part of an explanatory structure at all." They are locally coherent accounts, not investigations of the "cognitive tension between a well-founded theory and the states of affairs it has yet to account for" (239). In reading a text, we understand its meaning by relating it to possible senses of the words used, grammatical usage, historical situation, and social convention, and find significances through the application of psychological, sociological, philosophical, linguistic, and economic theories, but these ancillary activities do not explain the text.

COROLLARIES

The failure to recognize that the impossibility of constructing literary theories in the strict sense in no way denies the development and application of certain principles for certain purposes has produced an extraordinary schizophrenia. Literary theories of various partly competing, partly complementary kinds are still assumed, asserted, and debated on all sides. The essay that doesn't *sound* as though it has a theoretical foundation is very likely to be dismissed as hopelessly out of date. But at the same time, *au courant* critics and theorists are expected to know, and show that they know, that there are no valid foundations on which theories may be constructed. It is hard to imagine another field which could so happily embrace both theory and anti-theory, thus requiring in effect that the arguments of its adepts show due homage to the reign of theory without taking theory seriously. Theoretical foundations are still expected, but only admittedly cracked and crumbling ones qualify. Little wonder that from the point of view of many other disciplines literary criticism and theory are a kind of specially insulated playground on which games are played with great abandon just because nothing that happens there could have any consequences.

An apparent oddity in the current situation is that those commentators on literature most concerned about the practical effects of literature, about its power either to maintain or alter cultural attitudes, tend to look not to hermeneutic but to hermetic theorizing. Such writers seem to draw on the circumambient atmosphere of hermeticism to discredit all interpretations and readings except their own; they assure us that we nevertheless need not despair since they possess the one key. Most often the key is a Marxist one that unlocks the surprising secret that everything not written from a Marxist point of view is an apology for capitalism. But if, as Marxist, feminist, and politically concerned critics in general tend to argue, literature and commentary on it has been employed to maintain the power of males and/or a capitalist society and/or white (Caucasian) values and/or money-and-power elite, literature and literary commentary must have been sufficiently interpretable to convey those messages. Even if one says that many writers have not actually been aware of the cultural prejudices they have been supporting and transmitting, the unreflecting assumption of such prejudices by both authors and readers must have been operative in helping govern the intended (and presumably actual) responses of readers. Therefore politically oriented criticism requires the analysis and reconstruction of cultural contexts, and of the ways these act to assign reference, avoid ambiguity, and make the interpretation of indirect expression possible. Everything from the crudest of racial jokes to the subtlest reinforcement of assumptions of male superiority depends on the understanding of the interaction of discourse and context for which speech-act theory, studies in coherence and cohesion, discourse analysis, and the kind of philological scholarship that makes possible the reconstruction of historical context are the necessary tools.

In addition, it is hard to imagine an argument for a better society that does not assume that such a society is a worthy goal, that is, has ethical value. But just as the denial that language can be used to make a consistent argument denies the possibility of valid argument for the improvement of the society, the denial that language has reference to non-linguistic reality finally denies the grounds for any change. From the point of view of those who deny that language has access to reality, statistics evidencing that women are paid less than men for the same work and studies of male bias in the language would have nothing to do with each other.

The practical difference between hermetic and hermeneutic commentary is, then, all important. The consideration of the context assumed by the author, which includes knowledge of extra-linguistic reality, is not only necessary for interpretation of intention, but links intentions to realities existing outside the system of language. From this perspective, the charge that hermeneutics is too passive, that it does not sufficiently engage the problems of the world, is the result of one more confusion. The process of relating the words of the text to knowledge, attitudes, and beliefs that the author could assume to be shared, which is essential to interpretation, is a necessary step in moving toward an evaluation. The evaluation itself is extrinsic to the interpretation, and in fact is a matter of assigning significances, not discussing meaning, but if we would not let theorizing mislead us, the safe road is from the reconstruction of shared beliefs to their evaluation rather than from an already adopted evaluative scheme to a search for evidence to support that scheme.

FISSIPAROUSNESS AND PLURALISM

It is passing strange how threatening many have found E. D. Hirsch's distinction between meaning and significance. One of the more curious features of the hostile reaction to Hirsch's argument has been the assumption that he is the originator and major proponent of what seems to the hermeticist to be an artificial distinction. But a moment's thought about the meaning of meaning reminds us of its multiform ambiguity, an ambiguity that demands to be sorted out. For all their care in making discriminations in *The Meaning of Meaning* (1923), Ogden and Richards never recognized how often "meaning" is divorced from authorial intention in readers' responses to texts. On the other hand, distinctions between authorially intended and reader-induced meanings (the latter produced by the reader's assignment of analogies and patterns probably or certainly not foreseen by the author) have been made a number of times over the last forty years, although, as usual in literary commentary, different writers have chosen different terms with which to designate the distinction.

In addition to Grice's "non-natural" vs. "symptomatic," Richard McKeon, Elder Olsen, and R. S. Crane distinguished the "literal" from the "analogical" meaning, while Wayne Booth (*Critical Understanding*, chap. 6) has contrasted "understanding" with "overstanding."[4] Roger Scruton contrasts meaning (as intended) and association, a word to which he here gives a more formal meaning (43); Umberto Eco differentiates the intention of the text from the intention of the reader or, alternatively, "interpreting" from "using" a text (68). Richard Freadman and Seamus Miller's term for more or less what I call significance or symptomatic meaning is "inferred meaning," while Eugene Nassar's is "metacriticism."[5]

The second misconception, equally curious, but more damaging (held in the face of Hirsch's explicit development of the contrary position in the 1960 *PMLA* article in which he first argued the distinction as well as in the volume *Validity in Interpretation* in which he further developed it) is that Hirsch insists upon a single correct mode of response to the reading of a literary text. However, most critics who assert that a text has many meanings are actually arguing for a multiplicity of what Hirsch calls significances – the number of which he has no interest in limiting.

It is not my intention here to defend the precise terms in which Hirsch states and develops the distinction between meaning and significance. Rather, I want to insist once again – the point seems to require continual restatement – that the very nature of commentary on literature guarantees that a text of any interest will allow the assignment of multiple significances: one might well define the degree of potential interest of a text in terms of the extent to which it lends itself to the production of significances. The very process of reconstructing authorial meaning demands a process of excluding what the author could not have intended to express, which in turn implies the possibility, in fact unavoidability, of interest in what the author could not have said because to have said it would have demanded knowledge or systems of thought external to what the author and audience could have shared. Stated another way, in seeking the author's intention the mind works centripetally, moving as far into the context presumably anticipated by the author as possible while jettisoning as much as possible of what we know could not belong to that context. Having grasped what then seems the most probable intended meaning, we think centrifugally, carrying, perhaps forcing, the meaning beyond authorial intention or control. Thus while hermetic theory seeks to deny the possibility of the interpretation of authorial intention through the reconstruction of context and the assumption of the communicative contract as a guiding principle, hermeneutics much more generously accepts the legitimacy of pursuing any number of symptomatic readings, including contextless reading and the "teasing out" of contradictions.

Actually, the importance of significances remains the same whether one accepts authorial intention or not; the only difference is that the non-intentionalists tend to claim that the meanings (that is, significances) they discuss find their way into the text by a sort of osmosis from the culture – in which case it is hard to know why the same patterns of significance are not to be found in all texts written in the same general culture in the same general period (some critics do, in fact, discover the same significance in everything they read). If one rules out the interpretation of authorial intentions, the non-intended meaning which one finds in the text must just mysteriously "be there," or be the result of equally mysterious processes of language or culture that somehow constantly produce new texts by processes of change internal to themselves.

In any case, an intentionalist's interest in a literary text does not stop with the understanding of *meaning*: it is necessary to place, judge, compare, assign causal conditions for – in short to *use* – that meaning. Doing this requires removing it from the authorially assumed background and placing it within whatever systems of thought one has found useful for explaining the manifold of experience. There is no great mystery here; as argued previously we move easily enough from one network of concepts to another. We can understand a variety of disparate networks, theoretical frameworks, systems of concepts (whichever phrasing seems most appropriate) even though we can't *adhere* to two or more that we are aware are in conflict.

I have tried to suggest that the most satisfactory way of regarding significances or symptomatic meanings is as our personally situated evaluations of or reactions toward the author's intention as we understand it and the shared assumptions that made possible the conveying of that intention in the way it was conveyed. Whatever our beliefs about authorial intention, our discoveries of significances are of central importance to us. In large part we care what and how Chaucer or Donne or Pope or Coleridge said what they said and we care about the stories Fielding or Austen or Faulkner told because they can be given symptomatic meaning. That is one reason that even intentionalists often blur the distinction in the process of explicating a text. Even though one may clearly recognize the difference between an author's meaning and the use one wishes to make of it or the parallels that interest one, a natural way of setting out one's understanding of a text is precisely by drawing on anachronistic parallels or other modes of thought otherwise alien to the author and his or her expected audience. Literary hermeneutics leads one toward symptomatics; confusion arises only when the possibility of understanding intentional meaning is denied and symptomatic meaning is elevated to the position of primary or basic meaning.

Now since symptomatic meanings are evoked as a way of explaining, categorizing, or making manifest readers' reactions to a text, they almost always draw on systems of thought originating independently of the text which are at least provisionally accepted by the critic. They thus depend on the persuasive authority of figures like Freud, Marx, Lacan, Heidegger, or Jakobson. Such theories are psychoanalytic or socioeconomic or philosophical, not literary. They have not been developed out of conditions specific to the writing and reading of literature; literature as a whole cannot be subsumed under them; and they are not at all restricted to literature. And, as noted in Chapter 4, the fields on which literary theorists tend to draw are those in which competing, essentially unverified, theories struggle indecisively.

None of which means that perspectives these disciplines may suggest to the literary critic are in themselves invalid. What it does mean is that the interpretive practices derived from such theories are valid in ways that require careful definition. In the first place the vocabularies of such theories can have authoritative meaning only for those who fully recognize and accept the structure of theories behind them. Second, even though their apparent purpose is to explain, symptomatic meanings can never function as causal explanations even for those who fully accept the theory employed. (See the latter part of this chapter.) Even if the critic had access to the transcript of the full psychoanalysis of an author, and fully accepted the psychoanalyst's methods, all that could be argued would be that certain elements of the author's particular mental structure were contributing conditions to the production of the text. Or, to shift the field a bit, if a critic fully accepts Freudian psychology and wishes to argue that Hamlet's relationship to his mother is a result of Shakespeare's awareness of something like what Freud would later explain as the Oedipus complex, what is really being said is that Freud's theories provide a useful analogy. Evidently an indefinite number of analogies may be offered, none of which rules out any other. An essay that takes Hamlet's attitude toward his mother in the closet scene as analogous to the relation between one generation and the next, the younger always finding its principles superior to those of the older, does not necessarily clash with a strictly Freudian criticism – one can in fact accept a number of such analogies, though one can not give equal attention to them all simultaneously.

The play as a whole can equally yield any number of analogies. An example I always recall with pleasure, although unfortunately I am no longer sure of the speaker – perhaps George Winchester Stone – was a talk in which the situation in Hamlet was likened to that in English departments generally. The department chair will always seem a usurper to some, especially to someone who had hoped to occupy that position; there are always those who, like Gertrude, seem to others immoral in their willingness to comply with whoever is in power; few departments of any size lack a hot-headed Laertes or a tedious Polonius; and there is always a Fortinbras-like power (dean, provost, board of trustees) that may prove either menace or ally.

All such analogies are in effect hypothetical constructions. Books and essays do not generally proclaim their hypotheticality, but how many critical commentaries ought really to begin with something like, "If we were to regard Faulkner's *The Bear* as a Marxist analysis of the South," or "It will be illuminating if we think of Marlowe's 'To His Coy Mistress' as a satire on the *carpe diem* theme," etc. There is much virtue in your if, and where the critic has omitted it, the thoughtful reader ought to provide it. The role of such imported theorizing is pretty much what Walter Pater said was the role of philosophy generally: it awakes our interest by leading us to see selectively chosen patterns within texts and/or texts as parts of larger patterns. It should hardly be necessary to insist that to the extent interest is generated either in the text itself or the concept of the world the text is used to illuminate, such critical arguments are not only justified but central to our interest in literature. There being no objective limit to the number of such possible patterns, and often no reason except personal interest or predilection for preferring one over another, the realm of criticism, of the pursuit of significance, is necessarily a pluralistic domain. The wonder is that those who are so worried by the possibility of a single meaning have not embraced the advantages of the meaning/significance (intended/symptomatic meaning) distinction. Without requiring the denial of intention and the possibility of at least partial recovery of that intention (without which language would have no use), it allows one to recognize the multiplicity of significances that may interest a reader.

In a 1981 leader in the *Times Higher Education Supplement*, the author included English among the fissiparous disciplines.[6] I had not before encountered "fissiparous" – that which produces new individuals by fission – but it turns out to be a fine word to describe the necessary multivocality of criticism. The pursuit of new significances produces further new significances: psychological criticism divides because there are different psychological theories, these further divide as they are modified or applied differently by different critics. The same is true of all varieties of criticism: sociological, political, anthropological, feminist, or whatever. Fissiparousness is the unavoidable nature of literary response; it is also one that deserves celebration. The pluralism that seems to me the most profitable attitude with which to approach literary texts results from a conscious recognition of that nature. After all, our continuing interest in texts written in wholly other circumstances arises from the possibility of discovering new significances. Both Paisley Livingston (206–7) and James Battersby have used the analogy of the map to explain the necessity of pluralism. Maps are designed to answer specific questions. There are maps designed to answer questions about road networks, about population distribution, about topography, about growing seasons, about agricultural production, about the incidence of certain diseases, about the locations of everything from castles to campgrounds. Similarly one can map a text in answer to an almost infinite number of questions. What roles are assigned to women? What kind of socio-economic structure is portrayed? What evidence is there that the author favored certain views of religion, or politics, or human history? Battersby comments: "The pluralist view of maps is that they have many interests and that they are the way they are because they have the interests they have" (*PR*, 47). Or again, "the map is already a version and is the version it is because it has the interests it has" (*PR*, 52).

Such pluralism is precisely not that of Stanley Fish: it explicitly recognizes that one can move from one framework of significance to another while still recognizing that the employment of each of these is a different thing from the construction of intended meaning. R. S. Crane, who is among those who recognize the difference between interpretation of an author's intention and significances relevant to our own interests, uses the word criticism in the way in which I have been employing it in the following apt summary of what is the major point of his *The Languages of Criticism and the Structure of Poetry:*

> What I would propose . . . is that literary criticism is not, and never has been, a single discipline, to which successive writers have made partial and never wholly satisfactory contributions, but rather a collection of distinct and more or less incommensurable "frameworks" or "Languages," within any one of which a question like that of poetic structure necessarily takes on a different meaning and receives a different kind of answer from the meaning it has and the kind of answer it is properly given in any of the rival languages in which it is discussed. (*LCSP*, 13)

So long as there was a general belief that it was possible to identify something like Matthew Arnold's "the best that is known and thought," stably shifting, or perhaps shiftingly stable canons could exist. That is, to rationalize the oxymoron, certain works were added over time while certain others almost ceased to be read; certain works moved from a tentative position on the margin toward the center while others drifted toward the periphery. But at any given time there was general agreement about the composition of the "best" literature. But canons are in fact selected according to implicit or explicit purposes. The canon more or less accepted at the end of the nineteenth century had been selected because it was amenable to certain patterns of significance: that which had been found aesthetically pleasing over the centuries, that which seemed to embody particular forms of rationality, that which had been culturally influential (which the educated should recognize), etc. The works selected fit well with the purpose of illustrating and transmitting these significances. However, as the number of significances of interest to readers has increased as the result of sociological, psychological, anthropological, and political currents, so has the number of purposes according to which works are selected for discussion. The number of works thought to be worth careful reading and discussion has grown because very different types of texts are useful for considering the range of significances various critics, teachers, or readers think it important to pursue. I do not think this means that the role of authorial meaning has become insignificant, however, for among the works that seem useful for a particular purpose, whether that of a Marxist, feminist, Freudian, absurdist, humanist, or whatever other kind of reading, those in which the authorially intended meaning seems richest, most interesting, most thought-provoking will be those most often chosen, assigned, recommended, discussed.

TERMINOLOGICAL PROMISCUITY

Pluralism is one thing, the unavoidable misreadings and mutual incomprehensibility that increasingly accompany divergent critical approaches quite another. Not only is much of what has been published in the last ten years unintelligible to the amateur of literature (I intend amateur in the original sense of lover), but often pretty much so to professors of literature who happen to have a different set of interests from those of a particular set of critics and theorists or who have not been reading a particular journal. Some of this Babel-like situation is necessary, resulting from the very nature of literary discourse, but a good bit of it is not: the latter testifies only to the temptations of pretentiousness and laziness.

The difference in attitudes toward terminology in the physical and biological sciences and in literary commentary is in itself evidence of the distance between these disciplines. There are all sorts of sub-fields within any science that make use of procedures and terms that are peculiar to themselves and which an individual coming from another sub-field would have to master, but a biologist with, for instance, an interest in blue-green algae is unlikely to encounter a study on the subject that he cannot interpret, whereas an authority on William Faulkner may find a discussion from a Lacanian, or Althusserian, or Bakhtinian approach unintelligible. It is true that scientific terms obviously change their meanings as theories in which they are central change: gravitation is not the same thing after Einstein as it was after Newton. However, such changes are not the result of idiosyncratic uses by individuals but reflect a realignment of terminology across an entire field. Although the existence of "phlogiston" was part of the explanation of the phenomenon of burning and thus had attributed to it certain characteristics now associated with oxygen, when the entire system of thought of which phlogiston made a part was replaced by that of the atomic system, the term "phlogiston" obviously imported too much of the discredited system: one cannot now describe water as made up of hydrogen and phlogiston.

In contrast, literary critics and theorists employ established terms with new meanings as well as their traditional ones, new terms conveying hitherto unknown concepts, and new terms conveying senses previously associated with older terms. In addition to the terminological problems resulting from the importation of theories from other disciplines, writers of literary commentary tend to resist precise definitions, blithely assign new meanings to well established terms, and blur distinctions as soon as they are made. The degree to which a chaotic variety of senses is associated with key literary terms became clear to me in the course of compiling a dictionary of major literary concepts for a series of volumes treating different disciplines. The editor's suggestion that the discussion of each concept should proceed historically and conclude with current usage seemed reasonable enough, but it turned out that in literary-critical discourse much more often than in the social sciences, the latest use is only one of several competing senses that continue to have currency. Moreover, whereas in the social sciences a sense is authorized through its use by a writer the results of whose research are judged more accurate or complete than that of previous researchers, in literary study a particular sense of a term can be authorized simply through being used in an interesting manner by a critic who attracts sufficient attention. In such cases the new or modified sense takes its place beside the older ones; there is no imperative that it replace these. Senses tend to accumulate, to exist in a kind of jostling pack rather than supersede each other.

Thus "symbol" may designate a conventional sign, a sign that bears an indirect or figurative meaning, an image suggesting a concept or network of concepts, or an evocation of the transcendent (there are additional complications in "symbolic," which Julia Kristeva, for instance, employs to designate the human infant's responses to the acquisition of language). Another interesting example of a multiplicity of partially incompatible senses is "historicism," which can designate any one the following beliefs: that the meaning of a text is to be found through the reconstruction of the history of its reception, that the meaning of a text is to be found by reconstructing the historical context in which it appeared, that language and culture constantly change and therefore meanings are always relative, that history reveals laws or cycles from which predictions can be made, and that the diversity of the past and relativity of the observer's position make it impossible to reconstruct past meanings (although those who presently most strongly advocate this position tend to find one constant – the struggle for power). Clearly "historicism" sometimes carries the idea that past contexts are more or less homogeneous and can be reconstructed, and sometimes that they are not homogeneous and cannot be reconstructed; at times it embodies the premise that history can be of great use in understanding the present and predicting the future and at times the premise that the continuing relativity of everything to everything else invalidates projections into the future.

"Text" may designate any written or printed form of discourse; the most authoritative form of a written or printed discourse; the written or printed discourse specifically divorced from authorial intention or from readers' responses, or from both; the patterned words from which the reader constructs meanings; any cultural phenomena that may be interpreted or analyzed; and literary structures that are without closure, indefinitely deferring meaning as opposed to those that are regarded as univocal. "Code" is constantly employed to mean one of three quite different things: a system of rules for relating one set of phenomena to another; a system of symbols or signs (and thus a natural language); or the cultural information (background knowledge) that allows one to relate the dictionary senses of words to the larger context necessary to understand their use in a given situation. "Context" may be intended to designate the *total* situation relevant to understanding an instance of language use; the *internal* context (relations of words to each other within the discourse, the "cotext"); the wholly *external* context. Thus New Critics have been called contextualists because they advocate careful analysis of the structure of language within the text while Marxists are often called contextualists because they insist on the importance of understanding the cultural structure surrounding the text itself. And then there is the use suggested by I. A. Richards in which the term context designates the penumbra of words likely to be associated by sound or meaning with the words actually used.[7] "Criticism" as used in discourse about literature can designate evaluative judgment (as it does in general speech), close analysis designed to explicate the author's intended meaning, analysis of significances of the text outside or beyond the author's intention, or all commentary on literature of any sort.

The almost endemic ambiguity of key literary terms is matched by its obverse: the degree to which what is essentially the same concept comes to be designated by a number of terms the similarity of which is not generally perceived. For instance, the overall reconstruction of the author's meaning is commonly called explication, but also "understanding" by E. D. Hirsch, "interpretation" by Umberto Eco, "uptake" by Austin, and "reading out" by Seymour Chatman. Even concepts that have come under close investigation only in recent years have quickly acquired multiple designations. What Brian McHale calls indirect discourse is Dorrit Cohn's "narrated monologue" and Genette's "transposed speech"; it is also a form of what Bakhtin calls "double voicing." The difference between indirect discourse and direct discourse can also be profitably described as that between what J. L. Austin calls "phatic" and "rhetic" acts (95). What Wayne Booth calls dramatized and undramatized narrators are more or less Genette's intradiegetic and extradiegetic narrators. Lack of awareness of what is being written in other countries, problems of translation, and reluctance to incorporate terminology from another language lead to such examples of greater or lesser synonymy as story, *fabula*, *histoire*, narration, and *diégèse*. What is especially confusing is that terms pointing to the same general phenomena are often not exact synonyms but more like a set of largely but not wholly overlapping circles.

While seeming to write in an increasingly technical manner, critics have become less and less inclined to define the specific senses of the key terms they employ. Only those who are familiar with the author, or who know the full range of possible senses and can pin down the one intended by following such clues as which critics are cited with approval and which with disapproval or the unexpressed but necessary assumptions of the critic can be sure of the sense. Further complicating matters is the likelihood that the reader will be confronted with a considerable number of terms with multiple possible meanings within the same text. Necessarily, then, to an extent corresponding to the number of key terms employed but not specifically defined, each piece of literary commentary is implicitly if not explicitly addressed to a sub-coterie within the larger coterie made up of those engaged or interested in literary criticism in general – and even then only the writer who exercises constant vigilance over the consistency of the terms he or she chooses to use can hope to be logically consistent. That the concepts relevant to literary study need correspond to no entities in the physical world (that is, to no sense reports) allows terms to float and signifiers to be linked to new signifieds with impunity so far as practical checks are concerned.

In a field which draws so heavily on the theories of others, and in which newly important significances emerge from decade to decade, terminological consistency is hardly possible. Definitions and distinctions will continue to depend on purposes. Thus whether one wishes to differentiate symbolism from allegory depends on whether an interesting new perspective can be opened up by pursuing the distinction. One can equally argue that symbolism and allegory can be regarded as essentially the same – or that the traditional exaltation of symbolism at the expense of allegory can be reversed – so long as making such a claim proves a way of generating an interesting argument.

However, although the necessity of making use of an unstable vocabulary in a verbal landscape in which shapes shift and edges crumble is an occupational hazard for the commentator on literature, one cannot help feeling that confusion need not be granted quite so extensive a domain. There is no reason for not exercising all possible care in avoiding possible misunderstanding or sheer incomprehension – for not, in short, making sure that the reader of a critical essay is aware of the provenance of the vocabulary employed. There is something bizarre in the notion that the communicative contract should be less in force in writing about literature than elsewhere. In using a term that has a history of different senses, it ought to be common courtesy to stipulate the sense intended as precisely as possible. It used to be very much standard practice, for example, to stipulate the senses of key terms, often by citing the writer who first used or gave a specific sense to a term: "the symbol as Coleridge defined it" or "historicism in Auerbach's sense." For years after T. S. Eliot employed the phrase "objective correlative" or I. A. Richards introduced the terms "vehicle" and "tenor," critics continued to tie these terms back to their origins, as in "Eliot's objective correlative" or "that which Richards designates as the tenor." It ought to be equally incumbent on the critic or theorist to give an explicit definition of the new or modified use of a term adapted for the writer's own purposes. One tires of the constant citation by theorists of Humpty-Dumpty's announcement that a word means what he chooses it to mean. Of course a word means whatever one chooses so long as it is employed only in one's private thoughts (although failure to be clear about exactly what one does mean by certain words can easily muddle one's thoughts) and equally can mean whatever one explicitly stipulates it to mean (although more may be lost than gained by forcing inappropriate meanings). But the communicative contract requires that one's readers or hearers not be presented with unexplained idiosyncratic meanings.

Some confusions are undoubtedly due to simple ignorance of the precise senses in which terms have previously been employed – unfortunately the pressure to publish quickly through the application of some newly touted theoretical approach has very much increased instances of such failures of historical awareness. Yet worse, at times the avoidance of any precision in the use of terms appears to have the strategic functions either of covering up inconsistencies and illogicalities or smuggling in the authority associated with influential critics. Certain words recommend themselves because they have a vaguely professional sound. They have the right resonance, and thus serve as evidence that the writer has been feeding in the proper critical fields. An example is the use of "deploy," which has come into prominence over the last two decades. The word appears again and again where an older critic might have written "employ." To write "Eliot deployed the image of water," as opposed to

"Eliot employed the image of water" signals at least that one is swimming with the current. The actual differences are slight, the term "deployed" perhaps suggesting somewhat conscious strategy, and perhaps more important, game-playing (further suggesting a distance from any concern for extra-linguistic reality).

Such relatively innocuous turns of style can easily be transformed into a conscious strategy. Not a few critics and theorists seem to have come to feel that somehow the accretion of specialized jargon that makes so much literary commentary unreadable in substance and offensive in style has made it a more rigorous and respectable enterprise. That the arguments carried by such prose are as hard to imagine as quantum theory in physics or the astronomer's concept of an apparently infinitely expanding universe in itself suggests a distant alliance with science. For others such style is a demonstration of a radical anti-bourgeois stance (however difficult this is to understand in that political and cultural radicals might be expected to eschew elite language). Cedric Watts describes as "The Jargonish Fallacy" such writing in which "a critic claims or implies that to use a very difficult or obscure mode of expression is to demonstrate one's integrity (for one thereby opposes the controversial and therefore the ideologically conservative), whereas to express oneself clearly and intelligently is to compromise with the conventional and therefore to support the bourgeoisie" (31–2). A more skeptical remark is André Lefevere's that sufficiently heavy jargon is a way of "immunizing" one's statements against falsification (14); in effect the same unfalsifiable vagueness is achieved to which the logical positivists objected in traditional metaphysical language. The result is too often what James Battersby has referred to as "countless dark and dense essays in the allegorical mode favored by theory" (*PR*, 5).

Another problem too rarely recognized is that terms that have only recently entered the literary/critical argot, or that have long been absent and only recently been resuscitated, remain closely linked to the system of thought which introduced them for a considerable period of time. While R. S. Crane welcomed the variety of "languages" of criticism, he recognized that the specialized terminology of a particular theory-based approach must remain closely linked to the theory if it is to provide the particular kind of insight intended: "so . . . with many of the general words which critics themselves have used to designate the subjects or characteristics of subjects they are engaged in discussing – it can never be safely assumed

in advance that their common use by two different critics is a sign
that these critics have constituted the effective subject-matters of
their discussions in the same way, so that it is possible to make
direct comparisons between their conclusions . . . " (*LCSP*, 18). Or
again,

> "A critical language . . . is more than a finite set of basic and often
> implicit definitions which, as a conceptual scheme of a determi-
> nate sort, constitutes its literary objects as the particular subject-
> matter that is being talked about. It is also a special set of
> assumptions as to how the principles and distinctions needed in
> the discussion are to be derived and as to how they may be used
> to give a valid and relevant knowledge concerning whatever the
> subject-matter is taken to be" (*LCSP*, 19–20).

A word like "aporia" no longer simply designates a doubt or
perplexity, as it did for centuries, but for the present is strongly
associated with deconstructive practice. Since it is unlikely that a
critic would be using what had been quite a rare word in English
if it had not been revived by the deconstructive program, to use it
without explicit qualification is to bow in that direction, accepting
the unavoidability of contradiction that is guaranteed by deconstructive theory. The term "deferred," although still in general use
to mean simply "postponed," has become so clearly associated with
Derrida's coinage of "différance" that it must be used with similar
care. To say "Meaning is of course always deferred" will signal to
many readers acceptance of the whole of Derrida's reworking of
Saussure, a commitment that, in fact, fewer and fewer writers un-
reservedly care to make. Unfortunately this term in particular seems
often employed only in order to give the right sort of ring to statements that really mean no more than "a reader can never be sure
of a totally accurate reconstruction of meaning."

The situation is already clouding for the word "inscribe." The
first sense listed in the OED is "To write, mark, or delineate (words,
a name, characters, etc.) in or on something; esp. so as to be con-
spicuous or durable, as on a monument, tablet, etc." The quality of
durability is what deconstructionist criticism has tended to seize
upon, transmogrifying it into "necessarily always present," or in
Derrida's all-too-fashionable formulation, "always already." That
is, in inscribe as currently used, the notion of "always already"
combines with Derrida's use of "writing" as that which makes

language possible to create that which could not be otherwise, which language makes necessary. Since this sense is already being blurred by more careless writers who have taken it as simply the approved-by-the-best-poststructuralists word for "writing" or even "existing," its use invites considerable vagueness. To write in 1995 that "male dominance is inscribed in the culture" may be intended to mean simply that an assumption of male superiority is reflected in many customs, expressions, and modes of thought (and thus is durable but not necessarily unyielding), or it may carry the sense that it is so embedded in the structure of language as to be immutable without total destruction of the present culture.

Notes

1. Dowling points out that an obligation and a promise differ in that the promise is the *act* that produces a *state* of obligation (90–1). An author's intention may be understood as a state, or series of states, producing a series of acts (the encoding of the intended message in one form or another) that produces the final state of the text.
2. E. D. Hirsch's reply to Knapp and Michaels (entitled "Against Theory?") makes the point, as does Dowling's, in saying that intention is *formally* necessary. Dowling's excellent treatment of the basis of the New Critical intentionality argument seems however to oversimplify in placing intention only in the speaker internal to the text ("persona" and "implied author" may, I take it, be equivalent terms); even Wimsatt and Beardsley would admit that the external (flesh and blood) author intended that the reader attribute the appropriate intentions to the internal speaker.
3. Although Dilthey's distinction is as well known as useful, the contrast between understanding and interpretation has not always been developed in the same way by later writers. Thus the philosopher Paul Ricoeur writes, "By understanding I mean the ability to take up again within oneself the work of structuring that is performed by the text, and by explanation the second-order operation grafted onto this understanding that consists in bringing to light the codes underlying this work of structuring that is carried through in company with the reader" (OI, 378). For Ricoeur, explanation is the description of the linguistic rules, the semiotic system that must be employed in interpretation. But such an explanation is a description of procedures, not in fact the application of a theory that can be tested. A particularly fertile source of confusion is the tendency to conflate the distinction between understanding and explanation that I have outlined with a different sense that has arisen in the course of an extended debate between Jürgen Habermas and Hans-Georg Gadamer in which

explanation has come to be associated with the *use* of the understanding of a text or, more frequently, an aspect of the structure of society, to alter that structure.

4. In "In Defense of Overinterpretation," Jonathan Culler defends what Booth calls overstanding, the "pursuing of questions that the text does not pose to its model reader" (114). Precisely – but in contrasting this, the pursuit of symptomatic meaning, with the overinterpretation that Umberto Eco questions in an earlier essay in the same volume, Culler is confused: Eco's reservations are about imputing impossible or improbable *intentional* meanings.

5. Nassar defines metacriticism as "the assessment of the view of life of a work or its author by a critic who uses as his basis of judgment his own or other views of life" (*The Rape of Cinderella*, 133). The emphasis on assessment gives metacriticism a somewhat narrower sense than I assign to significance, but since statements of significance are rarely independent of implicit or explicit value judgments, the two terms are not far apart.

6. "Isolated Islands of Discontent," *Times Higher Education Supplement*, Feb. 13, 1981, p. 31.

7. A survey of the several meanings of "symbolism," "historicism," "text," "code," and "context" may be found in my *Dictionary of Concepts in Literary Criticism and Theory*.

7

Historical Scholarship and Literary History

The conscious implication of Flaubert's Parrot *is that since we cannot know everything about the past we cannot know anything; but its actual effect – and its success – is to suggest something different: that the relative confirms the idea of truth instead of dissipating it, that the difficulty of finding out how things were does not disprove those things but authenticates them.*

John Bayley, *The Order of Battle at Trafalgar*, 12.

"Literary history" is a phrase used so confidently one might think it neither problematical nor controversial, but it is in fact so particularly likely to lead the unwary into confusion as to deserve a chapter to itself. Indeed the last half-century has produced a cautionary series of attempts to bring order to this complexly recalcitrant topic.[1] The first difficulty is the same found pretty generally throughout literary commentary: the failure to take account of the different senses in which a key term is used. One finds many an essay seeking to contrast literary history with criticism, or dividing it into types, or giving warnings about its pursuit, but few of these offer an explicit definition of the thing itself. As most often used, the term mixes together several distinct kinds of activity while pronouncing generalizations about the whole that properly apply to only one of these activities. Jerzy Pelc does not exaggerate when he comments that "literary history" has been variously used to mean "'pure' literary history, literary theory, the sociology of literature, the psychology of literature, the semiotics of literature, the methodology of literary history, the methodology of literary theory, elements of aesthetics, elements of the history of culture, elements of the philosophy of culture, elements of ethics, elements of such disciplines as sociology, linguistics, psychology, political and economic history, etc." (90). Moreover, it has often meant one or another mixture of these.

The second difficulty arises from contemporary debates over the possibility of linguistic reference and the difficulty of writing history of any sort. If, as some of the most influential contemporary literary theorists seem to continue to hold, words cannot refer to an extra-linguistic reality, to speak of historical fact may seem naive. In the words of Terence Hawkes: "A language . . . does not construct its formations of words by reference to the patterns of 'reality,' but on the basis of its own internal and self-sufficient rules" (16–17).[2] Taken at face value, such a position would seem to reduce all attempts at literary history to unconfirmable linguistic constructions. As a result, many a contemporary literary essay manifests evident uneasiness over the difficulty of reconciling the attempt to say anything true or meaningful about any aspect of culture, and especially anything that has a historical dimension, with the argument that since there are no apodictic first principles all human judgments are relative and the truth of any belief incapable of determination. This conflict is far from being simply a philosophical conundrum; strong tensions arise from the incommensurability of such slogans as "all is language" with the desire to somehow use literature to combat perceived abuses in the social structure, a desire shared by many of those who subscribe to such a slogan.[3] If history is *nothing but* a narrative structure, total fictionality reigns – or would if the concept of fictionality were possible without the experience of fact. On the other hand, it is impossible to return to the naive view that the literary critic or the historians of literature present us with objects in themselves as they are.

However we need not remain entranced by such fashionable paradoxes as that stated by David Perkins: "My opinion is . . . that we cannot write literary history with intellectual conviction, but we must read it. The irony and paradox of this argument are themselves typical of our present moment in history" (17). That the prefatory announcement by the literary historian that the investigation he or she has undertaken and now offers, nicely printed, to the reader is an impossibility has become an almost obligatory gesture, as Robert Johnstone notes.

The first step in seeing more clearly the issues in which the subject of literary history is entangled – including the opposition between an anti-foundationalist relativism and the belief that it is not an oxymoron to speak of historical fact – is a simple exercise in desynonymization. There is considerable value in emphasizing the differences, first, between the *historical scholarship* that provides the basic data for *literary history* and, second, between literary histories

of two different kinds of scope, each of which – to further compli-
cate matters, may exhibit one of two primary orientations. I want to
argue that the historical scholarship which is the essential ground
of literary history is insulated from the kind of relativism insisted
upon by hermetic theorizing. However, the uses of the *results* of
that activity are, like all explorations of significance, reflections of
the contemporary preoccupations of particular discourse communities and thus necessarily relative, or, I should prefer to say, partial.

"Literary history" frequently has been, and continues to be, used
to designate the whole of linguistic, historical, and biographical
studies intended to provide the background for understanding
a literary work. As René Wellek phrases it, this wide sense is equivalent to "study of literature in the past" (LH, 115). For instance, in
Norman Foerster's "Literary Scholarship and Criticism" (1936) "literary scholarship" and "literary history" are used synonymously.
While R. S. Crane's influential "History versus Criticism in the Study
of Literature" (1935) carefully distinguished literary-historical study
in general from true literary history, in the debate between the New
Critics and advocates of older, more historically based methods of
study, "literary history" came to serve as a kind of shorthand for all
research intended to reconstruct one or more aspects of the context
in which a text was written. Thus Cleanth Brooks's "Literary History vs. Criticism" (1940) employed "literary history" and "historical scholarship" interchangeably in explaining that providing a vision
of the past "through eyes long turned to dust . . . is the function of
the historian" (LHC, 404). Forty-three years later in *The Rich Manifold* Brooks refers to literary history in the same way: it is the study
of "the background and genesis of a literary work" or "the genesis
and development of a literary work" (*RM*, 34).

Such usage roughly corresponds to the older sense of "philological," that which included not only the study of grammar (understood as both syntactical structure and the semantic possibilities of
individual words) but the exploration of the immediate situation
and the total cultural context in which a text was produced. This
broad sense lies halfway between the yet older usage exemplified
by Martianus Capella's designation of the whole of the seven liberal arts as "philology" and the much more restricted meaning of
"the study of languages" or even "the study of the history of change
in language" (diachronic linguistics) which it had come to have by
the end of the nineteenth century.[4] As "philology" in English usage
became increasingly identified with the study of the development

of language,[5] "literary history" seems to have begun to acquire the portion of philology's former meaning that was fading – an illustration of the Saussurian principle that a change in the value of one word in a language system will necessarily alter the values of others, especially near synonyms.[6]

HISTORICAL SCHOLARSHIP

However, "historical scholarship" is a much less confusing designation than "literary history" for the pursuit of facts outside or beyond the individual text. I have quite purposely chosen the word "facts"; at a time when commentary on literature seems built on shifting sands, it is well to recognize that literary scholarship treats factual questions that are for the most part open to determinate resolution.[7] The prevalence of tags and quotations in medieval literature; Wyatt's modification of the form of the Italian sonnet and Surrey's further modification of the form; the gradual decline in the popularity and composition of verse drama; the impossibility of Milton's having influenced Shakespeare; the rise and fall of the heroic couplet as a major verse form; the importance of the dramatic monologue in the Victorian period; the temporal priority of *In Memoriam* over Darwin's *On the Origin of Species*; the contemporary and continuing preference for Charles Dickens over George Meredith; the increase in the importance of free indirect speech in the novel from at least the middle of the nineteenth century; the diversification of the detective story in the second half of the present century; the enormous popularity of Louis L'Amour's westerns – all these are facts.

Some facts are more subject to possible correction than others, but if, for instance, an earlier author than Wyatt were found to have been the importer of the Italian sonnet, what had been thought to be fact would simply give way to a new fact. That is, such matters as the first writer to use a specific stanza form, or the date of publication of a poem, or the authorship of a particular text, are not in principle indeterminate (unknowable), although in particular cases the necessary data for a positive determination may not be available or new evidence may require corrections. Of course to say that *Paradise Lost* was written in 1667 is to employ at least three conventions: the very convention of measuring time in years, the convention of counting the years from a particular point in time, and the convention of Arabic numbers. But within these shared conventions, the fact *is* a fact, and one that can be translated into the calendars of other cultures and other numbering systems. The date 1667 may be absurd under the aspect of eternity, but that view is precisely what we don't and can't share. Similarly, key terms such as "detective novel" or even "popularity" may be redefined, but such redefinition does not affect the facts related to the term in its earlier use.

I was surprised to discover the following statements being made in a sober manner as late in the day as 1990.

> Truth is produced, not discovered, and is a property not of the world but of statements. To put the matter another way, statements do not refer to but rather constitute facts: what counts as a fact is determined not by its existence in the world but by the discursive practices that make it possible for something in the world to serve as a fact within a certain discourse.[8]

What is being confused here are of course a fact, belief in a fact, the significance attached to a fact, and the form of statement of a fact, a confusion the implications of which extend far beyond the study of literature. Let us take the statement "The German government's policy was to destroy all Jews." That is a fact for which there is a tremendous amount of evidence. Unless all that evidence can be plausibly reinterpreted, the statement will remain a fact. That within certain ideological communities the Holocaust is not accepted as a fact is also a fact, and one can conceive, barely, of a time in the history of the world when the Holocaust might no longer be accepted as fact. Even so, it would remain a fact and could always be rediscovered although whether it was or not would have no bearing on its facticity. The current significance of that fact is different for the average gentile, Jew, and neo-Nazi; its significance will almost certainly be different for the educated person of, for instance, AD 2100 and different yet again in AD 5000. The form of such a statement can always be quarrelled with – one can imagine an argument to the effect that what the Germans really wanted to do was simply rid the country of Jews – had they all moved elsewhere, that would have been perfectly acceptable. I don't believe that, and I don't know anyone who does, but even if it were true, it would not alter the fact of the killing of six million Jews; it would only render the form of the statement partially inaccurate, a matter that could be corrected by rewriting it more simply: "The German government was responsible for the death of six million Jews."

To return to the treatment of specifically literary phenomena by historical scholarship, the prevalence of blanket denials of the possibility or value of literary history makes it necessary to bear in mind that such denials can be viable only as directed against the pattern into which the literary historian organizes such facts, not against the possibility of historical facts per se. Historical scholarship is thus the most definitive activity of literary research. While no research is wholly objective – what one is able to find is governed largely by what one is looking for – historical scholarship seeks nothing but what is demonstrable in principle and, far more often than not, in actuality.

It may be worth repeating that it is very curious indeed how completely those who relish the notion of language as an arbitrary and autonomous system and consequently project this principle into a denial of the possibility of historical fact fail to see that Saussure's point that the very recognition that the same object is denominated by different words in different languages necessarily affirms that there are objects stable enough at least to be recognized and discriminated by speakers of these different languages. Of course Saussure also pointed out that words designating the same sort of object in various languages are frequently not fully synonymous – in his famous example the French *mouton* can designate both the sheep in the field and the mutton in the stew – but we could not know that that is the case if sheep and mutton were not discriminable objects. And what is true of objects of course is equally true of specific actions and events.

I have given so much space to historical scholarship because the habit of lumping it together with literary history in its more specific and useful senses falsifies both its status and its function. Historical scholarship in fact underlies almost the entire range of hermeneutical and critical activities, including "literary history" in its more restricted meanings, but it is not coterminous with any of these activities.[9] The distinctions between these endeavors are best understood in terms of a matrix of commonly accepted dichotomies that crosscut each other. The first is that between *synchronic* and *diachronic* focuses. Employed synchronically, the findings of historical scholarship may serve hermeneutics, the construction of *intended meaning*. The results of synchronically focussed historical scholarship may also be employed in the construction of symptomatic meanings: the tracing of patterns of cultural and/or psychological forces that seem to account for certain aspects of the text or responses to it. As noted earlier, because they almost always draw on external theories presumed to be well grounded, studies of significance are often thought by their authors to be more scientific than those which seek to interpret intended meaning. Thus Todorov describes such "scientific" endeavors which he contrasts with the "interpretive":

> [We] find here . . . psychological or psychoanalytic, sociological or ethnological studies, as well as those derived from philosophy or from the history of ideas. All deny the autonomous character of the literary work and regard it as the manifestation of laws that are external to it and that concern the psyche, or society, or even the "human mind." (6)

Hermeneutic interpretation having been explored in Chapter 5 and the significances pursued by criticism in the first portion of Chapter 7, they need not be further considered here.

It may be urged that materials gained through historical scholarship are at times employed simply for better understanding of the interrelationship between a literary text and the cultural milieu in which it was created. Such would seem to be a claim of certain New Historicists, although such explorations seem very often reducible to either intended meaning or symptomatic meaning, or perhaps a conflation of the two. If neither of these is the goal, it is hard to see what the relationship between the text and the facets of the historical context discussed in the same context might be. In any case it is worth noting that the "New Historicist" principle that literature acts on culture as well as culture on literature was long ago validated by an elder historicism and will be found exemplified in literary histories now often regarded as irremediably old-fashioned.

LITERARY HISTORY: INTERNAL VS. EXTERNAL

Diachronically applied historical scholarship, on the other hand, supports the study of the temporal sequence of a selected group of texts and the development of modifications or major innovations over time – in other words, *literary history*. Failure to distinguish between the several kinds of literary history produces as much misunderstanding as the failure to distinguish between literary history and historical scholarship. Literary history itself is best regarded in terms of two distinctions. The first is between studies that pursue primarily relations and influences *internal* to the succession of texts, and those that emphasize *external* influences.[10] Studies of either kind must again be subdivided into two categories of literary history as distinguished by their scopes. Studies of the sequence of appearance, changes in, and development of a specifically stipulated type of text (often a single genre) I will refer to simply as *histories of a type*. The second category consists of *histories of a literature*.

Internally oriented literary histories chronicle the facts of succession and change, the explanations of which changes are understood to lie primarily within the relations between author and author, text and text. The emphasis falls on deviations from and modifications of prior models. René Wellek championed such processes as "nearest to the specific task of the literary student" (SKLH, 122). "The literary historian in this sense has a task analogous to that of the historian of art or of music, who can trace the evolution of portrait painting or of the sonata without necessarily paying much attention to the biographies of painters or composers or to the audience for which the paintings and compositions were designed" (SKLH, 112). While external forces probably always exert some influence, there are a number of well-known theories of literary history which minimize them. The most obvious example is the Russian Formalists' description of literary history as a constant struggle against the "automatization" which causes experience to become stale, routine, and thus blind; new techniques of "making strange" thus become continually necessary. Harold Bloom's view of literary change as resulting from the misprision of earlier poets by "strong" poets who come after is also in its own way internal. (Neither of these theories explains the directions in which change occurs, only the fact of its necessity – as Medvedev/Bakhtin pointed out in the case of the Russian Formalists.) Hayden White adapts Jakobson's division of the structures of discourse into two great modes, the metaphoric and the metonymic, as an argument for the alternation of metaphoric and metonymic emphases in literature.[11] (This solves the problem of direction, at least on the highest level, by resolving it into an alternation, but does not address the question of the differences between one metaphoric or metonymic period and the next.)

Wellek himself, long a champion of the internal history of

literature, finally came to believe that "One work is the necessary condition of another one but one cannot say that it has caused it." He concluded that "The so-called laws of literary history boil down to some vague psychological generalities: action and reaction, convention and revolt, the 'form-fatigue' formulated by a German architect Adolf Göller in the 1880s" (FLH, 72). The Russian Formalists may indeed well have been right that the overarching internal force for change and development is simply the desire for novelty, an explanation which can account equally for new techniques, structures, and subject areas, and for authors' incorporation – and modification – of fresh new forms or subjects found in the works of other authors.

Many literary histories, especially histories of types or genres, try as much as possible to avoid looking toward external cultural forces. For example, John Heath-Stubbs announces in the beginning of his little volume on the pastoral, "We shall be dealing with a particular poetical convention, which had a definite historical origin in the work of certain Greek poets of the second century before Christ" (1). And that is the way the book proceeds: the concern is the succession and change within that succession, not the explanation of the changes. The following comes from David Fowler's *A Literary History of the Popular Ballad*:

> The approach which I have adopted for the present study is fundamentally a chronological one. I believe, with Hodgart, that there is an early history and a later history of the ballads, and that it is only through a rigorously chronological analysis, with careful identification of the sources of every ballad, that we can come to recognize a most important and impressive historical phenomenon: the evolution of ballad style. (4–5)

This evolution is traced, not explained.

Both examples I have cited successfully avoid the obvious temptation to identify change with progress. While change is rather naturally understood as "development," and development equally naturally suggests "improvement," neither development nor improvement necessarily means progress. A development may be an isolated change, an altering of direction, or an improvement – it is not necessarily progress. A remark by G. K. Chesterton is relevant: "Even when we improve we never progress. For progress, the metaphor of the road, implies a man leaving his home behind him:

but improvement means a man exalting the towers or extending the gardens of his home" (12). It is thus possible to speak of a poet finding ways to improve the handling of the heroic couplet, or a dramatist making monologues more realistic, or a novelist gaining subtlety in handling free indirect discourse without implying either that all improvements in heroic couplets, monologues, realistic effects, or the use of free indirect discourse must lie in the same direction or that the heroic couplet, stage realism, or free indirect discourse are in themselves necessarily preferable to blank verse, anti-realistic conventions, or tagged dialogue.

Although the literary history that looks primarily to the historical succession of developments within a genre or type of literature can be very useful, we know that literary texts are in part cultural artifacts. Emphasis on explaining the existence of the text produces the externally oriented literary history. A problem arises, however, when "explanation" is taken to mean "cause" in a strong sense. "Difference implies change. Change implies cause," writes Hayden White. "And where there is no discussion of cause, we must suppose a want of analytical rigor or a willed decision to halt analysis short of comprehensiveness in the interest of other, extra-literary or ideological, considerations" (PCLH, 100).[12] However, although to explain literary change on the basis of a single or primary cause has seemed to many almost a requirement of intellectual respectability, the difficulties scholars have encountered in achieving this goal, and the number of different causal explanations whose sponsors continually contend, has led to understandable skepticism about the possibility of literary history itself.

Much of the difficulty lies in a confusion between "cause" and "condition." Logic – a discipline with which literary study seems generally rather uncomfortable – distinguishes "necessary" and "sufficient" conditions: A is a sufficient condition for B if B is always produced by the presence of A; A is a necessary condition for B if B cannot occur without A.[13] To say that one thing is a "cause" of another is often assumed to be the same as saying that the first is a necessary *and* sufficient condition for the existence of the second, but in fact, it is rare that a condition is *both* necessary and sufficient. Although a literary history may suggest that Shaftesbury's philosophy, or Protestantism, or the power of the monarchy, or the capitalist system is a cause of important aspects of a given text (in the strong sense of cause), few would care to accept the challenge of proving that one of these explanations presents a condition that was both necessary and sufficient. Such conditions may indeed be merely contributing rather than either truly necessary or sufficient. A good deal of contention would evaporate if historians of literature never allowed themselves to speak of *the* cause, restricting themselves to forms like "*a* cause of . . ." or, better, "a likely influence on."

Thus, that there was a general shift away from syntactical figures to tropes at the end of the sixteenth century is a condition that helps explain Donne's poetry, but in itself it is neither necessary nor sufficient. The wider dissemination of texts through printing is perhaps a necessary condition of tighter presentational structure, but in itself it is hardly a sufficient one. The increasing need to disseminate information in the seventeenth century is perhaps a sufficient condition for the increasing practice of a plainer style of prose in the seventeenth century, but it is not a necessary one. To put the matter in a more comprehensive form, it is a misunderstanding to assume that literary history (as I have defined it), whether of a type or of a national literature, whether it looks to internal or external influences, offers strict cause-and-effect explanations.

WITH REGARD TO HISTORIES OF A LITERATURE

I have called all narratives of the changes in and development of the literature of a people sharing a language, culture, and geographical area "histories of a literature." For the most part the history of a literature is a mixture of bibliography, biography, cultural analysis, literary change, and critical commentary. "It must be admitted," wrote René Wellek, "that most histories of literature are either social histories or histories of thought as mirrored in literature, or a series of impressions and judgments on individual works of art arranged in a more or less chronological order" (LH, 115).

Although there are evidently histories of the literature of Nebraska, of York, of the American West, the paradigmatic model is the history of a national literature. It is quite possible to write the history of a national literature with a strongly internal orientation. Of particular interest are two recent histories of English literature that are almost wholly concerned with relationships of internal succession. One is Peter Conrad's *Everyman History of English Literature* (1985). "I wanted to show," writes Conrad, "that the works of the more than a thousand years that this narrative covers themselves comprise one indivisible, unending book" (vii). "I have not written an external history, aligning literature with social changes or political events; my aim is to demonstrate how history happens within the literature, which has its own chronology" (ix). Similarly, Alastair Fowler, making a distinction between literary contents and literary forms, writes in his Preface, "I mainly trace . . . changes in kinds and forms. Sometimes these have social or economic causes, but more often they are developments internal to literature – shifts of fashion, deeper movements, growth cycles, effects of compensation" (*HEL*, x). That two such histories of English literature could have been written by British scholars in the 1980s, a time of strong Marxist currents in British universities, is intriguing, especially in view of the social emphasis currently so much insisted upon in literary histories of American literature.[14]

In general, however, historians treating a national literature are even more strongly tempted to explain the narrative they present than those writing histories of literary types. Recent decades have seen a number of varieties of Marxist criticism which, with greater or lesser subtlety, link a national literature to social reality seen as a highly complex economic and political struggle. But of course Marxists are not the only commentators who have sought to explain literary change through such social structures. Sir Sydney Lee wrote in 1913, "In literary history we seek the external circumstances – political, social, economic – in which literature is produced" (8). Broader yet is Hippolyte Taine's 1863 formula of *race, milieu,* and *moment.*

Since the changes chronicled in a national literary history are almost necessarily assumed to be identified in part with the character of the nation or people, the more ambitious the attempt to achieve a unified view, the stronger the imposition of quasi-teleological patterns. In Robert Johnstone's happy phrase, the history of a national literature is "a genre of the cultural imagination" (31). The narrative constructed is assumed not only to cast light on the historical development of the literature, but to use the literature to illustrate the present happy or sad state of the culture. Thus the national literary history tends to combine the assignment of symptomatic meaning to synchronic slices of the history with the history of diachronic changes. At the same time earlier literature is at least partly understood and evaluated in terms of the present state of things. This is true even when great emphasis is placed on cultural currents traced so far back as to seem inherent in a culture. Douglas Hyde states in the introduction to *A Literary History of Ireland*,

> The love for literature of a more traditional type, in song, in poem, in saga, was, I think, more nearly universal in Ireland than in any country of Western Europe, and hence that which appears to me to be of most value in ancient Irish literature is not that whose authorship is known, but rather the mass of traditional matter which seems to have grown up almost spontaneously, and slowly shaped itself into the literary possession of an entire nation. (x)

The claim may well be accurate, but the emphasis it receives here and elsewhere in the book is called forth by Hyde's indignation over the education in Ireland at that time which drove out the Irish language and lore to replace them with a shaky knowledge of English.

As we have been reminded by a flood of articles on the revision of American literary history, the *Literary History of the United States* edited by Spiller (1948) seeks primarily to reflect the "American way of life – which really means the American way of thinking and feeling" (xv) and a literature "intensely conscious of the needs of the common man, and equally conscious of the aspirations of the individual in such a democracy as we have known here" (xvi). On the other hand, Emory Elliott, the editor of the *Columbia Literary History of the United States* (1988) emphasizes diversity, writing that "concurrence remains impossible at this time. There is today no unifying vision of a national identity like that shared by many scholars at the closings of the two world wars" (xii). It might have been thought that growing recognition of the role of cultural differences in the history of the United States together with the contemporary emphasis on the value of the multicultural nature of the country would have suggested that a history of American literature per se was hardly a viable project, but the imperative to describe the literature of a nation in a way congruent with current modes of thought evidently remains strong. (It is perhaps worth asking if, at this point in history, "literature in English" is not a more profitable topic than the national literature of any single English-speaking country.)[15]

A history of a national literature is more often than not *expected* to serve cultural purposes, which is not to say that such a history is necessarily consciously intended to support a political or ideological agenda. For example, E. G. Brown writes on the first page of his four-volume *Literary History of Persia*:

> This book, as its title implies, is a history, not of different dynasties, which have ruled in Persia and of the kings who composed those dynasties, but of the Persian people. It is, moreover, the history of that people written from a particular point of view – the literary. In other words, it is an attempt to portray the subjective – that is to say the religious, intellectual, aesthetic – characteristics of the Persians as manifested in their own writings, or sometimes, when they fail, in those of their neighbours. (I: 3)

The farther the historian of literature moves toward cultural analysis, the greater is the tendency to use literature to illustrate aspects of the society as much as to use the social/cultural context to explain literary development. To look in both directions is to reflect the central principle of the "old" historicism (stretching from Herder to Ranke to Auerbach) that all aspects of a culture are mutually illuminating. Thus Erich Auerbach: "If we assume with Vico that every age has its characteristic unity, every text must provide a partial view on the basis of which a synthesis is possible" (19).

.

DATA AND USE; SYMPTOMATIC AND INTENTIONAL MEANING

Historical scholarship is the source of facts which are then employed in the service of determining possible intended meaning, of writing literary histories of all four permutations, and, to a lesser extent, of inducing symptomatic (extra-authorial) meanings. The order in which I have listed these three uses seems to me roughly to correspond to the degrees of their relativity. That is, as we move from interpretation of authorial meaning to internal and then external literary history and on to symptomatic meanings, the foregrounding of specially chosen conditions increases. The interpretation of authorial meaning can never be more than probable, and correct interpretation is always threatened by readers' failures to recognize operative elements of context, but in fact the degree of probability is high and errors always potentially corrigible by the discovery of further elements of context. Internal literary histories are subject to inadequacy in the selection of examples considered, and there is often a wider field from which such examples must be chosen, but errors are again corrigible. External literary histories are likely to ignore or suppress some explanatory conditions in the interest of emphasizing others – interesting narrativity or "tellability" requires this. Symptomatic meanings induced by recourse to imported theories – the potential number of which is without discernible limit – necessarily foreground specially chosen conditions. Each construction of symptomatic meaning is to be judged in relation to the external pattern on which it draws and thus is wholly relative in that meanings induced by the application of separate externally derived modes of explanation cannot conflict.

In recent years, the narratologist's distinction between story and narrative (or story and discourse) has frequently been applied to literary history. What historical scholarship makes available is the story; the literary historian creates a narrative out of the story materials – internal histories nevertheless remaining more story than narrative while external histories are at least as much narrative as story. Although, as in the writing of fiction, the less the story is presented as a simple succession of events, the more interesting it is likely to be, the analogue can be pushed too far. For instance, as Cynthia Chase and Jonathan Culler (*PS*, 172–83) have suggested, in fiction one can think either of the narrative as a function of the story events or the story events as a function of the narrative structure. Actually, neither relational order is fixed for the novelist or short-story writer, who may in fact constantly adjust one to the other. But in the writing of literary history, whatever facts are known at the time of writing constitute the only story there is: the historian as historian is presumed not to have tampered with these, however much they may have been narrativized through the selection, ordering, and emphasis that constitutes their "emplotment." To put the matter another way, it has long been recognized that "history" may designate either the subject of study (events, aspects of the past as revealed by whatever evidence exists) or the specific presentations of the results of such study. The first is the data, the second the narrative commentary. The issue that necessarily arises is whether what we call data are actually artifacts of the narrative commentary. To which the answer is pretty clearly, "Yes and No." The totality of, say, American nineteenth-century texts and documents has a "brute reality" – these exist (or have existed) and can be altered or added to only by forgery. On the other hand, what a given narrative commentary calls into prominence and what it ignores from this totality, what it defines as literature and what relations it points to, are *processed* data.

Finally, it may be worthwhile to point out that in so far as literary history seeks to uncover the causes – more properly, the conditions – which produced new genres, themes, techniques, or other literary qualities, it is either not pursuing meanings or pursuing symptomatic ones. However, to the degree that authors can be assumed to have expected readers to respond to contrasts between their works and the readers' expectations, aspects of intentional meaning are introduced. In recognizing a parody, we recognize an indirect illocutionary force that alters our interpretation of the author's perlocutionary intent. A harsh treatment of a situation that has almost always been treated sentimentally will suggest that the author intends the reader to think about the situation in a different way.

Notes

1. René Wellek's "Six Kinds of Literary History" (1946) and "The Fall of Literary History" (1973), R. S. Crane's "Critical and Historical Principles of Literary History" (1967), Geoffrey Hartman's "Toward Literary History" (1970), Hans Robert Jauss's "Literary History as a Challenge to Literary Theory" (1970), Robert Weimann's *Structure and Society in Literary History* (1976; Epilogue, 1984), and David Perkins's *Is Literary History Possible?* (1992) approach the issues from different perspectives that interestingly illuminate changes in literary theory over four decades.

2. A similar comment from a somewhat more centrist critic is Robert Scholes's "Criticism. . . . has taught us that language is tautological, if it is not nonsense, and to the extent that it is about anything it is about itself" (FCF, 233). Scholes's and Hawkes's statements date from more than 15 years ago (a long time given the present rate of critical revolution), but that such summary statements are less often made in the 1990s seems to reflect not the repudiation of the view they encapsulate but the degree to which it has been absorbed into the general intellectual milieu.

3. It is all very well to say that the multiform structures of society are nothing but the creatures of language, but, to make another use of Saussure's famous example, raising and slaughtering sheep, or sitting down to a meal of saddle of mutton, or starving for lack of anything to eat are not linguistic acts, even though they may be described in language and regarded metaphorically as signs in a gestural language.

4.   Bacon thinks of literary history in a no less comprehensive way in the *Advancement of Learning* (1605). "History is Natural, Civil, Ecclesiastical, and Literary; whereof the three first I allow as extant, the fourth I note as deficient. For no man hath propounded to himself the general state of learning to be described and represented from age to age . . ." (183).

5.   The 1892 edition of *Chambers's Encyclopaedia* gives interesting evidence of the change: "within recent years, philology has entered upon a new phase, or rather a new study has sprung up alongside the old. As the naturalist investigates a class of objects not with a view to turn them to use, but to understand their nature, and classify them, so the new school of philologists examine and compare the structures of the various languages, and arrange them in classes and families, with the ultimate view of arriving at some theory of language in general – its mode of origin and growth."

6.   The broader meaning of "philology" was, however, maintained in Germany: both Erich Auerbach and Leo Spitzer could claim allegiance to "romance philology." For a useful discussion of the comprehensiveness possible to the conception of romance philology see Geoffrey Green's *Literary Criticism and the Structures of History: Erich Auerbach and Leo Spitzer*.

7.   The continuing skittishness about seeming to assume any sort of factuality is nicely indicated in a single sentence from Jerome McGann's useful essay "History, Herstory, Theirstory, Ourstory": "Every so-called fact or event in history is imbedded in an indeterminate set of multiple and overlapping networks" (197). That there are any number of overlapping networks is indeed the reason that no one history can be definitive, but why must the word "facts" be preceded by "so-called"?

8.   This appears in Lee Patterson's "Literary History" in *Critical Terms for Literary Study*, p. 257.

9.   Alastair Fowler's way of putting this is: "In each discipline there is an 'outside' of superficial facts, more or less certain, and an 'inside' of patterns, myths, themes, and laws, more or less interpretable and debatable" (TH, 120). From the context in which this sentence appears, I take superficial to be a synonym for external, not an attribution of insignificance.

10. The terms "intrinsic" and "extrinsic" are frequently used to mark this difference, but because of the well-known application of those terms by Wellek and Warren to modes of interpreting meaning, I have preferred "internal" and "external" to designate different modes of constructing literary history.

11. See also David Lodge, *The Modes of Modern Writing: Metaphor, Metonymy, and the Typology of Modern Literature* (1977) and chapter I of *Working With Structuralism* (1981). Jakobson's exploration of metaphor and metonymy in relation of speech disorders is to be found in "The Metaphoric and Metonymic Poles."

12. Similar is R. S. Crane's 1967 comment, "the historian of literature is the chronicler and interpreter of change; he is fulfilling his function

only when the knowledge he has of the literary past is integrated into an explanatory narrative of the transformations undergone, during some determinate period . . ." (CHP, 6).

13. More formally, to quote Morris Cohen and Ernest Nagel's *Logic and Scientific Method*, "A proposition *p* states a *sufficient condition* for another proposition *q* if '*p* implies *q*' is true. A proposition *p* states a *necessary condition* for another proposition *q* if '*not-p* implies *not-q*' is true" (388).

14. Perhaps the much longer history and greater variety of English literature is less encouraging to the writing of a history oriented toward a current social agenda. Again, although both were published in 1948, the well-known *Literary History of England* edited by A. C. Baugh presents a much less consistently held cultural overview than the *Literary History of the United States* of which R. E. Spiller was the primary editor.

15. A cogent argument that the "concept of 'national literatures' in English has outlived its usefulness and should be abandoned" will be found in Christopher Clausen's "'National Literatures' in English: Towards a New Paradigm."

A Note on New Historicism

The uses of the word historicism are as confusing as those of any of the important concepts in the humanities, but within literary study the most common sense has been the belief that a text cannot be understood apart from the conventions, beliefs, concerns, values, and interests of the culture in which it was produced. Obviously the defense of the logical (not necessarily psychological or intellectual) primacy of intended meaning that I have tried to make assumes the importance of historical approaches while at the same time recognizing that the beliefs and attitudes that an author consciously or unconsciously assumed to be immanent in a culture to which anticipated readers belonged may reveal a great deal about the culture; the resulting silences may indeed cast light on the author's intentions.

A reaction against excessive preoccupation with cultural history combined with the kind of misinterpretation of just what was meant by the "intentional fallacy" (discussed in Chapter 5) decreased the historical emphasis in literary studies (even though many scholars happily carried on the tradition); the structuralist emphasis on the autonomy, reflexiveness, or lack of external reference in literature or in all discourse (theorists phrase the matter variously) further seemed to deny the validity of a historical approach. As the sterility resulting from the reduction of all texts to examples of the same abyss became apparent, the importance of historical milieu began to be recognized anew. But a direct call for a return to an older principle or practice is seldom a successful strategy – especially where defects in the older approach have in fact become evident. Enter, then, the New Historicism announced by Stephen Greenblatt (see *PFER*, 5–6). The New Historicism saw itself as new in several ways. First, whereas the older historicism had seen each age as a unified system, the emerging type of historicism would emphasize the tensions within a culture at any given period. Second, the new type would recognize that the historian's view of a past culture is a product of the historian's own perspective and interests. Third, the new historicism would emphasize the tension in a culture as instances of a political struggle. Fourth, the "organic unity" of literary works would be explicitly questioned. Now the first point is something of an exaggeration – for instance, how many literary scholars considering the nineteenth century have overlooked the struggle between the landed aristocracy and the manufacturing interests, or between the philosophical radicals and the prosperous conservatives, or the philosophical contest between Coleridgean transcendentalism and the Benthamite Utilitarians? Nevertheless, it is true that political oppositions were given new emphasis under the influence of both Michel Foucault and Marxism.

Of course all human actions can be regarded as the result of political forces; they can equally be regarded in relation to gender, geography, love, or jealousy. None of these perspectives wholly subsumes the others. The degree to which it is profitable to consider a text from the perspective of political (or any other) forces will depend on both the text and the reader's purpose. There has been a shift toward speaking of "struggles for power" rather than political oppositions, but although "power" is perhaps a broader term than politics, the more it is stretched to apply to human motivation in general, the less specific its meaning and the greater the degree to which it conceals differences between varying human situations and relations. Struggles for power between parents and children, husbands and wives, the poor and the rich, employers and workers, and candidates for the same political office are hardly the same in kind.

As for the emphasis on the commentator's own situatedness, the issue had been clearly raised in hermeneutics by Dilthey; it can equally be seen as an extension of the philosophical historicism that argued from the differences in beliefs and values found over time and across cultures that all values and at least certain kinds of belief are wholly relative. And finally, to speak of the unity of a text is not to speak of the author's achievement of an ideological consistency; once again it is necessary to insist that a sense of unity is simply what the reader assumes the author assumed the reader would seek as a guide in constructing his or her interpretation. In any case, few of those regarded as New Historicists have betrayed any uncomfortableness about setting out their readings as correct ones – correct presumably for readers of the commentator's own time and culture, although even that is too strong a statement given the differences of perspective to be found everywhere at all times.

The rapidity with which literary theories shift, divide, and metamorphose can be seen in the little more than a decade since the birth of the New Historicism was proclaimed. The term has already become old-fashioned, something to be repudiated by those on the march to ever-new vantage points. Nevertheless, it has not yet become wholly antique, despite the anxiousness of the practitioners of (at least) three different forms to establish their own forms of practice.

Stephen Greenblatt, who almost by accident bestowed the name New Historicism upon the returning legitimacy of taking account of historical circumstance, has given the name "cultural poetics" to his own personal approach, "the study of the collective making of distinct social practices and inquiry into the relations among the practices" (*SN*, 5). The distinguishing feature of this approach is the sheer ingenuity with which he is able to bring a non-literary text into conjunction with a literary one with which it has parallels (the parallel, not surprisingly, is usually a power struggle). This strategy avoids the temptation to construct a monolithic structure against which to set the text, but if the chosen "non-literary" text is not exemplary of at least a major current within the culture, its relation to the literary text it presumably parallels is either fortuitous, and thus unilluminating however interesting as a coincidence, or both texts must be seen as part of a major contemporary mode of thought or belief – in which case a good deal more evidence than the existence of the two texts is necessary. The major feature of the second group, the Marxists whose criticism is generally designated as "cultural materialism," is, as one would expect, the unmasking of the action of the capitalist ideology as a force maintaining the hegemony of the already powerful. Rather strangely, although the ever-present class struggle is central in such analyses, the very power of the capitalist ideology explored makes it seem almost as all-pervasive, as universal, as the system of thought set out by the older historicists and deprecated by the new.

By 1983 Jerome McGann was already urging an historicism which, while recognizing the relationship of the literary work to the historical moment in which it was created, recognizes the ideology of the past and sees it as illusion, but also, presumably, by awareness of the difference, recognizes its own forms of thought. Thus,

> the abstractions and ideologies of the present are thereby laid open to critique from another human world, and one which – by the privilege of its historical backwardness, as it were – can know nothing of our current historical illusions. Our own forms of thought thereby begin to enter our consciousness via the critique developed out of certain past forms of feeling. (13)

In this way McGann preserves the Marxist emphasis on the cultural perspectives of the past as ideological, as the product of false consciousness, and admits that this view is produced by his adherence to a Marxist perspective. However, it is not clear that Marxism's illusions are thereby made evident – assuming that a Marxist can recognize the possibility of illusion in whatever variety of Marxism he or she believes.

The kind of movement of mind that McGann is suggesting is very nicely supplied by Marjorie Levinson's long essay on "Tintern Abbey" in *Wordsworth's Great Period Poems* (1986). Much richer than a straightforward Marxist analysis, it insists that Wordsworth had to deny the encroachment of industry, the pollution of the river Wye, and the beggars and vagrants who camped about the Abbey in order to create the vision he seeks. " 'Tintern Abbey's suppression of a historical consciousness is precisely what makes it so Romantic a poem" (45). The poem's brilliance is a result of suppressing the reality presented to Wordsworth's actual eye; but Levinson sees this as a tragedy: "In beholding *from* this green earth, in seeing *into* the life of things, the poet lost the ground he stood on and the teeming life of things" (46). What happens in the course of the essay is a shift from an analysis of what Wordsworth emphasized and what he omitted to a judgment about what he should have included if he had a social conscience – at least the social conscience of a liberal (leftist) of the 1990s. It is in short a judgment based on socio-political criteria – and presumably valid enough so long as one gives pride of place to those criteria. It is also worth noting that while Levinson emphasizes the actual title, her own approach questions why a poem usually cited as "Tintern Abbey" says so little about Tintern Abbey. The poem's actual title is, of course, "Lines Composed a Few Miles above Tintern Abbey, on Revisiting the Banks of the Wye during a Tour, July 13, 1798." I haven't made the experiment, but I'm not at all sure that one can even see the Abbey from "a few miles" above (or below, which is where Levinson thinks the poet must actually have been).

In any case, Hayden White is probably quite on the mark in writing of the New Historicism, "What they have specifically discovered . . . is that there is no such thing as a specifically historical approach to the study of history, but a variety of such approaches, at least as many as the positions on the ideological spectrum" (NH, 302).

8

Professionally Speaking: Rhetoricity and Mimesis in the Classroom

We talk about the tyranny of words, but we like to tyrannize over them too; we are fond of having a large superfluous establishment of words to wait upon us on great occasions; we think it looks important, and sounds well. As we are not particular about the meaning of our liveries on state occasions, if they be but fine and numerous enough, so the meaning or necessity of our words is a secondary consideration, if there be but a great parade of them.

David Copperfield, chap. 52.

Our ideal definition of a novel is helpful if we consider it an ideal towards which certain kinds of fiction tend; but if we allow it to determine in advance what we are going to see in a novel, it will end by obscuring the reasons why fiction is in fact enjoyed, and thus divorcing the critic wholly from the appreciative reader. A critic so divorced is engaged merely in a kind of pedantic play, which may be amusing to himself and his fellow professionals but has no further function.

David Daiches, "The Criticism of Fiction: Some Second Thoughts," 190.

THE OLD QUESTION

Teaching literature has never been easy – the old Oxford skeptics were not altogether wrong in thinking literature unteachable. Despite undergraduates' ever-lessening knowledge of the cultural information necessarily assumed by writers of every age, it is not the body of students but the subject that is, in an important sense, unteachable. Facts, conventions, and the expectations of writers can be taught. But the process of assembling what is necessary to understand what is read is purely heuristic; the value of literature lies

179

in the experience of understanding it and then exploring its significance within one's own mental milieu. The classroom lecture can
point the way, but the experience is an event (an event which need
not end when the final sentence of a text has been read), not the
sum of preparatory information.

The experience of reading can be all too easily short-circuited by
classroom insistence on symptomatic meanings – however interesting, such meanings are necessarily reductive, and the validity and
adequacy of the use to which they are put can only be judged in
relation to as full an understanding of authorial meaning as possible. Whether triggered by doubts about the philosophical respectability of seeking authorial meaning, or discomfort with the notion
that anyone can establish the best that has been known and thought,
or discomfort with the fragmentation of goals within literature departments, some thoughtful faculty members fear that the enterprise on which they have been embarked is adrift pedagogically;
others fear that it is being driven all too forcefully by certain narrow ideological currents. Six reactions predominate.

(1) There are those who, recognizing that the study of literature
is far from being a science, seek ways of making it more scientific.
I am fully sympathetic with André Lefevere's concern to make literature accessible by "codifying the repertory of literary procedures
in its historical evolution" (77). However, his attempt to argue for
the testability of hypotheses about meaning seems to me to make
only figurative use of such words drawn from the realm of science
as "prediction," "hypothesis," and "falsification." Paisley Livingston
argues that the study of literature can be made scientific by moving
away from an emphasis on interpretation toward "a reintegration
of the study of literary works within a realist sociohistorical framework of analysis" and "a more properly epistemological and cognitive role for literature" through "a reintegration of literary work
within the ongoing project of hypothesis formation within the human and social sciences" (244–5). Livingston clarifies this rather
vague terminology by suggesting the kinds of questions that should
be asked: Not "What does a particular text mean?" Rather, "What
are the consequences of an utterance in the context of the interaction in which it occurs?" "What systems of interaction are the proxi-
mate conditions of the emergence of an utterance?" "What is the
meaning of a text in the context of a particular program of research?
(249, 255, 260). All of which are perfectly valid questions, but, again,
questions the answers to which do not seem specifically scientific.

(2) Some, while not convinced that the study of literature can be a science, have wished to move from the messiness of interpretation and criticism to the investigation of poetics and semiotics as does Jonathan Culler in the first chapter – titled "Beyond Interpretation" – in *The Pursuit of Signs*. In his structural phase Culler advocated "a poetics which stands to literature as linguistics stands to language" (*SP*, 257), the goal of which would be "to understand how we make sense of a text" (*SP*, 259). In a recent essay, Culler argues that "the idea of literary study as a discipline is precisely the attempt to develop a systematic understanding of the semiotic mechanisms of literature, the various strategies of its forms" (IDO, 117). Well, in so far as the mechanisms that make interpretation possible are concerned, what is being described is simply hermeneutics. But the hermeneutical principle requires that to *practice* hermeneutics, one must know a good bit about cultural and literary history (the development of genres for instance). And as for symptomatics, the elucidation of significances depends on the manifold systems of thought that may be brought to bear on a text – and these of course are contingent on the culture of the moment.

(3) On the ground that literature is a product of the culture, the cultural materialists see literary commentary as a critique of that culture (many see this as a new role for criticism, although it is, *mutatis mutandis*, what Arnold had in mind in "The Function of Criticism"). But although culture provides the absolutely necessary context for the existence of literature, and responses to literature have real effects on the culture, Cultural Studies study culture, not literature. Moreover, it is impossible to imagine Cultural Studies without a theory of culture, a theory that will necessarily be economic, political, psychological, philosophical, etc. Literature becomes just one of the sources of evidence, not an experience. The New Critics may be faulted for giving insufficient attention to context and for appearing to equate the understanding of meaning with the whole of readers' responses to literature. But they were right in seeing that it is the experience of literature, not its use as a confirming example of some theory, that gives literature sufficient interest to make it worth while to use it for the purpose of illuminating the culture.

(4) At least one scholar/critic, recognizing that literature departments are already heavily committed to the application of theories of culture, suggests that that activity be properly recognized by the creation of a department of Cultural Studies – for which staff could

readily be found in English departments – and that the study of literature proper become the study of poetry. Bernard Bergonzi presents this option in a straightforward if somewhat resigned way:

> If Cultural Studies goes its own way, what happens to what is left? I would certainly not favor a rump version of one of the current forms of English degree, with their recurring arguments about canons and coverage, the definition of literature and the place of theory. Instead, I propose taking the logic of generic concentration as far as it can go, with a degree which would study, in detail, a single genre, poetry. (194)

The aim would be to consider poems as aesthetically organized formal structures; that they can be considered from other perspectives would not be denied – but such other perspectives would not figure in the discipline Bergonzi calls "the art of poetry." The novel would be excluded because "as soon as we have finished reading a novel we begin to forget it, and what is left to talk about is a vague cloud of fading impressions" (195). The suggestion is not as radical as it may seem: in the beginning the study of vernacular literature was evidently intended to center on poetry; certainly it is poetry with which students have the greatest difficulty, and a familiarity with tropes and figures is probably more easily gained from a study of poetry than of prose. But would one really wish to exclude the essay or the short story? Would drama in verse be included but not that in prose? And would one wish to relinquish the consideration of all symptomatic meaning to Cultural Studies? I would hardly think the last desirable, since symptomatic meaning provides so large a part of the interest of reading, but if not, where and how would the line be drawn?

(5) On the ground that we simply do what we do and nothing we do is more defensible than anything else, certain "new pragmatists" may be said to be content to sail before the wind. That may seem a reductive summation, but the steps are clear – and nowhere more repeatedly and directly set forth than by Stanley Fish. Three of his statements ought to make the point (I have chosen what seem to me particularly succinct and clearly phrased examples; although these come from essays of different dates, equivalents of each are to be found in almost every one of his essays since his 1975 discovery of the presumably all-sufficient explanatory power of interpretive communities). The anti-foundationalism which he espouses "teaches

that questions of fact, truth, correctness, validity, and clarity can neither be posed nor answered in reference to some extracontextual, ahistorical, nonsituational reality, or rule, or law, or value; rather, anti-foundationalism asserts, all these matters are intelligible and debatable only within the precincts of the contexts or paradigms or communities that give them their local and changeable shape" (A-F, 344). "The fact that a standard of truth is never available independently of a set of beliefs does not mean that we can never know for certain what is true but that we *always* know for certain what is true (because we are always in the grip of some belief or other), even though what we certainly know may change if and when our beliefs change" (DvP, 365). Thus, "anti-foundationalist thought deprives us of nothing; all it offers is an alternative account of how the certainties that will still grip us when we are persuaded to it come to be in place" (*DWCN*, 26). What Fish is arguing – that our knowing that everything is relative has no consequences on what we nevertheless believe – also implies that although action taken as a result of one's belief *may* have consequences, there is no way to judge those consequences except in terms of what we believe. Fish's final words at the end of what is probably his best known essay, "Is There a Text in This Class?" are necessarily "not to worry" (ITTC, 321). But if no one can actually live by such a doctrine, which is what Fish happily asserts, there seems little point in teaching students to read by it.

(6) Perhaps the most frequent prescription is to reorganize the teaching of literature as the teaching of rhetoric, although a closer look reveals not only diversity but incompatibility among the advocates of a "return to rhetoric." There are those who wish simply to identify literature and rhetoric and others who insist that all commentary on literature is rhetorical in the sense of being epideictic. Followers of Paul de Man equate the rhetoricity of language with that they regard as the inescapability of misreading, indecidability, and textual self-undoing. For others denial of the possibility of rational thought as a reasoned balancing of alternatives becomes encapsulated in the slogan, applied to both literature and commentary on literature, "All discourse is rhetoric." What is meant by this is not simply that what one says and writes is partly governed by the desire to say something effectively, but that the something one wishes to say is supported by nothing more than an argument or perspective that one has chosen to accept. To speak of teaching rhetoric in this sense is thus an extension of Fishean

anti-foundationalism, an extension that Fish himself has made explicit. "Whenever we are asked to state what we take to be the case about this or that, we will always respond in the context of what seems to us at the time to be indisputably true, even if we know, as a general truth, that everything can be disputed. *One who has learned the lesson of rhetoricity does not thereby escape the condition it names*" (WMP, 552).

There is a kind of seductiveness about such absolutist reductions as "All is rhetoric." However, the premise that all discourse is rhetorical is self-undermining – which gives it a special attractiveness to the hermetically oriented mind. If, as Stanley Fish is happy enough to point out, belief is produced only by persuasion, that is, by skillful rhetoric not demonstration, the belief that belief is produced only by such persuasion is itself the result of the skillful rhetoric of the presenter. If rhetorical power is derived from logos, pathos, and ethos and yet logic is sterile, pathos the result of culturally induced attitudes, and ethos an illusion since there is no stable subject, it is hard to see how it has maintained its power.

The Marxist Terry Eagleton, having proven to his own satisfaction that there is no such thing as literature (since there is no definite criterion by which it may be defined), urges the study of rhetoric as a way of understanding how a capitalist discourse embodied in both the literary text and critical commentary on the text deceives us.[1] But an interesting problem emerges when one puts Fish's insistence on the necessarily ungroundable rhetoric of literary commentary beside Eagleton's insistence on the necessarily ideological structure of literary texts. If Fish is correct, Eagleton's analysis of literature must be as groundless as any other; if Eagleton is correct, a literary text must have specific rhetorical effects, and therefore Fish must be wrong. Of course if all discourse is rhetorical in Fish's sense, neither can be right or wrong; if Eagleton is correct that literature and literary criticism are both necessarily ideological, neither can be other than the enunciator of a given ideology. The great problem with taking the views of either Fish or Eagleton in the extreme forms to which they push them is that they reduce the meaning of "rhetoric" to that under which it too long suffered: it becomes simply a set of techniques for persuading others to accept that which is false.

Now the return to a recognition that the ability to employ and analyze rhetoric is an important part of the education of the only animal that uses language has been one of the valuable outcomes of recent decades: I want to build on it by arguing for a rhetorical perspective distinct from all those I have listed. All texts seek to persuade; it is just that the degree of overtness of the persuasive strategies varies. Since there is no doubt that authors depend on shared background, it is easy enough to see dependence on shared assumptions as a kind of reinforcement of them. On the other hand, although the rhetoric of argument necessarily moves – at least when effective – from a ground of shared agreement, to assume that authors cannot use shared assumptions to go beyond them is a fallacy against which one need only instance Socrates. It is equally a fallacy to think that shared assumptions can be questioned without relying on yet other assumptions. I should like to propose that the relation between both rhetoric and literature and rhetoric and commentary on literature be thought somewhat differently. Let me begin with the first pair.

LITERATURE AS RHETORIC

Walter Pater opens his essay "Style" by remarking that it is "surely the stupidest of losses . . . to lose the sense of achieved distinctions." In practice the abolition of distinctions is most often accomplished by reducing one term to another, a kind of verbal play which immediately generates pressure for the reestablishment of something like the original distinction. That is why, although I think literature, commentary on literature, and rhetoric have a good deal to do with one another, I don't want to say that literature *is* rhetoric. Perhaps the most useful way of putting it is that it is well worth while to regard literature *under the aspect of rhetoric*.

Wilbur Samuel Howell, one of the most distinguished historians of rhetoric, insists strongly on the importance of maintaining Aristotle's distinction between persuasion as the purpose of rhetoric and mimesis as the purpose of poetry (and, by extension, of prose drama and prose fiction). Nevertheless, instances immediately arise to mind to suggest that it is best not to hold to this contrast too firmly and Howell's own concern to include non-fiction prose in the category of literature in itself indicates the need for rapprochement. A good bit of mimetic literature seems to be intended to persuade while all sorts of rhetorical argument make use of mimesis in the form of narratives. If rhetoric is the study of the best means of persuasion, certainly representation of human experience

is one of the most effective means. Many a sermon would be considerably less powerful or interesting if deprived of narrative
examples.

On the other hand, if we consider the first-order purposes – that
is, the usual perlocutionary intentions – of mimesis and rhetoric,
two poles, if not two distinct endeavors, are clearly evident. If we
ask not whether a discourse seems intended to persuade, but what
it seems to intend to persuade its audience to do, rhetoric in its
traditional sense can be said to have a definite end in view: those
to whom it is addressed are to find a person guilty or innocent, vote
for or against a motion, prefer this candidate over that, storm the
barricades, or buy a certain detergent. In contrast, literature, I wish
to argue, seeks to cause the reader to see something freshly, which
may lead to a mental refurbishing, a reorganizing of one's habitual
mode of thought. The process may indeed lead on to actions of
some sort, but action is not the immediate perlocutionary intent.
The Russian Formalists had it right when they emphasized the primary function of literature as being defamiliarization. As did
Wolfgang Iser in emphasizing the novel's capacity to cause readers
to recognize gaps in their mental schemes or imbalances between
what they thought they thought and what they find themselves
thinking as they read.[2] Actually it is pretty much what Matthew
Arnold meant in "The Function of Criticism at the Present Time" –
literature is one of the sources of fresh currents that may "float"
problems and issues.

As soon as one thinks of the matter in this way, one sees that the
relationship is best understood as a continuum. The old category
of epideictic or display rhetoric which pretends to attempt to
persuade in order to give pleasure (while actually persuading the
audience of the cleverness of the rhetor) is close to the literary pole,
while the poem, play, or novel with a thesis is close to the rhetorical
pole. While a novelist may be presumed to wish to persuade the
reader to accept to some degree his or her view of life, that view
may be anything from almost invisible to unmistakable, and range
from being very general to being strongly focused on a specific
issue. One need only think of the differences among Agatha Christie,
Anthony Trollope, Jane Austen, Henry James, Ernest Hemingway,
Harriett Stowe, and George Orwell. But the broad center of the
genre, at least in terms of those novels that continue to be read and
talked about, consists of novels that ask one to look freshly not
at single issues but at a range of cultural values and human

experiences. In the same way the briefest of lyrics tends to take an incident or scene as the occasion for asking, "have you thought about flowers, or stones, or love, or immortality in this way?" To the degree that a literary text is persuasive, it persuades us to look at something once again.

We can widen the meaning of rhetoric without losing what has been its central meaning if we think of "persuasion" as any mode of encouraging recognition. To persuade is presumably to change or alter another's view, but where "persuade" suggests moving from opinion or position *A* to opinion or position *B*, altering includes the possibility of enlarging one's view. Possible new perspectives appear. One may then choose perspective *X* over perspective *Y* or *Z*, but one may also simply recognize that a fuller understanding of some aspect of human life arises if one accepts that all three perspectives have some degree of validity.

Rather, then, than defining rhetoric by what it does (persuade), it may be more useful to describe how it does what it does. For that purpose I want to draw on Henry Johnstone: when successful, rhetoric drives a wedge between ourselves and that which we are being presented with.[3] Or, to put it more clearly, it drives a wedge between habitual modes of thought and the new order of conceptualization that is being presented to us, producing a new, or clearer, or more complex perspective. André Lefevere offers a straightforward statement of the point in saying that insight may come from "the comparisons readers make between the way in which they deal, have dealt, might deal with a certain common human experience and the way writers they happen to read suggest it might be dealt with" (69). The metaphor of the wedge gives us a useful way of thinking about literature. Literature is notoriously difficult to define – every specific definition seems to depend on criteria that exclude some kind of writing that someone will wish to include. I simply want to argue that the class of texts that is found to reward extended thought and discussion – that most often finds its way into a syllabus or learned essay – is almost certain to be rhetorical as Johnstone defines rhetoric. It will be found to drive a wedge, to encourage reexamination of the customary.

The wedge metaphor is a helpful way of thinking about rhetoric, but in itself it doesn't help us understand how mimesis functions. To begin with, it is not intended to deny the more usual metaphor of mimesis as a mirror. The simplistic dismissal of mimesis on the ground that since we can't know ultimate reality – if there is such

– no author can reflect it, is hardly worth noting inasmuch as (1) humanly constructed versions of reality are partial reflections of brute reality and (2) the literary text is a peculiarly selective mirror. Catherine Belsey indulges in a curious piece of logic in writing the following. "The claim that a literary form reflects the world is simply tautological. If by 'the world' we understand the world we experience, the world differentiated by language, then the claim that realism reflects the world means that realism reflects the world constructed in language" (46). But language constructs no one world and is used to construct many. The question is: whose *parole*, in the words of what discursive community, spoken in what context, and constructed as a reflection of what set of beliefs has produced a given text? "London is an exciting compendium of architectural history, where ghosts of a picturesque past may share space with today's men and women enjoying a green park or going about their business in one of London's famous squares." "London is a grimy, trashy, often cruel city where nasty new buildings, looking half-derelict after twenty years, strive to cancel the charm of the old, and the homeless wait for the theatres to close so they can sleep under the sheltering marquees." Both statements describe London (at least in my experience) and both describe a real, that is, experienced, world in standard English.

It is worth while to see how complex a notion mimesis really comprises. The model I want in fact to propose is suggested by Paul Ricoeur's distinction between three forms of mimesis, of representation, although I don't know that he would endorse the uses I make of his distinction. In any case, mimesis has had a bad press, which Ricoeur may help us to counter.

Let us then begin where in fact Saussure begins: with primitive sense data or reports. Saussure speaks of language as transforming the chaos of sense reports into nameable chunks: here a tree, there a tiger, over there a mountain (see especially pp. 111–12). Presumably we add something to these perturbations of the senses to transform them into objects of perception. The perception of an object as Saussure understands it involves the attaching of a name, but even if it is possible to perceive and distinguish individual objects without naming them, our ability to think and communicate about things requires names. Kant of course had already argued that our minds add both space and time and categories such as quality, quantity, and relation; C. S. Peirce speaks of perceptions as produced by an act of judgment performed on sense data (or what he calls "percepts").[4] Kant, Peirce, and Saussure all assume that our minds add and/or subtract qualities in order to turn sense reports into perceptions. As noted in Chapter 2, from this point of view it is wholly correct to say that language is arbitrary because there is no reason a certain sound should designate a certain sense impression, and words are mutually defining in the sense that impressions are divided by the human imposition of language. *However*, to say that language is arbitrary is not to say that there are no sense data to which it is related or that I cannot correlate my sense data with another person's, and to say that it is mutually defining is not, again, to say that language is independent of sense data. The resistance to our assumptions, hopes, and desires by bare percepts or sense data assures us that there exists a structured physical reality, that there exists what Peirce called "irrational insistency" and Burke "the unanswerable opponent" (Peirce, 6.340; Burke, *PLF*, 92). Again, the same consideration also applies to Thomas Kuhn's concept of science. A prevailing scientific paradigm, he argues, breaks down when the accumulation of phenomena it cannot explain becomes too great; for Kuhn, the result is not simply a change in the theories understood but in the world understood by those theories.[5] But the causes of those unexplainable phenomena are extra-linguistic sense data or percepts.

My point is that this entire process is a kind of mimesis. That is, the mind "copies" what is after all produced by something external – by brute or unmediated reality – that stimulates it. It "copies" in such a way as to impose order on that which it copies and make it identifiable. This can be called mimesis₁. It is important to recognize that the operations of this first-order mimesis call upon both language and communal modes of conceptualization, but that their basis is the involuntary percept produced by stimuli beyond either language or society. It is equally important to recognize that the operations of this first mimetic action are not themselves wholly involuntary. Whatever the mind may do in a Kantian, Saussurian, or Peircean sort of way to render sense reports amenable to its apparatus is evidently beyond our intervention. However, even at the level of naming, one has choices among which one chooses on the basis of one's intentions: the cat on the mat can also be a feline, a kitty, a puss, a mouser, a Siamese, a grimalkin.

Certainly at the level of assigning connotations, attributes, and evaluations – that is, of moving from simple indexing names to attributive ones and on to constructing explanatory narratives –

individuals are aware of competing possibilities. Here it is that basic differences in individual experience, the result of both the specific percepts (sense reports) received by individuals and the segments of culture that most influence them, determine the choices. Those different percepts (the different contacts we have had with brute reality and to which we usually give the ambiguous name "experience") have their chance to help determine construction of what that reality is like. There is a constant interplay or mediation between previous constructions and the reception of percepts that don't fit those constructions. The uniformity we encounter assures us of stable underlying structures; the surprises and novelties we encounter assure us that this uniformity is not the mere creation of our own minds, language, or social community. Robert Scholes uses the kangaroo, a signified without a signifier when first sighted by English sailors, as an example of the discovery of a set of percepts quite stable, if inclined to hop strangely, prior to linguistic denomination (*TP*, 97–8). The creation of discourse I'll call mimesis$_2$. All discourse mimesis$_2$ depends on the relation of language to reality; that is, mimesis$_2$ depends on mimesis$_1$. While all communication depends on the incorporation of large amounts of socially constructed reality (if it did not, we would not be able to understand it), what we think of as literature, with its greater degree of freedom from actual sequences of events and from ordinary syntactic structures and semantic usage, is especially susceptible to individual structuring. The very concentration of attention by the author of literary discourse is likely to cause a clarification of the relation of discourse to brute (non-linguistic) reality in the author's own mind. The negotiation or mediation here is between the form the author elects and the author's own sense of reality. I do not wish to propose a definition of literature since I hold by Louise Rosenblatt's view that any text *may* be read as literature or not (though the odds are a great deal better for some texts than others). However, the mimetic impulse tends to summon up the particulars, the concrete details, that forbid reducing texts to universal types or abstract propositions.

Mimesis$_3$ is the reader's response to the text, the reader's attempt to fit the product of mimesis$_2$ to the results of that reader's mimesis$_1$. Again the attempts at accommodation of the text – the text produced by the author's second-order mimesis operating on that author's own first-order mimesis occur through the accommodation of that text to the results of the *reader's* first-order mimesis. The efforts of such accommodation may well shift the ultimate response away from the conventions structuring social reality. That is one way of looking at Wolfgang Iser's notion of the power of literature to produce new perspectives through inducing conflicting norms. However, Iser does not argue, as I wish to do, that the ultimate criterion of judgment will be the degree of consonance with the brute reality underlying all percepts and thus all mimesis. I will dare to be so unfashionable as to cite a New Critic, R. P. Blackmur, for support: "Poetry is the game we play with reality; and it is the game and the play – the game by history and training, the play by instinct and need – which make it possible to catch hold of reality at all" (423).

As I have urged earlier, we are almost never in doubt about the facts of physical reality that an author wishes us either to imagine or regard under a new aspect. We know what appearances in the physical world Iago caused Othello to misinterpret, we know that they *were* misinterpreted, we know what physical acts by Desdemona would constitute unfaithfulness, we know that she was not guilty of these, and we know that Othello kills Desdemona by smothering her. We know, to take non-fiction, that in *The Stones of Venice* John Ruskin is writing of actual buildings in a locale to which we can actually transport ourselves, and that when he says that there are thirty-six pillars in the first level of the Ducal Palace in Venice, we can verify that. What in truth the critical reader of literature questions is not the concept of mimesis, but the *functioning* of that mimesis.

— We may question whether the patterning is interesting enough to give pleasure, or enough pleasure relative to that which we think possible.
— We may question the cognitive adequacy of what is said or implied.
— We may question the accuracy of the description.
— We may debate analogies either implied by the author or asserted by other readers.
— We may challenge the author's apparent ideological assumptions on the basis of symptomatic analyses, or we may challenge another person's symptomatic analyses of the text.

All such challenges arise from the mimetic operation of our individual minds.

Now what is operative to some degree all the way through this sequence of acts of mimesis is *dissonance*, a difference between human responses that must be mediated. Thus difference is essential to thought, although in a different way than it is essential to the structure of the language system. Hermeticists and anti-foundationalists move too readily from what is true of language as a system of potentialities to the actual instance of use. Once again, it is the differences in language use, in attributives, in narrative constructions produced by individuals speaking from different perceptions, not the differences between contiguous terms in the structure of language as a whole, that both produce strong differences in response and give language power by keeping it in relation to reality and preserving it from convention and cultural pieties. Literature allows one to gain new perspectives simply through the encounter with statements in different words, with new analogues, with alternative narratives. It can do this with less friction than ordinary discourse because the dialogue between the text and the reader does not have to become a debate – the text may well offer a challenge, but it is not a challenge that has to be met in a certain form, at a certain time, in front of any other person. Monroe Beardsley defends the cognitive value of literature as a source not of evidence but of "new hypotheses about human nature or society or the world" (*Aesthetics*, 430). The distinction between hypotheses and evidence is perfectly obvious but, I think, insufficiently remembered in criticism: the evidence that might support a hypothesis must come from extra-literary experience. More recently Robert de Beaugrande has defined literature in terms of those texts that promote "alternativity" – that is, texts which, while eliciting a world somehow related to our experience, bring us alternative or additional perspectives (8–9).

"Perspectives" and "hypotheses" are vague words – what kind of perspective or hypothesis? And on what? And so what? What follows is a rather traditional list of the variety of ways in which literature can serve thought. My presentation of these functions is, I fear, quite a prosaic one: I have tried to avoid pretentious, paradoxical, pseudo-philosophical, and consciously ingenious phrasing. Clarity seems to me of special importance in this matter. I should add that each of these modes in which a literary text may function is influenced by symptomatic meanings; indeed, in general the degree to which symptomatic meanings support each function increases as one goes down the list.

(1) The first and most necessary function is purely hedonic, the provision of pleasure. The parallel with rhetoric is evident here – the rhetor unable to hold the audience's interest will not get much of a hearing. Interest and pleasure are of course not synonymous, but that which gives pleasure clearly interests us, while the pursuit of that which interests us tends to give us pleasure. One hardly need dwell on this function except to recognize that pleasure is provided through many different avenues, which for short can be called imaginative patternings; we respond with pleasure to patternings of incident, description, figures, imagery, sound, syntax, character, thought, and emotion. Such pleasure is the basis of all the other functions of literature: without it, we would presumably take our thought straight in the form of philosophy, sociology, psychology, political rhetoric, and so on. Of course, the complication here is that many of what I have called imaginative patternings are the means by which other functions or services are performed at the same time.

(2) The second service is the transmission of insights. At least since Aristotle's statement that poetry is "more philosophical than history," literature has been regarded as the mode of speaking most likely to lay whatever wisdom one has before a broad audience – and I rather doubt that the speculations of our century are capable of wholly invalidating that notion. However, the term "wisdom" is so unfashionable today as to seem almost archaic. (We praise individuals now by calling them brilliant, or clever, or astute, but hardly ever do we call them wise.) We are much more comfortable speaking of insights than wisdom. It is easy enough to assemble a variety of insights that have seemed relevant to a wide variety of situations. Theophrastus's comment that time is the most valuable thing a person can spend; or Samuel Johnson's warning to pedants that "Life is surely given for higher purposes than to gather what our ancestors have wisely thrown away"; or Hamlet's "the readiness is all"; or Hawthorne's warning against the seeking of absolute perfection in "The Birthmark."

But it is at least arguable that what we think of as a wise insight may simply be an apt expression of something already widely believed if not always acted upon. "What oft was thought, but ne'er so well express'd." One can take the lower ground and argue that what literature can offer in the way of making us think better need not be what an author *knows* but what he or she shows us about the ways of thought. That is, perhaps the greater part of the insights that literature can bring consists not in expressions of authorial profundity but in demonstrations of the relatively few *modes of thought* that lie behind the infinite number of *things that can be thought*. One can reasonably argue that such modes are presented in their most concrete and persuasive form in literature. Greek tragedy, Plato's dialogues, Montaigne's essays, Bunyan's *Pilgrim's Progress*, Wordsworth's poems on nature, Austen's novels, Newman's *Apologia*, Wallace Steven's poetry and Scott Momaday's *The Way to Rainy Mountain* represent greatly varied but ever-recurring modes of thought.

(3) The next service is part of the traditional definition of literature: entry into the vicarious experience. The degree to which one can understand the life experience of a member of a different culture, the other sex, or even a different social class or different vocation is a matter of debate, but no one doubts that literature at least allows glimpses of the world that would never have been generated by one's own experience.

(4) The fourth service is the third writ large: the provision of perspective-giving contrast through representation of the social, political, and economic arrangements of other cultures and times. Again, how accurately such writers as Hesiod, Teika, Chaucer, Fielding, Goethe, Balzac, and George Eliot portrayed their own times and cultures, and how fully we can understand those portrayals, are matters of contention, but it is hard to deny that different social arrangements are found in different periods and different countries, and that these are reflected with some accuracy in the corresponding literary works. That social structures are largely arbitrary but purposive, changing and changeable but often possessed of a high degree of inertia becomes evident to the wide-ranging reader in concrete rather than abstract ways.

(5) The fifth function is the analytic. That is, literature very frequently provides a more accurate, or at least contrasting, perspective to the general assumptions or beliefs of a group or a culture. Obvious examples are the satires of a Juvenal or a Swift, Dickens on the condition of the poor, *Heart of Darkness* on colonialist exploitation, and Charlotte Perkins Gilman's *The Yellow Wallpaper* on the disastrous effects of male arrogance and stupidity.

(6) The next service, one into which the analytic merges, is the diagnostic. Partly because of their mimetic qualities, literary texts can be searched for symptoms of the cultural forces, tensions, and assumptions that lie beneath the form and explicit insights of a text.

Prejudices of all kinds lurk in almost every text, some of which are likely to be the self-serving assumptions of the more fortunate and powerful groups in a society. The ability to recognize those assumptions is as important for gaining historical perspective as knowledge of changing customs and practices.

(7) The last service I'll mention is the analogical. That is, literature provides conceptual analogues: we comprehend more quickly and can explain to others more effectively those phenomena and personal experiences for which we can find narrative analogues and descriptive metaphors. Many a contemporary political leader can be analyzed from the perspective of Greek tragedy; Dickens's *Little Dorrit* mimes much more than the financial bubbles of Victorian England – it continues to speak rather directly to a country that has yet to extricate itself fully from the Savings and Loan debacle; Isaac Asimov's tales of robots and colossal computers are transparent parables of the way technological advances raise wholly unforeseen problems. Certain works thus come to be part of a kind of cultural short hand: *Oedipus, King Lear,* the *Divine Comedy, Candide, Pride and Prejudice,* and *Moby Dick* become no small part of cultural literacy (a term which, properly understood, can be used without apology). The more analogues that can be drawn from a work, the more substantial the place it occupies in the structure of that literacy.

Of course, these functions are hardly separable. The wonderful description of the fog surrounding and seeping into the Court of Chancery in the opening pages of *Bleak House* is delightful in itself; intriguing as a metaphor that can be traced through the novel; analytic in suggesting the fogginess of the aristocracy, the law courts, and much organized philanthropy; diagnostic in reminding us that it is perennially in the interest of more than those who practice law to befog issues (one fears that Dickens's parliamentary leaders Boodle, Coodle, Doodle, and Foodle would feel perfectly at home in any known legislative body); and richly analogical. To transfer analogically the self-serving practices of the Court of Chancery as represented by that fog to the field of literary studies, a fog that is not wholly unpurposive lies heavily on the pages of many a journal of literary criticism these days, an increasing number of which go largely unread for the excellent reason that they are largely unreadable. All of these functions can be understood through the metaphor of the wedge. This is true even of the purely hedonic for the interests and mental pleasures of literature – unlike those of physical pleasures – are produced by the unexpected, the different, that which contrasts with our routine.

It may be worth while considering the nature of wedginess. The essence of a wedge is that it is sharp or thin on one end and considerably broader on the other. In a text, what corresponds to the sharp end is a surprising event, an unexpected point of view, a striking image, a seeming paradox, an apparent anomaly. These effect an entry between the object and habitual associations, while the gradual recognition of the total structure of the work is like the action of a wedge in widening the separation. The wedge may be driven between one's beliefs and a depiction of life that one accepts, that is, between the author's habitual construction of reality and the reader's reconstitutive recognition of the plausibility or attractiveness of an author's reconstruction of reality as embodied in the text. An obvious example is the conflict between the socially accepted view of the beneficial operation of poor laws and Dickens's plausible illustrations of their actual effect. The mimetic process of reading may on the other hand cause the reader to recognize a conflict between two generally received opinions: Trollope's Barsetshire novels bring the general respect for representatives of the church up against the equally general knowledge that humans are unlikely to be able to transcend normal human nature. Unlike straightforward rhetorical argument, very frequently the reader is not being asked to judge that A is wrong and B is right, but rather to realize the complexity of the human situation. Certain hermeticists are fond of using the word solicitation in its sense of "shaking up" to refer to their challenges to the reference of language, and to concepts of the author and reader as individuals. However, the word can more usefully be employed to refer to the shifting of a reader's habitual modes of thinking as the result of unaccustomed perspectives or relationships encountered in reading literature.

That both individuals and cultures fall into routinized ways of perceiving and evaluating experience need not be evidence of human perversity, or laziness, or the influence of a powerful elite that imposes a specific perspective. The experienced world is simply too complex, too full of a number of things, too rich in possibilities, too lavish of viewpoints for any discourse to be comprehensive. Every utterance is a selection from innumerable possibilities – "Shall we go to the concert tonight?" may elicit any number of relevant (and perhaps irrelevant) responses. A lengthy text can be seen as a sequence consisting of countless decisions, some of which the author consciously understands to be choices between equally relevant or significant or interesting possibilities. The choices add up to a set of perspectives that are interpretable because the choices that led to them can be retrospectively seen to have a reasonable degree of compatibility (unity) though prospectively they were not predictable. To say anything is to move something to the foreground – which means to move or leave a great number of things in the background. (I should say here that one of my colleagues who has studied with Derrida tells me that Derrida's central point is just this: that all discourse falsifies by foregrounding certain concepts while relegating equally important ones to the background. To which I can only reply that I am happy to hear it – but that the French *savant* seems to have taken a very long and tortuous path to his goal.)

Lyric, narrative, and drama alike are capable of driving wedges between what Carlyle liked to call use-and-wont and the object, concept, or experience with its many customarily ignored facets. All are capable of causing the reader to ask "Is (this aspect of) the world like this?" "Could it be like this?" "Should it be like this?" But the wedge is not driven, the new perspectives entered upon, until the authorial meaning is understood. That is the importance of the specifically hermeneutical activity.

It is notorious that the New Critics tended to equate complexity with value. This has been seen as a purely aesthetic assumption by those who dismiss the aesthetic as artificial, as an illusion somehow fostered by capitalism, or simply as a kind of pleasure comparable to that of solving a puzzle. Finding an interpretation that confers unity on a text does yield a kind of satisfaction like that felt when a puzzle has been successfully addressed, but it seems reasonable that the text which mimes something of the complexity of the world is more interesting – and thus more valuable as a rhetorical wedge – than that which simply presents one perspective, even a new or unfamiliar one. Certainly it will seem more interesting and useful once the new perspective is no longer new.

In thinking of literature as a form of rhetoric a number of strands of thought set out in the discussion of the common hermetic fallacies come together. Being mimetic of human experience, literature represents aspects of the only kind of experience available to human thought. In considering meaning we are considering what is said and why it is said as it is, the interpretation of which must consider both internal and external context. The parallel here is with the full understanding of a single sentence, its successful "up-take" in J. L. Austin's words. Just as "uptake" requires an under-standing both of the proposition and its illocutionary force, in considering what the speaker of a poem, or the narrator of or char-acters in a novel say, and what the characters in a novel or play do, we consider what is said and done and why it was said and done in that way in that context in order to arrive at the total meaning. To ask why an author chose to express that meaning is to go be-yond the question of meaning and enter the realm of significance. The total meaning – what is said and told and the implied perspec-tive on what is said and told – constitutes the miming of experi-ence, for everything we experience, including what we read, is accompanied by our responsive attitude to what we experience. The variety of responses to human experience is reflected by the number of ways it may be mimed, each of which corresponds to the achieved authorial meaning of a text; the reader responds to the mimesis that originated in the author's response to his or her experience.

The first goal to be pursued by English departments should then be the accurate interpretation of literary texts of all genres. George Steiner is right. "The job to be done is not one of 'critical theory,' of the 'sociology of literature,' or *mirabile dictu*, 'creative writing.' If we are serious about our business, *we shall have to teach reading*. We shall have to teach it from the humblest levels of rectitude, the parsing of a sentence, the grammatical diagnosis of a proposition, the scanning of a line of verse, through its many layers of perfor-mative means and referential assumptions" (T&C, 16). As urged earlier, such understanding requires a knowledge of genre, an alert-ness to tropes and figures, a sensitivity to the way that the cotext orients the reader to the probably intended sense of a given word, a familiarity with narratological devices and strategies, and a knowl-edge of what an author would seem to have presumed that a reader would know, that is, the operative cultural context. Given motiva-tion to tackle a variety of literary texts, practice in interpreting these and encouragement to pursue what then strikes them as interesting significances, readers can go it alone. The goal of the classroom then is presumably to give practice in relating the text to its appro-priate context so that the reader is not baffled in seeking to under-stand the authorially intended meaning, and to encourage relating the result to personal experience, extra-linguistic theories, and whatever else a reader finds of interest.

The understanding of the cultural context is never of course complete, but without a degree of familiarity with the background, and practice in untangling certain kinds of time-obscured allusions and assumptions, readers will necessarily remain locked in their own time and place. That is the reason it is important for at least some faculty members to be as deeply conversant with the culture of a particular locale and span of history as possible. The "mere" understanding of meaning is too easily dismissed by those who teach literature, either as old fashioned because it is what the New Criticism concentrated on or boring because the meaning has become so obvious to them that they no longer find it interesting. But the author's meaning is precisely what the average undergraduate is trying to get hold of. This is easy to forget; the reminder often takes the form of the discovery that a discussion of the author's possible perlocutionary intentions or of possible symptomatic meanings has been derailed by the failure of a significant portion of the class to understand what happened in the plot of the novel or the meaning of certain lines in a poem.

Jonathan Culler speaks of theory as the "logic of signification" and as providing "persuasive accounts of signification." I have to admit that I am not at all sure what the fancy phrase "logic of signification" might mean other than the ways in which authorial meaning is conveyed and significances explored. Finally the author's meaning is of interest to us because of the significance we assign it – but it does shift the balance toward interpretation. A discussion of *Bleak House* is hardly complete, I should think, without some consideration of Dickens's treatment of women, the possible significances of taking Esther as the ideal of womanhood, Dickens's dependence on improbable personal benevolence and individual philanthropy to bring happiness out of misery, and his sentimentalization of Jo. But it begins with the re-creation of what the original readers' responses are most likely to have been.

My version of the primary goal of literature is of course directly opposed to that of a theorist like Hillis Miller. I can agree, subject to certain practical reservations, with a statement like the following in the penultimate paragraph of Miller's "The Function of Literary Theory at the Present Time":

> Courses in the literature departments should become primarily training in reading and writing, the reading of great works of literature, yes, but with a much broader notion of the canon, and

along with that training in reading all the signs; paintings, mov-
ies, television, the newspaper, historical data, the data of material
culture. An educated people these days, an informed electorate,
is a people who can read, who can read all the signs, no easy
thing to learn. (FLT, 392)

Given the difficulty of interpreting texts whose meaning depends
on irony or indirection of any sort, allusion, complex structuring, or
the dialogical interplay of perspectives – all features frequently found
in literary works – Miller's expansion of the responsibilities of an
English department demands that an impossible amount be crowded
into a few courses. But the principle seems reasonable enough, even
if its practice is hardly so. Again defining the sort of "noncanonical"
reading he recommends in "The Ethics of Reading," Miller writes:

I mean a response to the demand made by the words on the
page, an ability, unfortunately not all that common, to respond to
what the words on the page say rather than to what we wish they
said or came to the book expecting them to say. (ER, 338)

But such counsel assumes a very different countenance when read
against Miller's statements elsewhere – these suggest again and
again that what he actually expects reading to be is, always and ever,
the discovery of aporias, contradictions, and undecidabilities as in
the following passage from "Deconstructing the Deconstructors."

My account of deconstruction has been misleading ... if it has
suggested that the dismantling is performed from the outside by
the critic on a piece of language which remains innocently mys-
tified about its own status. ... The text performs on itself the act
of deconstruction without any help from the critic. The text expresses its own aporia ... (DD, 108).

The final paragraph of the essay from which the above comes reads:
"The critic, then, still has his uses, though this use may be no more
than to identify an act of deconstruction which has always already,
in each case differently, been performed by the text on itself" (DD,
109). Or again, the last sentence of "The Imperative to Teach" defines teaching as the "iterated, and reiterated demonstration, out
there in the open, whatever the teacher may think he or she is
doing, of the impasse [of undecidability] I have tried to define"

(IT, 308). To which conceptions of the roles of critic and teacher the entire perspective I have tried to create cries NO.

The rhetorical work of the literary text depends on the reader's comparison of the world created by the novel with that experienced by the reader and mapped by contemporary conceptual schemes. Beyond that we can hardly go. What, precisely, are the effects of reading literature and how beneficial to the individual are these likely to be? I have tried to suggest a number of effects that I believe beneficial, but none can be guaranteed. Bernard Bergonzi is salutarily honest about this matter. "The humanizing and moral effects of reading literature must be left to occur as and when they will, which will be different in every individual. They certainly cannot be turned into the stated goal of an academic program" (200).

THE RHETORIC OF LITERARY COMMENTARY

Writing about literature belongs to the province of non-mimetic rhetoric. However, rather than Stanley Fish's elaborate arguments for the omnipresence of rhetoric, which rely on an absolutist antifoundationalism, I would prefer to draw on a rough version of positions taken by Chaim Perelman in *The Realm of Rhetoric* and by Kenneth Burke in a number of his books; both writers assume a continual rhetorical pressure. Perelman writes: "In contrast to ancient rhetoric, the new rhetoric is concerned with discourse addressed to *any sort of audience*.... The theory of argumentation, conceived as a new rhetoric or dialectic, covers the whole range of discourse that aims at persuasion and conviction, whatever the audience addressed and whatever the subject matter" (*RR*, 5). Perelman's book as a whole appears to me clearly to regard as rhetoric the use of any technique that may persuade an audience to consider alternatives to presently held views. I particularly like Burke's definition of rhetoric as "rooted in an essential function of language itself ... the use of language as a symbolic means of inducing cooperation in beings that by nature respond to symbols" (*RM*, 43). The rhetorical dimension of course exists in varying degrees – in literary criticism, as I use the term, it is so important that I'm tempted to dub such writing "critoric." Traditional rhetoric has been divided into three types, forensic for arguing before a court, deliberative for persuading an assembly to a course of action, and epideictic for the purpose either of strengthening adherence to something already generally accepted or simply displaying one's cleverness and power of persuasion. It is not unreasonable, if a bit simplistic, to apply all three to literary commentary. The counterpart of forensic rhetoric would be attempts to persuade others of the significance one finds in a text. "Is there evidence of such a pattern?" becomes the question rather than "Is there evidence that a person acted in violation of a law?" That of deliberative would be evaluative arguments: "This text rates high or low judged by the following criteria" rather than "this course of action is the better or worse."

At one time a great deal of criticism was explicitly evaluative; the decline of judicial criticism is the result of the disintegration of agreement on criteria – or at least certain kinds of criteria. *"Paradise Lost* is the greatest English poem" or "George Eliot's novels reveal the true human condition" are the kinds of assertions unlikely now to be met with, while "Nadine Gordimer's novels represent the immense difficulties of South African Whites and Blacks in understanding each other" or "Peter Shaffer's plays dramatically display the complexity of human motivation" are of the kind still explicitly stated. No less than the grander assertions, the latter are assertions of value: the works referred to are believed *good because* of the quality ascribed to them. The existence of the quality itself is almost necessarily based on social, psychological, political views where formerly the more sweeping evaluations tended to be based on assumptions about aesthetic value; in either case there is no distinct line between deliberative judgments and forensic arguments. On the other hand, however, these days the existence of symptomatic meanings may or may not be seen as bestowing value. That a textual pattern explicable on Freudian, Lacanian, or Marxist terms can be argued to exist in a given novel may be of interest to critics of the appropriate persuasion without a claim for any sort of value being made even by such critics.

In the scheme I've outlined, epideictic criticism becomes simply the display of one's abilities to argue interestingly – even to give pleasure by the subtlety of one's argument. This explains the existence of a good many books and essays that seem to have little to do with the literary text presumably under discussion or, indeed, with human experience. Often one is expected simply to marvel at the unexpectedness of the associations made, or the audacious paradoxicality of the conclusions reached. Michael Carter's "Scholarship as Rhetoric of Display; or, Why is Everybody Saying all Those Terrible Things about Us?" presents a vigorous argument that literary scholarship is all epideictic, specifically the kind of epideictic rhetoric intended "to amuse and impress" (305). Such rhetoric, says Carter, has no extrinsic value (changes nothing in the world external to the text) but he believes it does have intrinsic value – it gives insight (it is not clear to me into what such insight is presumably penetrating) and defines an ever-changing community. It "is a discourse that a community uses to reveal itself to itself" (307). The conclusion is that

> The goal is simply to participate, to enjoy being a part of a conversation about language that has been going on for twenty-five centuries. It has been, and continues to be, a most stimulating conversation. But let's stop taking it so seriously. It is, after all, a form of play. (312)

I hope I have already made sufficiently clear my own reaction to the production of such effects through playing with evident fallacies and obscurantist strategies; fortunately the display of wit, cleverness, and the unexpected insight is not necessarily dependent on eristic means. If literary texts are indeed capable of freshening our thought through rhetoric in the mimetic form of persuasion, so in fact are commentaries on literature. Their role is to invite us to realign what has become habitual, to reexamine the customary. Rather than seeking to be definitive, to replace other perspectives, they invite us to consider adding an additional perspective. They may well be purely hypothetical; many should be read as such, whether they admit to it or not. Cathy Popkin has adroitly challenged the aura of all-knowing certainty with which so many critics and scholars seek to surround their pronouncements. Noting that fiction is assumed to begin "with a tacit 'as if,'" she suggests that literary commentary might well begin with a "what about...?" (181). She is quite on target; a good many literary essays are most properly read as beginning with a tacit "as if" or "as though."

On the other hand, if the reading of literature is only a pastime like stamp-collecting and interpretation and criticism only a competitive game like chess, what is written about need only be addressed to a small band of interested *aficionados*. But if an argument can be made that it is something more, something that justifies its place in the curriculum, there is little excuse for making the bulk of commentary on it esoteric.

Notes

1. See, for instance, Chapter 1 and the Conclusion in Eagleton's *Literary Theory: An Introduction.*
2. *The Implied Reader.* See pages xii and 53–5 for succinct summaries of the point.
3. See especially pp. 124–5 in Henry Johnstone, *The Problem of the Self.*
4. Peirce's most succinct statement on the subject is perhaps that found in the essay "Pearson's Grammar of Science," *Popular Science Monthly* 58 (1900–1901), 301–2; rptd. *Collected Papers*, 8: 144–5.
5. Kuhn: "I have so far argued only that paradigms are constitutive of science. Now I wish to display a sense in which they are constitutive of nature as well" (*SSR*, 110).

9

Publishing the (Highly) Perishable

Every now and then, a sense of the futility of their daily endeavors falling suddenly upon them, the critics of Christendom turn to a somewhat sour and depressing consideration of the nature and objects of their own craft. That is to say, they turn to criticizing criticism. What is it in plain words . . . How far can it go? What good can it do?
H. L. Mencken, "Criticism of Criticism of Criticism," 3.

But dissertations have to be submitted, and (where promotion is at stake), books have to be published. You can spread your insights thin (many a long-drawn-out thesis could be compressed into a tolerably interesting article). You can choose an unexplored subject – and as time goes on, those that remain are bound to be more and more trivial. Or you can strain after false originality. One way or another, the books that result, and which multiply at an increasing rate, are likely to mean as little to posterity as most nineteenth-century collections or sermons do to a modern reader. (312)
John Gross, *The Rise and Fall of the Man of Letters*, 312.

No essay of which I am aware so accurately sums up the ethos of contemporary departments of literature as the first chapter of Jonathan Culler's *Framing the Sign: Criticism and its Institutions*. If there has been any change in the discipline in the five years since the essay appeared, it has been in the nature of intensification of the situation he describes. And yet thoughtful reading of that essay is likely to induce schizophrenia. Evidently intended to set the stage for the remainder of the volume, the chapter provides a valuably concise history of the development and, especially, expansion of the study of literature in American universities in the twentieth century. A quick reading suggests that Culler is attempting to give a relatively objective account, one that does not omit cross-currents and conflicts. Nevertheless, the essay as a whole is an apologia for, even a celebration of, literary departments as they are. Are university teachers of literature as a whole so satisfied with themselves? Should they be?

The major motif which emerges from the essay's combination of candor and complacency is praise for the discipline as it is and is likely to become. On the first page Culler notes that "many might argue that literary criticism has ceased to be a modest and judicious activity serving literature and its readers and become pretentious and chaotic, a domain of competing, often abstruse theories, demanding the attention that might be devoted to literature itself" (*FS*, 3). Well, yes, many might argue something like that, though the word "modest" is rather loaded – one would hardly think of Arnold, Leavis, or Blackmur, all of whom sought to avoid falling into theorizing, as advocating a modest role for literature or its critics. Similarly the innocent-seeming phrase "serving literature and its readers" operates dismissively to suggest that those who think literary criticism has become pretentious and its theories quite unnecessarily abstruse see "serving literature and its readers" as having no end beyond, perhaps, satisfying readers' curiosity about an occasional obscure passage.

In the course of the essay Culler duly notes that the expansion of universities has required an increase in the number of faculty members in English and foreign language departments; that the adoption of the sciences as the model for true professionalism racheted up the expectations for publication; and that the scramble to add new graduate programs and expand existing ones, which resulted in far too many PhDs for the jobs available, made it necessary for members of literature and language departments to devote more and more time to finding something to say in print. Moreover, he is very clear that what is submitted to journal and book editors and referees for grants must be strongly innovative. Taken by themselves, many sentences sound distinctly like indictments. "In the academy, professionalism ties one's identity to an expertise. . . . This induces a proliferation of sub-fields: writers of letters of recommendation find that they have a stake in defining some area – say, psychoanalytic interpretation of Shakespeare – such that their candidate may be deemed one of its most accomplished experts" (*FS*, 29). "Provosts and deans apply pressure that makes even conservative chairpersons willing to encourage publication that will attract attention. For deans in the American system, 'visibility' may become more important than what is called 'soundness'" (*FS*, 31).

"This over-expansion [of PhD programs] . . . led to the job crisis of the 1970s and 1980s, whose effect was to stimulate the production of critical writing, since, as current wisdom has it, more publications are needed to get a job interview today than were required twenty years ago for tenure" (*FS*, 27). Yet, somehow all this is set out as though it constituted unquestionable evidence of the operation of the best of all possible academic worlds. There is a smugness in many of the comments on how things are that seems to say, "And a good thing too."

It would be hard to dispute the facts Culler presents – indeed the chapter probably ought to be required reading for students contemplating entering a PhD program in literature. The question is how one ought to react to these facts; whether the present state of the discipline ought to be accepted with equanimity. Culler's optimism appears to derive from his apparently unquestioning equation of literary criticism with the production of knowledge, a word he uses without any qualification. This assumption also makes possible Culler's contrast of two models of the university, and specifically of literary studies. "The first makes the university the transmitter of a cultural heritage, gives it the ideological function of reproducing culture and the social order" (*FS*, 33). One may pause to note that the assumption that familiarity with what has been, or is at the moment, thought valuable and important in a culture can only lead to production of more of the same is a common, if constantly disconfirmed, belief. Nietzsche, Marx, Freud, Saussure, Peirce, Heidegger, Wittgenstein, and Camus, for instance, were hardly among the culturally ignorant. "The other model," writes Culler, "casts the university as producer of knowledge" (*FS*, 34). This second model "gives criticism no specific educational function, but makes cultural progress or innovation the goal of teachers of literature. Critical investigation, in this second model, is simply what professors do: to write criticism is to generate knowledge . . ." (*FS*, 35). To make quite sure that this second model is perceived as wholly superior, a concern for teaching is cast in the role of dog in the manger. "For the most part, appeal to teaching is a conservative, even reactionary gesture: the suggestion that thinking and writing about literature ought to be controlled by the possibilities of classroom presentation is usually an attempt to dismiss new lines of investigation or abstruse critical writings without confronting them directly" (*FS*, 37). Here is a straw man indeed. Concern that too great a share of effort is given to publication the primary purpose of which is to increase one's reputation at the expense of teaching effectively (which includes finding the best ways of presenting new knowledge) is hardly the same thing as wishing to limit thinking and writing about literature to what can be presented in the classroom.

But the central question is, "to what extent *does* the writing of literary criticism represent a contribution to new knowledge?" Not directly to face that question in the 1990s is especially odd: no one knows that better than Culler, whose *On Deconstruction*, while striving vigorously to defend deconstruction, sympathetically sets out such arguments as the following.

> Since no reading can escape correction, all readings are misreadings; but this leaves not a monism but a double movement. Against the claim that, if there are only misreadings, then anything goes, one affirms that misreadings are errors; but against the positivist claim that they are errors because they strive toward but fail to attain a true reading, one maintains that true readings are only particular misreadings: misreadings whose misses have been missed" (*OD*, 178).

Such passages evidence a delight in playing with thought, but Culler himself sets out eristic as a set of strategies of argument, not methods of gaining knowledge (except of course knowledge of how to produce such eristic). In any case, for the reasons given earlier, it is impossible to equate what literary critics publish with the kind of knowledge (always corrigible as it may be) pursued by physical science, although the temptation is always there.

THE ACCUMULATION OF THE NON-CUMULATIVE

As I have argued earlier, the distinction between scholarship and criticism is real. Scholarship does constantly add to the store of facts for which the evidence is such that they may be taken as established even though they may later be overturned: dates of composition, details of the contemporary reception of works, printers' errors. Interpretations of texts may be contributions to knowledge, but the opportunities for making important contributions here are limited. Moreover, while the New Criticism gave an enormous impetus to literary studies by its insistence on close reading, it proved all too successful, so successful that it began to exhaust the field of its application, at least so far as the publication of explications was useful. It took some four decades, but eventually it began to be evident that there were a limited number of cruxes or hitherto unsuspected semantic wonders in the finite number of poems, short stories, novels, and plays that readers of critical journals regarded as of sufficient importance to be interesting. Once the habit of close reading, of seeking to understand as fully as possible rather than simply extracting an overall impression, became general, formal explication of texts that were not especially demanding became superfluous.

But literary criticism (by which Culler seems to have in mind pretty much the sense I have given it throughout this volume, that is, the exploration of symptomatic meaning), necessarily produces possible perspectives rather than knowledge. What a reader of criticism comes to know is that T. S. Eliot, J. Hillis Miller, Jonathan Culler, or Joe Z. Smith has said that it is useful, stimulating, or thought-provoking to look at poem X from a particular aesthetic, moral, religious, philosophical, psychological, or political point of view. It is rather forcing language to say, to take a major critic on a major poem, that Geoffrey Hartman's "Adam on the Grass with Balsamum" conveys knowledge of *Paradise Lost.* Neither, of course, does Addison's view of Milton or Coleridge's of Wordsworth, or Pater's of *Measure for Measure.* The succession of purely critical comments on a text is cumulative in the sense simply that the number of things said has grown, not in the sense that erroneous views are being definitively rejected, correct views are being given greater probability through being verified in new ways, or a more comprehensive, internally consistent understanding is being achieved.

Criticism is not cumulative: it cannot be so as long as there is no possibility of testing literary theories, incorporating those verified into a relatively consistent structure, and dismissing the others. That may seem a hard saying in the face of the long history of literary criticism, or the apparent dependence of most critical discussions on theoretical arguments, or the convention of citing critics of recognized reputation for corroboration. However, what cumulation there is is essentially superficial. One assumes that the critic writing on Shakespeare knows what Johnson, Coleridge, and Bradley had to say, but these earlier writers may equally well be cited as examples of error as of cogent insight. The conventions – indeed the expectations – of the discipline are that a case can be made in either direction; after all, one cannot be very seriously embarrassed by statements that are by their very nature unfalsifiable. While one critic may receive stimulation from another, it is just not the case that critics build on the verified results of previous critics. For instance, in reading the forty-eight general critical comments that the editor of the 1980 New Variorum Edition of *Measure for Measure* thought it worthwhile to include (from Dryden in 1672 to Hunter in 1965), one has no sense that the later critics are building on the earlier ones; that is, they are not acknowledging what has been verified to that point and pushing on to new discoveries that may be verified in their turn.[1] That some critical commentaries are better (more plausible, more interesting) than others everyone would grant; but if by chance we could agree on which they are, they would not constitute a chain of advancing knowledge. Nor would I argue that the insights of others with whom I most agree constitute pieces of knowledge. James Cameron's observations that for Dickens "private happiness overcomes public despair" and that Dickens seeks "the creation of small impregnable oases of private happiness" (18) seem to me especially happy, but what a pedant one would be to insist that students accept these as items of knowledge, or facts, about Dickens's novels. Randall Jarrell very incisively hits off a characteristic of Wallace Stevens that I find well worth considering when he says:

> His poetry is obsessed with lack, a lack at least almost taken for granted, that he himself automatically supplies; if sometimes he has restored by imagination or abstraction or re-creation, at other times he has restored by collection, almost as J. P. Morgan did – Stevens likes something, buys it (at the expense of a little spirit), and ships it home in a poem. (125)

However, Jarrell's comment hardly represents a discovery of which all succeeding readers of Stevens should know. Culler's notion of "critical progress" is mysterious, if not empty.

It is undeniable that one of the great attractions of the New Criticism was the opportunity for additional publication. The recognition that published explications of every literary text that seemed to have merit is not necessary more or less coincided with the enormous expansion in the number of students seeking topics for doctoral dissertations and approaches amenable to a continued program of research that would establish them as worthy of their places in the profession. At the same time more and more colleges and universities tried to capitalize on their growth by making themselves recognized as centers of research; deans and academic vice-presidents, taking the sciences as their model, were increasingly demanding that faculty in the humanities find more to say about their subjects, and say it in print. That outlets increased correspondingly is hardly surprising. Harry Levin noted in 1988, "It has been twenty years . . . since I had occasion to notice: 'Learned journals multiply for the advancement, not of learning, but of assistant professors'" (CI, 35). As one might expect, more and more explications and "close readings" came to seem labored or trivial. As more and more explicators explicated, it became evident that each new explication was in competition with all earlier ones, although the later ones most often were able to add or alter very little, a buttress here, a finial there. "What A, B, C, and D have pointed out is on the whole correct, but what they have failed to note is. . . ."

The structuralist and poststructuralist revolution was the answer to many a prayer. As Bernard Bergonzi notes, "The advent of poststructuralism has given a great impetus to interpretive productivity, since all the literary texts that were once interpreted to show organic unity and complexity of meaning can now be interpreted [read symptomatically, in my terms] to reveal underlying clashes" (167). Frederick Crews comments that "the inquisitive sociologist cannot avoid noticing that the deconstructionist program promises to allay one of the besetting self-doubts of academic critics, a fear that the things worth saying about the finite number of authors in one's field have already been said" (119). Moreover, where one apparent advantage of the New Criticism for the graduate student or probationary faculty member had been that explication did not necessarily depend on a broad knowledge of the cultural context (although the most impressive interpreters brought such information to bear), hermetic commentary, which is most frequently produced by the application of a theory to a very small, carefully selected portion of a text, requires even less knowledge of anything but the chosen theory. If application of the theory to yet more and more works seems too tame or unprofitable, one can always try turning the theory on its head. As René Girard has noted, "[i]t is relatively easy . . . to simulate originality by saying the opposite of what your immediate predecessors have said, especially if they are the only people you have read and studied" (238). The pressure for innovation can in fact make ignorance of previous discussion a virtue. On the other hand, such pressure, in Richard Levin's words, creates "a choice between publishable novelty and unpublishable credulity" – in effect, Hobson's choice. The problem is exacerbated by the demand, especially in American universities, that young faculty members get one or more books in print within a few years of the completion of their graduate work – every graduate student knows that the dissertation should therefore be regarded as the draft of his or her first book. Departments of literature, understandably seeking to give their students the best possible start in the discipline as it is, have tended to narrow the breadth of reading, the diversity of literature with which students must be familiar, in order to give them the opportunity to concentrate on the area of the dissertation. It is hardly surprising that the resulting dissertations are often claustrophobic applications of whatever theory is fashionable at the moment. George Steiner is more likely right than wrong in commenting that the "notion that a dissertation should be a piece of literary criticism, that a young man or woman in the very early twenties should have something fresh or profound or decisive to say about Shakespeare or Keats or Dickens is . . . perplexing. Few people are ever able to say anything very new about major literature, and the idea that one can do so when one is young is almost paradoxical" (TCG, 76). One might gloss Steiner's comment by picking up that final word "paradoxical" and noting an additional application: it is precisely by saying something paradoxical that the feat of saying something new is most often achieved these days. Although one might think that only so many arguments that meaning is indeterminate, or that all thought is culturally constrained, or that the evidently direct is ironic or vice versa can be read without impatience, nevertheless even the tiredest demonstration of paradoxicality seems still largely taken to be equivalent to freshness. Naturally enough in such circumstances, criticism that is "profound or decisive" remains particularly rare.

Experienced critics become bolder yet: thus one learns from Terry Eagleton (the present tolerance for manifest absurdities is a particular boon to Marxist critics) that in *Macbeth* "The witches are the heroines of the piece, however little the play itself recognizes the fact, and however much the critics may have set out to defame them. It is they who, by releasing ambitious thoughts in Macbeth, expose a reverence for hierarchical social order for what it is, as the pious self-deception of a society based on routine oppression and incessant warfare" (WS, 2).[2] We also discover that Lady Macbeth is a "bourgeois individualist" (*WS*, 4). In 1974, after discussing a passage from Samuel Butler's *Erewhon*, Wayne Booth commented:

> No party to the various discussions will take any originator seriously who suggests that Butler was really defending the church or really a Satanist alluding to Beelzebub with his reference to Providence; or that for Butler Providence suggests Fate and Fate suggests Karma. . . . yet I suspect that if I worked up an article defending any one of these absurd readings, I could get it published, as things stand, so confused have we become about what makes a contribution to meaning. (RI, 21)

Or again, André Lefevere wrote in 1977, "As it is . . . the uneasy coexistence of rival ideologies, combined with the huge increase in bread and butter 'scholarship,' have all but eliminated the practice of natural selection. We are left with 'criticism' . . . designed to highlight the critic rather than the work. . . . The 'pluralism' that is the pride of literary studies in fact creates a climate that actually protects recessive mutations" (62). (My own position in no way opposes pluralism – it is just that not every text requires a Freudian, Lacanian, new historicist, Marxist, essentialist feminist, non-essentialist feminist, and deconstructionist reading, especially readings that consciously seek a greater degree of radicalness).

What Booth and Lerner lament, Culler celebrates: "Interpretation itself needs no defense; it is with us always, but like most intellectual activities, interpretation is interesting only when it is extreme" (IDO, 110). One must agree with Stanley Fish that "The greatest rewards of our profession are reserved for those who challenge the assumptions within which ordinary practices go on" (DvP, 366), while nevertheless wondering whether every *outré* assertion is to be taken as a useful or legitimate challenge.

If the only questionable result of the flood of publication, and the strategies that make it possible, were the difficulty of finding the grain amidst the chaff, it might seem ungrateful to complain, especially if one were to take the excessively optimistic view that the amount of grain increases at the same rate as the chaff. Even so, however, the problem of knowing what is worthwhile, of using one's time more profitably than by sifting continually through ever-increasing amounts of critical comment, is hardly negligible. The increase, one must recognize, is in no small measure the result of vita-dressing. If deans, department chairs, and personnel committees automatically assign more points for books than articles, more for articles than notes, and more for two articles than one, the academic who squanders his capital, enriching an article or book with more good insights than is necessary, is clearly a profligate. What the ordinary intelligent but less than brilliant academic must seek in order to stay in the game is the "MPI," the minimal publishable idea, or, as others call it, the "LPU," the least publishable unit. Many a book would be better as an article or two; many an article ought to be a note.[3] John Gross asked in 1969, "How can anyone who tries to keep up with Wordsworthian studies find the time to read Wordsworth?" (310) Since then the situation has gotten much worse – although graduate students are presumably still warned to know thoroughly the critical writing that surrounds the topic they propose to write about, it is much to be doubted that many who are beyond graduate school conscientiously work through the relevant bibliography before beginning to write their own critical essays. Certainly, only those with a primary commitment to literary theory can keep up with even a small portion of that domain. That modern technology has made it much more convenient to discover what has been written probably serves more to make one feel guilty about how much one has skipped than to increase the amount of relevant material that one reads. The winnowing process itself gives pause: the task of sorting through recent critical books and essays is most often narrowed, one cannot but suspect, by restricting one's reading to what the best-known critics of the time have written and what has been published by the major journals and more prestigious presses. The more a critic is cited, the more it becomes necessary to cite that critic. But if the most useful and enlightening commentary is to be found only in the major journals and the writing of critics whose hyperbolic modes of assertion have made them best known, one wonders just what the use of all the other journals may be. In fact, of course, essays of importance *do* appear in the less prestigious journals, and critics one has never heard of are often as cogent and incisive as those whose names are, as it were, in lights.[4]

More worrying is the speed with which much theory-based criticism goes out of date – one is weary of the old phrase "publish or perish" even though it is a great deal more accurate now than when it was coined, but the amount of what has been published that quickly perishes as the theory from which it is suspended fades suggests an alternative meaning. Emblematic is a letter received by a colleague from the editor of a journal rejecting a submission

challenging an essay by a well-known critic that had been published a few years earlier; though the challenged essay had never
been questioned, it now represented a position, wrote the editor,
that was "no longer of particular interest." Indeed, when a critical
theory or approach begins to be dropped, it is most often because
it is no longer novel – its potential for surprise has been used up –
rather than because it has proven to be unsound. The argumentation behind many a theoretical approach can be shown to partake
of fallacious reasoning, but that carries weight only with those who
still believe that there are principles governing sound reasoning.
That the pursuit of novelty is the force that drives many a critic
from one theoretical formulation to another is further evidenced by
the rarity with which a critic announces that his or her previous
views were in error. The professionally clever critic just abandons
the exhausted field – and his or her accumulated errors and now
hollow pronouncements – to seek another. Among the few honorable
exceptions are Frederick Crews's essays on what he now finds
unacceptable in the Freudian criticism for which he was once a
major spokesman. Of course Stanley Fish has the best of both worlds
in presenting the shifts in his position as a saga in which he has
step-by-step mounted to the true theory – one which denies the
possibility of a true theory.

   Yet more troubling is the degree to which literary criticism and
theory is addressed solely to other literary critics and theorists –
actually to specialized subsets of critics and theorists. Some journals – I have in mind especially the prestigious *Critical Inquiry* –
seem to conduct a continual colloquy with themselves. In Jacques
Barzun's words, our learned journals have become "safe-deposit
boxes, double-locked against outsiders" (172). No one would wish
to deny that there is a place for theory and criticism written by
professionals for professionals: certainly not all that a thoughtful
and experienced critic wishes to comment on will be of interest to
the ordinary educated reader. Moreover, quite esoteric essays have
a role in keeping the profession alive – encouraging professors of
literature not to fall into modes of thought as routinized as those
out of which they strive to lift their students. But we are pretty
clearly over-supplied with the arcane, insistently paradoxical, and
resolutely impenetrable. If in fact it were the case that most publication results when and only when someone who has been teaching and thinking about an author, text, historical period, or genre
for some years finds, say, a stimulating analogy between a text and

a sociological theory, or delightedly discovers a particularly illuminating way of thinking about metaphor or satire, all would be well – and we all might have time to read a larger percentage of the published commentary on literature, and indeed more time to read and reread the literature itself.

Most worrying of all is the tendency of theory-based criticism to divorce the text from the human experience it – partially, inadequately, but necessarily and usefully – seeks to mime. The New Critical tendency to emphasize the symbolic at the expense of the mimetic has something to answer for here. When Hemingway's Frederic Henry escapes the firing squad by diving into the river, it is obvious to the symbolically oriented mind that Frederick undergoes a baptism into a new life; countless undergraduates must have dutifully noted this down in their lecture notes. Given the cultural background in which Hemingway wrote, it is possible to take the baptism as an intended rather than a symptomatic meaning, just as it is possible, again considering the cultural background, to take Faulkner's bear, Old Ben, as a symbol of a complex relationship between men and nature fast disappearing. And in such examples, the interpretation, necessarily arguable, is supported by other aspects of the story: despite obvious ironies, Frederick does enter a new life and nostalgia permeates the narration of *The Bear*. But what is one to say of W. B. Warner's reading of *Clarissa* as a game played with counters in which the rape of Clarissa is, like indeterminacy-celebrating hermeticism, simply a repudiation of limits judged to be artificial and arbitrary. For Warner, Lovelace has as goal "to undo the body's integrity, its system of self-enclosed meanings, and open it to new meanings, his own meanings" (67). (Quentin Kraft ironically comments, "Clarissa must be a narrow-minded young woman, indeed, and a spoilsport as well, to resist such a favor, at least to resist it in anything other than a playful way," OCN, 42). Such a reading as Warner's not only transgresses the hermeneutic principle of interpretation that requires taking account of the anticipated reader's presumed values, but, given the cultural background values of the present, it can only operate by denying the mimetic relationship between literature and human experience. Or, phrased differently, it is another example of the de Manian reduction of literature to a game with no consequences beyond the interest of tracing how a complex system cancels itself.

Professors of literature have perhaps asked themselves about the value of what they do more often than their colleagues in other disciplines – which may reflect either a salutary conscientiousness engendered by their studies, or the uneasy recognition that those who objected to the institutionalization of the university study of literature a hundred years ago were not altogether intellectual Luddites. Although most questioners have executed a sort of Cartesian maneuver, using doubt to clear the ground for the erection of stronger defenses, the doubts persist. That protests against the swelling flow of publication for the sake of well-filled vitas have been raised for decades might suggest that, after all, nothing has really changed. But the quantitative change in what is expected of members of the faculty of literature departments amounts to a qualitative one, as does the increasingly intractable result of all this activity. One notes wryly that in 1928 Douglas Bush disagreed with Henry Seidel Canby's concern about the volume of publication on grounds now long swept away: "After all there is only a handful of learned journals in literary fields, and there are thousands of college teachers" (476–7).

There must be something wrong when so many members of literature departments will admit that they feel guilty when they take time to read something that is not intended immediately to become grist for their own publication mill. There is something equally wrong when, as Culler reports, teaching is so widely regarded as a disagreeable burden, especially since it does not seem to be dislike of teaching but jealousy of time spent in something other than forwarding one's own publishing career that makes teaching seem a burden. Not less a symptom of something amiss is the deadly seriousness and increasing coterie-consciousness of much criticism and theory that carefully conceals any pleasure the critic may have found in the work. Randall Jarrell was complaining in 1955 about the critics whose demeanor seemed to say, "Good Lord, you don't think I *like* to read, do you? Reading is serious business, not something you fool around with in your spare time" (79–80). In the good old times of 1961, C. S. Lewis could still contrast the university teacher of literature in England with the luckless ones over the water who were being forced to become "mere professionals."

> Perhaps they once had the full response, but the 'hammer, hammer, hammer on the hard, high road' has long since dinned it out of them. I am thinking of unfortunate scholars in foreign universities who cannot 'hold down their jobs' unless they repeatedly publish articles each of which must say, or seem to say, something

new about some literary work. . . . For such people reading often becomes mere work. The text before them exists not in its own right but simply as raw material; clay out of which they can complete their tale of bricks." (6–7)

English university traditions have protected them from publication for the vita's sake longer than might have been expected, but that defense is now much diminished. The loss is not confined to the individual academic – the field of literary study becomes bleaker, its value to the culture less.[5]

Doubts about whether the primary activity of professional literary study should in fact be the publication of interpretation, criticism, and theory grow when one is willing to admit that criticism is not cumulative in any substantive sense, stands a considerable chance of not being read by others pursuing the same general topic, and is quite likely to be shortly outdated (not superseded by something which builds on its results but simply regarded as unprofitable). To find oneself reflecting on the value of one's vocation is disturbing, so disturbing that defenses arise immediately. There are multiple strategic reasons for accepting the status quo. To begin with, who can effectively protest? Older faculty who have published little (and whose rank and tenure would have been unattainable under the present dispensation) can be dismissed as simply seeking to justify themselves; senior faculty with a solid record of publication would seem to be indicting the basis of their own success; younger faculty would be seen as announcing their unsuitability for the present system. Moreover, as has been put to me forcefully more than once, it is in the interest of no one who has attained a niche in the system to protest. As Culler points out accurately enough, the discipline of English has done very well by outwardly imitating the model of the sciences.

After all, a successful protest would mean demotion of the study of literature from the exalted role of the discovery of ever new knowledge to that of the teaching of skills – on the whole, teachers of literature might well be no more highly regarded, receive no better pay than the teachers of the fine arts – and we know how hard they work and how comparatively poorly they are paid. Tenured professors of literature might even end up being exploited like the hired help who teach so many of the freshman composition courses. No one who knows what makes a successful academic administrator these days is likely to see much hope in persuading a dean that literature departments are engaged in a different kind of activity, one that requires as much knowledge, demands as much effort, and deserves the same rewards as disciplines with quite different missions. Recognition of this is probably why most protests against the absurdities of expecting the discipline to make the production of criticism its goal are made only in passing and not pursued. Nevertheless, while to criticize and at the same time admit that one sees no practical way of going about putting matters right is disagreeably like churlish carping, I can't help thinking that those who love and teach literature have, to put it minimally, no less responsibility to try to see things as they are and consider seriously if they are as they should be than those who pursue other disciplines.

THE COUNTER-ARGUMENT

There is perhaps no better way to conclude a critique of the profession than by citing Stanley Fish once more – this time two essays from *Doing What Comes Naturally*, "Profession Despise Thyself: Fear and Self-Loathing in Literary Studies" and "Anti-Professionalism." The experienced reader of Fish will already pretty much expect some variation on what has become the core Fishean Formula. This can be described as a combination of the always/already and always/not strategies: it is never possible to do X because X implies opposing Y but X is only possible because of Y. And then there is the coda: it doesn't make any difference because one will always think one is doing X; moreover it is the attempt to do X that creates the Y that makes X possible.

The bulk of "Profession Despise Thyself" consists of polemic critiques of certain writers who have questioned what they believe to be the undesirable directions the profession is taking (Peter Jay, Jonathan Yardley, Donald Davies, Walter Jackson Bate, and, more sympathetically treated, Edward Said). However, the core of this essay, and of "Anti-Professionalism" as well, lies in the following argument:

> While one can certainly say anti-professional things, one cannot be an anti-professional in the strong sense of operating independently of the profession. The things one might say become available only within the profession's present shape and would have the effect, if they were harkened to, not of eliminating the profession but of giving it and its objects another, no less professional

shape. To put it another way, insofar as it can have any consequences (apart from the impossible consequence of bypassing the
profession), anti-professionalism is a form of professional behavior
engaged in for the purpose of furthering some professional project.
(PDT, 206–7)

Well, yes, what one criticizes in a profession depends upon one's
conception of the profession as a whole. Criticizing a medical procedure because it is an ineffective cure requires the belief that it is
the responsibility of medical practitioners to cure physical and/or
psychological problems, etc. But one can still distinguish between
trying to change the shape of certain aspects of a profession as they
exist at a given time and supporting or even being neutral toward
those aspects.

Fish opens the way to the specific form of his argument by recognizing two views of professionalism, one described honorifically
and the other pejoratively, and then identifying literary anti-
professionalism with the latter. The pejorative view regards professionalism as another word for self-serving stratagems, among which
specialization is prominent. Any attack on specialization, then, is an
example of anti-professionalism, but, as instanced above, anti-
professionalism can only exist within a set of assumptions that
belongs to the profession. However, it could just as easily be asserted that anti-specialization is professionalism because it assumes
the profession, and then argue that it should really be called anti-
professionalism because it questions certain assumptions or practices of strategies of the profession. What would be lost in this
alternative mode of thinking about the matter is of course the sense
of paradox, since this second mode is more or less the way most
persons would normally think about it. Either way, however, the
distinction between applauding and deploring specialization (or any
other activity, aspect, or quality) of the profession remains important. In short, if one does not begin by calling the desire to change
the shape of the profession "anti-professional," one can remain with
the original issue rather than becoming sidetracked in the specious
argument that anti-specialization = anti-professionalism = being
professional = being self-contradictory.

Actually, Fish at one point approaches a more straightforward
conclusion:

If my argument is that there can be no literary criticism or peda-
gogy that is not a form of professionalism, it is also that there can

be no form of professionalism that is not an extension of some value or set of values. Whereas before one was asked to choose between professionalism and some category of pure value . . . the choice can now be seen as a choice between different versions of professionalism, each with its attendant values. (PDT, 211)

Right enough (though we have arrived at this perspective after an odd series of detours), but Fish then curiously continues:

To say that anti-professionalism is a form of professional behavior (and is therefore in a philosophical sense incoherent) is not to have closed the discussion but to have identified the basis on which it can continue by identifying the questions that now should be asked: "What kind of professional behavior is anti-professionalism? and What are its consequences?" (PDT, 211)

But, the important questions to be asked are rather different. "What values should literary study pursue?" "How can it best pursue them?" One can see why Fish would not wish to ask those questions.

One finds at the end of "Anti-Professionalism" a repetition of Fish's core argument: "even if one is convinced (as I am) that the world he sees and the values he espouses are constructions, or, as some say, 'effects of discourse,' that conviction will in no way render that world any less perspicuous or those values any less compelling" (A-P, 245–6). One can well turn this around and say, "even though the anti-foundationalist continues to make certain value judgments (as, for instance, that Jay, Yardley, Bate, et al. are wrong), he or she will try to avoid making overt statements about value." It is equally evident that Fish's argument is constantly haunted, like hermetic criticism, by the spectre of absolutism. To seek to alter the profession, whether much or little, is seen as being anti-professional; to be anti-professional is to be absolutely anti-professional. Once again the possibility of real change, of actual improvement, is made to seem impossible or at least illusory. But change is occurring constantly and, surely, there are better and worse directions of change.

CODA

I opened this volume by citing the late nineteenth-century arguments over including the study of literature in English at Oxford and Cambridge, but there is a bit of much earlier history that is perhaps even more emblematic of the problems lying at the heart of the teaching, critique, or analysis of literature. I refer to the all-too-human story of the establishment of the Oxford Chair of Poetry.

The Chair of Poetry was established in 1708 as the result of Henry Birkhead's last will and testament, a document much more specific about the character of the woman who was not to benefit from his estate than the responsibilities of the professors who were. The executors were surely given pause in reading that "Jane Stevenson whom I have formerly called and written to as my wife to save her credit in the world though I was never married to her nor betrothed to her" and who has "been extreem false and many ways exceeding injurious to me" was to receive one shilling while all Birkhead's "lands, tenements, and hereditaments" were to make up a trust "to maintain as far as it can for ever a Publick Professor of Poetry in the University of Oxford" (see Mackail). The Oxford Chair of Poetry in fact came into being without anyone knowing quite what a Professor of Poetry ought to be or do, and it was eleven years before anyone was appointed to the post. Even then, as J. W. Mackail's intriguing little history of the Chair of Poetry tells us, a good many of the occupants of the chair remained unsure about what they had been called to do – some apparently were so unsure that they did nothing at all. It can be plausibly argued that we are not much more certain about what a professor of literature professes to profess. We all have cause to be grateful to Matthew Arnold for using the Oxford Chair of Poetry to state the function of criticism as a source of fresh perspectives and incisive modes of thought, but he began at the far end – the obvious initial step is to understand the meaning of the literature one reads. The New Critics were right about that even though too many of their disciples failed to acknowledge the importance of going beyond that step. Now, two hundred years after Birkhead saw, however vaguely, the value of a professor of poetry, we ought to be able to see the value of professors of interpretation.

Notes

1. *A New Variorum Edition of Shakespeare: Measure for Measure*, ed. Mark Eccles (New York: Modern Language Association, of America, 1980).

2. That oppression was routine and warfare incessant in the time in which *Macbeth* is set is hardly arguable, but if the second sentence quoted means anything, it excuses the murder of Duncan as not only justifiable but heroic – that is clearly a significance induced purely by reference to Eagleton's brand of Marxism. One clue to our being given a meaning not only far from any authorial intention but far from anything an audience might recognize is the phrase, "however little the play itself recognizes the fact" – that is, there is little or nothing in the play itself to support this reading.

3. Yes of course administrators and personnel committees can give attention to quality – assuming they are willing to take time from their own work to read what their colleagues publish, and assuming they don't judge what they read solely by the light of their own theories and perspectives – but although the making of better informed judgments deserves strong praise, the definition of what a professor of literature is responsible for requires extensive rethinking.

4. W. V. Quine comments in "Paradoxes of Plenty" (*Theories and Things*): "The mass of professional journals is so indigestible and so little worth digesting that the good papers, though more numerous than ever, are increasingly in danger of being overlooked. We cope with the problem partly by ignoring the worst journals and partly by scanning tables of contents for respected names. Since the stratification of the journals from good to bad is imperfect, this procedure will miss an occasional good paper by an unknown author" (197). The last sentence is, I think, rather an understatement.

5. Thirty years ago in *The Rise of English Studies*, D. J. Palmer wrote: "The academic orientation of literary scholarship has had its advantages, chiefly because it seems to appropriate the great writers of the past within a small professional circle, where the level of discussion makes little contact with the interests of that now rather melancholy figure, 'the general reader.' Few outside the universities can follow the highly-specialized and technical methods of academic criticism, and small wonder when even the academics for whose benefit it is supposedly written find so much of this critical writing pedestrian or trivial, too often published only for the sake of publication. We shall soon have two distinct levels of literary experience existing side by side; where there is perhaps already an academic Shakespeare and a popular Shakespeare, there will also be two Dr. Johnsons and even two Dickens – a fate neither would have contemplated with equanimity." (169–70)

Works Cited

The following list has been constructed with an eye to the ways in which authors and volumes are cited in the text rather than to sheer consistency.

Abrams, M. H. *Doing Things with Texts.* New York: Norton, 1989.
Against Theory, ed. W. J. T. Mitchell. Chicago: University of Chicago Press, 1985.
Althusser, Louis. *For Marx* (1965). Trans. Ben Brewster. London: Allen Lane, 1969. Cited as *FM*.
——. "Ideology and Ideological State Apparatuses (Notes towards an Investigation)" in *Essays on Ideology.* London: Verso, 1984. Cited as ISA.
——. *Reading Capital,* Trans. Ben Brewster. London: NLB, 1970. Cited as RC.
Arbib, Michael and Mary B. Hesse. *The Construction of Reality.* Cambridge University Press, 1986. Cited as *CR.*
Aristotle. *Aristotle on Fallacies, or the Sophistic Elenchi.* Trans. Edward Poste. London: Macmillan, 1866; rptd. New York: Garland, 1987.
Arnold, Matthew. *The Complete Prose Works of Matthew Arnold.* Ed. R. H. Super. Ann Arbor: University of Michigan Press, 1960–77.
——. "The Function of Criticism at the Present Time" in vol. 3 of the *Complete Prose Works.*
——. "Literature and Science" in vol. 10 of the *Complete Prose Works.*
Auerbach, Erich. *Literary Language and Its Public in Late Latin Antiquity and in the Middle Ages.* Trans. R. Manheim. New York: Pantheon, 1965.
Austin, J. L. *How to Do Things with Words.* Eds. J. O. Urmson and Marina Sabisá. Cambridge, Mass.: Harvard University Press, 1975.
Ayer, A. J., editor. *Logical Positivism.* Glencoe, Ill.: Free Press, 1959. Cited as LP.
——. *Philosophy and Language.* Oxford: Clarendon, 1960. Cited as *P&L.*
Bach, Kent and Robert Harnish, *Linguistic Communication and Speech Acts.* Cambridge, Mass., MIT Press, 1979.
Bacon, Francis. *Advancement of Learning.* (1605) vol. 6 of *The Works of Francis Bacon.* Ed. J. Spedding, R. L. Ellis, and Douglas Denon Heath. Boston: Taggard & Thompson, 1863.
Bain, Alexander. "On Teaching English." *Fortnightly Review* n.s. 6 (August 1969), 200–14.
Bakhtin, Mikhail M. "Discourse in the Novel" in *The Dialogic Imagination.* Ed. Michael Holquist. Trans. Caryl Emerson and Michael Holquist. Austin: University of Texas Press, 1981.
——. *See also* Medvedev.
Barthes, Roland. "The Death of the Author" (1968) in *Image – Music – Text.* Cited as DA.
——. *Image – Music – Text.* Trans. Stephen Heath. London: Fontana, 1977. Cited as *IMT.*

——. "Introduction to Structural Analysis of Narrative" in *IMT*. Cited as ISA.

——. *The Pleasures of the Text*. Trans. Richard Miller. New York: Hill & Wang, 1975. Cited as PT.

——. "Science versus Literature." *TLS*, Sept. 28, 1967, 897–8. Cited as SvL.

——. *S/Z*, trans. Richard Miller. New York: Hill & Wang, 1974. Original French version, 1970.

——. "From Work to Text" (1971) in *Image – Music – Text*. Cited as WT.

——. *Writing Degree Zero* (1953). Trans. Annette Lavers and Colin Smith. New York: Hill & Wang, 1968. Cited as WDZ.

Barzun, Jacques. *Begin Here: The Forgotten Conditions of Teaching and Learning*. Ed. Morris Philipson. Chicago: University of Chicago Press, 1991.

Battersby, James L. *Paradigms Regained*. Philadelphia: University of Pennsylvania Press, 1991. Cited as PR.

——. "Professionalism, Relativism, and Rationality." *PMLA* 107 (January, 1992), 51–64. Cited as PRR.

Bayley, John. *The Order of Battle at Trafalgar*. London: Collins Harvill, 1987.

Beardsley, Monroe C. *Aesthetics: Problems in the Philosophy of Criticism*. New York: Harcourt, Brace, 1958. Cited as *Aesthetics*.

——. "The Intentional Fallacy." See Wimsatt.

Belsey, Catherine. *Critical Practice*. London: Methuen, 1980.

Bergonzi, Bernard. *Exploding English*. Oxford: Clarendon Press, 1990.

Blackmur, R. P. "Lord Tennyson's Scissors" in *Language as Gesture*. New York: Harcourt, Brace, 1952.

Bloom, Harold. *The Anxiety of Influence*. Oxford: Oxford University Press, 1973.

Boeckh, August. *On Interpretation and Criticism*. Trans. J. P. Pritchard. Norman: University of Oklahoma Press, 1968.

Booth, Wayne. *Critical Understanding*. Chicago: University of Chicago Press, 1979.

——. *The Rhetoric of Fiction*. Chicago: University of Chicago Press, 1961.

——. *A Rhetoric of Irony*. University of Chicago Press, 1974. Cited as RI.

Borges, Jorge Luis. *Labyrinths*. New York: New Directions, 1964.

Bordwell, David. *Making Meaning: Inference and Rhetoric in the Interpretation of Cinema*. Cambridge, Mass.: Harvard University Press, 1989.

Brooks, Cleanth. "Literary History vs. Criticism." *Kenyon Review* 2 (Fall, 1940), 403–412. Cited as LHC.

——. *The Rich Manifold*. Columbia: The Missouri Review, 1983. Cited as RM.

Brown, E. G. *A Literary History of Persia*. 4 vols. Cambridge: Cambridge University Press, 1929–30.

Bruss, Elizabeth. *Beautiful Theories: The Spectacle of Discourse in Contemporary Criticism*. Baltimore: Johns Hopkins University Press, 1982.

Burke, Kenneth. *The Philosophy of Literary Form*. Baton Rouge: Louisiana State University Press, 1941. Cited as PLF.

——. *A Rhetoric of Motives*. Berkeley: University of California Press, 1969. Cited as RM.

Bush, Douglas. "Scholars and Others." *Sewanee Review* 36 (1928), 475–85.

Cameron, James. "Problems of Literary History." *New Literary History* 1 (October 1969), 7–20.

Carnap, Rudolf. "The Elimination of Metaphysics through Logical Analysis of Language" in *Logical Positivism*, ed. A. J. Ayer. Cited as EMLA.

——. "Psychology in Physical Language" in *Logical Positivism*, ed. A. J. Ayer. Cited as PPL.

Carter, Michael. "Scholarship as Rhetoric of Display; Or, Why Is Everybody Saying All Those Terrible Things About Us?" *College English* 54 (March 1992), 303–12.

Chambers's Encyclopaedia. 9 vols. New York: Collier, 1892.

Chalmers, A. F. *What Is This Thing Called Science?* Milton Keynes: Open University Press, 1982.

Chase, Cynthia. "The Decomposition of the Elephants: Double-Reading *Daniel Deronda*." *PMLA* 93 (March, 1978), 215–27.

Chesterton, G. K. "The Invisible Man" in *The Innocence of Father Brown*. London: Cassell, 1926.

——. *The Victorian Age in Literature*. London: Williams & Norgate, n.d.

Clausen, Christopher. "National Literatures in English: Towards a New Paradigm." *New Literary History* 25 (Winter, 1994), 61–72.

Cohen, Morris and Ernest Nagel. *An Introduction to Logic and Scientific Method*. New York: Harcourt, Brace, 1934.

Coleridge, Samuel T. *The Statesman's Manual* (1816) in *Lay Sermons*, ed. R. J. White. Vol. 6 in *The Collected Works*, ed. Kathleen Coburn. 16 vols. London: Routledge & Kegan Paul, 1969–84.

Columbia Literary History of the United States. General editor, Emory Elliott. New York: Columbia University Press, 1988.

Comte, Auguste. *Cours de philosophie positive*. Ed. E. Littré. 2nd edition. Paris: J. B. Baillière et Fils, 1864. The first number given in the parenthetical citation refers to the translation given by F. A. Hayek in *The Counter-Revolution of Science*; the second to the original French in the above edition.

Conrad, Peter. *The Everyman History of English Literature*. London: Dent, 1985.

Crane, R. S. "Critical and Historical Principles of Literary History" in *The Idea of the Humanities*, vol. 2. Chicago: University of Chicago Press, 1967. Cited as CHP.

——. "History versus Criticism in the Study of Literature" in *The Idea of the Humanities*, vol. 2 (Chicago: University of Chicago Press, 1967). Originally published in the *English Journal* (College Edition), 24 (1935).

——. *The Languages of Criticism and the Structure of Poetry*. University of Toronto Press, 1953. Cited as LCSP.

Crews, Frederick. *Skeptical Engagements*. New York: Oxford, 1986.

Critical Terms for Literary Study. Ed. Frank Lentricchia and Thomas McLaughlin. Chicago: University of Chicago Press, 1990.

Culler, Jonathan. *Framing the Sign: Criticism and Its Institutions*. Oxford: Basil Blackwell, 1988, Cited as FS.

——. "In Defense of Overinterpretation" in Eco, *Interpretation and Overinterpretation*. Cited as IDO.

——. *On Deconstruction*. Ithaca: Cornell University Press, 1982. Cited as OD.

——. *The Pursuit of Signs*. Ithaca: Cornell University Press, 1981. Cited as PS.

——. *Structuralist Poetics*. Ithaca: Cornell University Press, 1975. Cited as *SP*.

Daiches, David. "The Criticism of Fiction: Some Second Thoughts" in *Literary Essays*. Edinburgh: Oliver & Boyd, 1956.

Davidson, Donald. "The Method of Truth in Metaphysics" in *After Philosophy: End or Transformation?* Ed. Kenneth Baynes, James Bohman, and Thomas McCarthy. Cambridge, Mass.: MIT Press, 1987.

de Beaugrande, Robert. *Critical Discourse: A Survey of Literary Theorists*. Norwood, N.J.: Ablex, 1988.

de Man, Paul. *Allegories of Reading*. New Haven: Yale University Press, 1979. Cited as *AR*.

——. *Blindness and Insight*. New York: Oxford University Press, 1971; 1983. Cited as *BI*.

——. "The Resistance to Theory" in *The Resistance to Theory*. Minneapolis: University of Minnesota Press, 1986.

Derrida, Jacques. "Limited Inc. abc . . . ," *Glyph* 2 (1977), 162–254. Cited as *LI*.

——. *Of Grammatology* (1967). Trans. Gayatri Spivak. Baltimore: Johns Hopkins University Press, 1976. Cited as *OG*.

——. "Signature Event Context," *Glyph* 1 (1977), 172–97. Cited as *SEC*.

——. "Structure, Sign and Play in the Discourse of the Human Sciences" in *The Language of Criticism and the Sciences of Man*, ed. Richard Macksey and Eugenio Donato. Baltimore: Johns Hopkins University Press, 1970. Cited as *SSP*.

Descombes, Vincent. "The Quandaries of the Referent" in *The Limits of Theory*. Stanford: Stanford University Press, 1989.

Dowling, William. "Intentionless Meaning" in *Against Theory*, ed. W. J. T. Mitchell. Originally appeared in *Critical Inquiry* 9 (June 1983), 784–89.

Dray, William. *Laws and Explanations in History*. Oxford: Oxford University Press, 1957.

Duff, J. Wright. *A Literary History of Rome: From the Origins to the Close of the Golden Age*. London: T. F. Unwin, 1910.

Eagleton, Terry. *Literary Theory: An Introduction*. Minneapolis: University of Minnesota Press, 1983.

——. *The Significance of Theory*. Oxford: Blackwell, 1990. Cited as *ST*.

——. *William Shakespeare*. Oxford: Basil Blackwell, 1986. Cited as *WS*.

Eco, Umberto, with Richard Rorty, Jonathan Culler, and Christine Brooke-Rose. *Interpretation and Overinterpretation*. Ed. Stefan Collini. Cambridge: Cambridge University Press, 1992.

Encyclopedic Dictionary of Semiotics. Ed. T. A. Sebeok. 3 vols. Berlin: New York: Mouton, 1986.

Encyclopedia of Philosophy. Ed. Paul Edwards. 8 vols. New York: Macmillan, 1967.

Fish, Stanley. "Anti-Foundationalism, Theory Hope, and the Teaching of Composition" in *DWCN*. Cited as A-F.

——. "Anti-Professionalism" (1985) in *DWCN*. Cited as "A-P."

——. "Change" (1985) in *Doing What Comes Naturally*. Cited as Ch.

——. "Consequences" (1985) in *Doing What Comes Naturally*. Originally appeared in *Critical Inquiry* 11 (March 1985), 433–58. Cited as Con.

——. "Demonstration vs. Persuasion: Two Models of Critical Activity" in *ITTC*. Cited as DvP.

——. *Doing What Comes Naturally*. Durham: Duke University Press, 1989. Cited as *DWCN*.

——. "Interpreting the Variorum" (1976) in *ITTC*. Cited as IV.

——. "Profession Despise Thyself: Fear and Self-Loathing in Literary Studies" (1983) in *DWCN*. Cited as PDT.

——. *Is There a Text in This Class?* Cambridge, Mass.: Harvard University Press, 1980. Cited as *ITTC*.

——. Is There a Text in This Class? in *ITTC*. Cited as ITTC.

——. "Witholding the Missing Portion: Psychoanalysis and Rhetoric" (1986) in *DWCN*. Cited as WMP.

Foerster, Norman. "Literary Scholarship and Criticism." *English Journal* (College Edition) 25 (1936), 224–32.

Foucault, Michel. "What Is an Author?" in *Language, Counter-Memory, Practice*. Oxford: Basil Blackwell, 1977.

Fowler, Alastair. *A History of English Literature*. Cambridge, Mass.: Harvard University Press, 1989. Cited as *HEL*.

——. "The Two Histories" in *Theoretical Issues in Literary History*. Ed. David Perkins. Cambridge, Mass.: Harvard University Press, 1991. Cited as TH.

Fowler, David. *A Literary History of the Popular Ballad*. Durham: Duke University Press, 1968.

Freadman, Richard and Seumas Miller. *Re-thinking Theory*. Cambridge: Cambridge University Press, 1992.

Frege, Gottlob. "On Sense and Reference" (1892). Trans. Max Black in *Translations from the Philosophical Writings of Gottlob Frege*. Ed. Peter Geach and Max Black. Oxford: Basil Blackwell, 1952.

Gadamer, Hans-Georg. *Truth and Method*. Trans. and ed. G. Barden and J. Cumming. New York: Seabury Press, 1975.

Girard, René. "Theory and its Terrors" in *The Limits of Theory*, ed. Thomas Kavanaugh.

Graff, Gerald. *Beyond the Culture Wars: How Teaching the Conflicts Can Revitalize American Education*. New York: Norton, 1992.

——. *Literature Against Itself*. Chicago: University of Chicago Press, 1979.

——. *Professing Literature: An Institutional History*. Chicago: University of Chicago Press, 1987. Cited as *PL*.

Green, Geoffrey. *Literary Criticism and the Structures of History: Erich Auerbach and Leo Spitzer*. Lincoln: University of Nebraska Press, 1982.

Greenblatt, Stephen, ed. *The Power of Forms in the English Renaissance*. Norman, Okla.: Pilgrim Books, 1982. Cited as *PFER*.

——. *Shakespearean Negotiations*. Berkeley: University of California Press, 1988. Cited as *SN*.

Grice, H. P. "Logic and Conversation" in *SWW*. Originally appeared in *Syntax and Semantics* 3. New York: Academic Press, 1975. Cited as L&C.

——. "Meaning" in *SWW*. Originally appeared in *The Philosophical Review* 66 (1957), 377–88.

——. *Studies in the Way of Words*. Cambridge, Mass.: Harvard University Press, 1989. Cited as *SWW*.

——. "Utterer's Meaning, Sentence-Meaning, and Word-Meaning" in *SWW*. Originally appeared in *Foundations of Language* 4 (August 1968), 225–42.

Gross, John. *The Rise and Fall of the Man of Letters* (1969); new edition, London: Penguin, 1991.

Harris, Wendell V. *A Dictionary of Concepts in Literary Criticism and Theory.* Westport, Conn.: Greenwood, 1992.

———. *Interpretive Acts: In Search of Meaning.* Oxford: Clarendon, 1988.

Hartman, Geoffrey. "Toward Literary History" in *Beyond Formalism.* New Haven: Yale University Press, 1970.

Hawkes, Terence. *Structuralism and Semiotics.* Berkeley: University of California Press, 1976.

Hayek, F. A. *The Counter-Revolution of Science.* Glencoe. Ill.: Free Press, 1952.

Heath-Stubbs, John. *The Pastoral.* Oxford: Oxford University Press, 1969.

Heidegger, Martin. "Letter on Humanism" (1947), trans. F. A. Capuzzi and J. G. Gray. In *Martin Heidegger: Basic Writings.* Ed. David Krell. New York: Harper & Row, 1977.

The Hermeneutics Reader. See Mueller-Vollmer.

Hesse, Mary. *The Construction of Reality.* See Arbib.

———. *Revolutions and Reconstructions in the Philosophy of Science.* Brighton: Harvester, 1980. Cited as *RR.*

Hirsch, E. D., Jr. "Against Theory?" in *Against Theory,* ed. Mitchell. Originally appeared in *Critical Inquiry* 9 (June 1983), 743–7. Cited as AT.

———. "Objective Interpretation," *PMLA* 75 (September 1960), 463–79.

———. *Validity in Interpretation.* New Haven: Yale University Press, 1967. Cited as *VI.*

Holloway, John. "Language, Realism, Subjectivity, Objectivity" in *Reconstructing Literature,* ed. Laurence Lerner.

Howell, Wilbur Samuel. *Poetics, Rhetoric, and Logic.* Ithaca: Cornell University Press, 1975.

Huxley, T. H. "Science and Culture" (1880) in *Science and Culture and Other Essays.* New York: Appleton, 1899.

Hyde, Douglas. *A Literary History of Ireland.* London: T. F. Unwin, 1906.

Interpretation and Overinterpretation. See Eco.

Iser, Wolfgang. *The Implied Reader* (1972). Baltimore: Johns Hopkins University Press, 1974.

"Isolated Islands of Discontent," *Times Higher Education Supplement,* February 13, 1981, p. 31.

Jakobson, Roman. "Closing Statement: Linguistics and Poetics" in *Style in Language,* ed. T. A. Sebeok. Cambridge, Mass.: MIT Press, 1960. Cited as L&P.

———. "The Metaphoric and Metonymic Poles" in *Fundamentals of Language* 1. The Hague: Mouton, 1956.

James, William. *Pragmatism: A New Name for Some Old Ways of Thinking* (1907). London: Longmans, Green, 1940.

Jameson, Fredric. *The Political Unconscious.* Ithaca: Cornell University Press, 1981. Cited as PU.

———. *The Prison-House of Language.* Princeton: Princeton University Press, 1972. Cited as P-HL.

Jarrell, Randall. *Poetry and the Age.* New York: Noonday Press, 1953.

Jauss, Hans Robert. "Literary History as a Challenge to Literary Theory." *New Literary History* 2 (Autumn 1970), 7–37.

Johnstone, Henry. *The Problem of the Self*. University Park: Penn State University Press, 1970.

Johnstone, Robert. "The Impossible Genre: Reading Comprehensive Literary History." *PMLA* 107 (January 1992), 26–37.

Kipling, Rudyard. "Thrown Away" in *Plain Tales from the Hills*. Calcutta, 1888.

Knapp, Steven and Walter Benn Michaels. "Against Theory: Hermeneutics and Deconstruction" in *Against Theory*, ed. Mitchell. Originally published in *Critical Inquiry* 8 (Autumn 1982), 723–42.

Kraft, Quentin G. "Science and Poetics, Old and New" *College English* 37 (October 1975), 167–75.

———. "On Character in the Novel: William Beatty Warner Versus Samuel Richardson and the Humanists." *College English* 50 (January 1988), 32–47. Cited as OCN.

———. "Toward a Critical Renewal: At the Corner of Camus and Bloom Streets," *College English* 54 (January 1992), 46–63. Cited as TCR.

Kripke, Saul. *Wittgenstein on Private Language*. Oxford: Basil Blackwell, 1982.

Kuhn, Thomas. "Reflections on My Critics" in *Criticism and the Growth of Knowledge*. Ed. Imre Lakatos and Alan Musgrave. Cambridge: Cambridge University Press, 1970. Cited as RMC.

———. *The Structure of Scientific Revolutions*. Chicago: University of Chicago Press, 1962; 1970. Cited as SSR.

Laplace, Pierre Simon de. "Essai philosophique sur les probabilités" (1814) in *Les Maitres de la pensée scientifique*. Ed. M. Solovine. Paris: 1921.

Lee, Sir Sidney. "The Place of English Literature in the Modern University" (1913), rptd. *Elizabethan and Other Essays*. Oxford: Clarendon Press, 1929.

Lefevere, André. *Literary Knowledge*. Amsterdam: Jan Gorcum, 1977.

Lerner, Laurence, ed. *Reconstructing Literature*. Oxford: Basil Blackwell, 1983.

Levin, Harry. "The Crisis of Interpretation" in *Teaching Literature: What Is Needed Now*. Ed. James Engell and David Perkins. Cambridge, Mass.: Harvard University Press, 1988. Cited as CI.

Levin, Richard L. "The Cultural Materialist Attack on Artistic Unity, and the Problem of Ideological Criticism" in *Ideological Approaches to Shakespeare: The Practice of Theory*. Ed. Robert Merrix and Nicholas Ranson. Lewiston, NY: E. Mellen, 1992. Cited as CMA.

———. *New Readings vs. Old Plays*. University of Chicago Press, 1979. Cited as NRvOP.

Levinson, Marjorie. *Wordsworth's Great Period Poems*. Cambridge: Cambridge University Press, 1986.

The Limits of Theory, Ed. Thomas M. Kavanaugh. Stanford: Stanford University Press, 1989.

A Literary History of England. Ed. Albert Baugh. New York: Appleton-Century-Crofts, 1948.

Literary History of the United States. Ed. R. E. Spiller, W. Thorp, T. H. Jackson and H. S. Canby. New York: Macmillan, 1948.

Livingston, Paisley. *Literary Knowledge: Humanistic Inquiry and the Philosophy of Science*. Ithaca: Cornell University Press, 1988.

Lodge, David. "Historicism and Literary History: Mapping the Modern

Period" in *Working with Structuralism*. London: Routledge & Kegan Paul, 1981.

———. *The Modes of Modern Writing: Metaphor, Metonymy, and the Typology of Modern Literature*. Ithaca: Cornell University Press, 1977.

Logical Positivism. See Ayer.

Longacre, Robert. *The Grammar of Discourse*. New York: Plenum Press, 1983.

Lovejoy, A. O. *The Thirteen Pragmatisms and Other Essays*. Johns Hopkins University Press, 1963.

MacCannell, Dean and Juliet Flower MacCannell. *The Time of the Sign*. Bloomington: Indiana University Press, 1982.

Mackail, J. W. "Henry Birkhead and the Foundation of the Oxford Chair of Poetry" in *Studies in Humanism*. London: Longmans, Green, 1938.

McGann, Jerome. "History, Herstory, Theirstory, Ourstory" in *Theoretical Issues in Literary History*. Ed. David Perkins. Cambridge: Harvard University Press, 1991.

———. *Romantic Ideology*. Chicago: University of Chicago Press, 1983.

McKeon, Richard. "The Philosophic Bases of Art and Criticism" in *Critics and Criticism: Ancient and Modern*. Ed. R. S. Crane, et al. Chicago: University of Chicago Press, 1952.

The Languages of Criticism and the Sciences of Man. Eds. Richard Macksey and Eugenio Donato. Baltimore: Johns Hopkins University Press, 1970.

Mailloux, Steven. *Interpretive Conventions*. Ithaca: Cornell University Press, 1982.

Martianus Capella. *De nuptiis Philologiae et Mercurii*. Ed. Adolfus Dick. Stuttgart: B. G. Teubner, 1925.

Medvedev, P. N./M. M. Bakhtin. *The Formal Method in Literary Scholarship*. Trans. Albert J. Wehrle. Baltimore: Johns Hopkins University Press, 1978. (It remains moot whether this volume was written by Bakhtin, Medvedev, or both.)

Mencken, H. L. "Criticism of Criticism of Criticism" in *Prejudices: A Selection*. Ed. James T. Farrell. New York: Random House (Vintage), 1958. Originally published as "Critics and their Ways," *New York Evening Mail*, July 1, 1918, p. 6.

Merquior, J. G. *From Prague to Paris*. London: Verso, 1986.

Miller, J. Hillis. "The Critic as Host" in *Theory Then and Now*. Originally appeared in *Critical Inquiry* 3 (Spring, 1977), 439–47.

———. "Deconstructing the Deconstructors" in *Theory Then and Now*. Originally appeared in *Diacritics* (Summer, 1975). Cited as DD.

———. "The Ethics of Reading" in *Theory Then and Now*. Originally appeared in *Style* 21 (Summer, 1987). Cited as ER.

———. "The Function of Literary Theory" in *Theory Then and Now*. Originally published in *The Future of Literary Theory*. Ed. Ralph Cohen. London: Routledge, 1989. Cited as FLT.

"The Imperative to Teach" in *Theory Then and Now*. Originally published in *Qui Parle* I (Spring, 1987). Cited as IT.

———. "On Edge: The Crossways of Contemporary Criticism" (1979) in *Theory Then and Now*. Originally published in *Bulletin of the American Academy of Sciences* 32 (January 1979). Rptd. with a "Postscript" in *Romanticism and*

Contemporary Criticism, ed. Morris Eaves and Michael Fischer (Cornell University Press, 1986). Cited as OE.

——. *Theory Then and Now*. London: Harvester Wheatsheaf, 1991. Cited as *TTN*.

Morris, Charles. *Foundations of the Theory of Signs*. Vol. 1, no. 2 of the *International Encyclopedia of Unified Sciences* (1938); Chicago: University of Chicago Press, 1960.

Mueller-Vollmer, Kurt, ed. *The Hermeneutics Reader*. Oxford: Basil Blackwell, 1986. Cited as *HR*.

——. "Understanding and Interpretation: Toward a Defence of Literary Hermeneutics" in *Literary Criticism and Philosophy*, ed. Joseph Strelka. University Park: Penn State University Press, 1983. Cited as U&I.

Nassar, Eugene Paul. *The Rape of Cinderella: Essays in Literary Continuity*. Bloomington: Indiana University Press, 1970.

Nuttall, A. D. *A New Mimesis*. London: Methuen, 1983.

Ogden, C. K. and I. A. Richards. *The Meaning of Meaning*. London: Kegan Paul, Trench, Trubner, 1938.

Olsen, Elder. "The Dialectical Foundations of Critical Pluralism" (1966) in *On Value Judgments in the Arts*. Chicago: Chicago University Press, 1976.

Palmer, D. J. *The Rise of English Studies*. Oxford: Oxford University Press, 1965.

Parrinder, Patrick. *The Failure of Theory: Essays on Criticism and Contemporary Fiction*. Brighton: Harvester, 1987.

Pater, Walter. *Appreciations*. London: Macmillan, 1889.

——. *The Renaissance*. London: Macmillan, 1888.

Pattison, Robert. "Trollope among the Textuaries" in *Reconstructing Literature*, ed. Laurence Lerner.

Peirce, Charles Sanders. *Collected Papers of Charles Sanders Peirce*, eds. Charles Hartshorne and Paul Weiss, vols. 1–6, and A. W. Burks, vols. 7–8. Cambridge, Mass.: Harvard University Press, 1931–35; 1958. The papers are conventionally cited by volume and paragraph, as: 6.340.

Pelc, Jerzy. "Some Methodological Problems in Literary History," *New Literary History* 7 (Autumn 1975), 89–96.

Percy, Walker. "The Delta Factor" (1975) in *MB*. Cited as DF.

——. *The Message in the Bottle*. New York: Farrar, Straus & Giroux, 1975. Cited as *MB*.

——. "The Mystery of Language" (1957) in *The Message in the Bottle*. Cited as ML.

——. "Semiotic and a Theory of Knowledge" (1957) in *The Message in the Bottle*. Cited as STK.

Perelman, Chaim and L. Olbrechts-Tyteca. *The New Rhetoric*. Trans. John Wilkinson and Purcell Weaver. Notre Dame: University of Notre Dame Press, 1969.

Perelman, Chaim. *The Realm of Rhetoric*. Trans. W. Kluback. Notre Dame: University of Notre Dame Press, 1982. Cited as RR.

Perkins, David. *Is Literary History Possible?* Baltimore: Johns Hopkins University Press, 1992.

Popkin, Cathy. "A Plea to Wielders of Academic Dis(of)course," *College English* 54 (February 1992), 173–81.

Popper, Karl. *Conjectures and Refutations: The Growth of Scientific Knowledge.* New York: Harper & Row, 1965. Cited as C&R.

——. *The Logic of Scientific Discovery.* London: Hutchinson, 1968. Cited as LSD.

——. *The Myth of the Framework.* Occasional Paper No. 14. London Association of Comparative Educationists. Cited as MF.

Pound, Ezra. *The Spirit of Romance.* Norfolk, Conn.: J. McLaughlin, 1952.

Quine, W. V. "Paradoxes of Plenty" in *Theories and Things.* Cambridge, Mass.: Harvard University Press, 1981.

Reconstructing Literature. See Lerner.

Richards, I. A. *Principles of Literary Criticism.* London: Routledge & Kegan Paul, 1925. Cited as PLC.

Ricoeur, Paul. "On Interpretation" in *After Philosophy, End or Transformation.* Ed. Kenneth Baynes, James Bohman, and Thomas McCarthy. Cambridge, Mass.: MIT Press, 1987. Cited as OI.

——. *Time and Narrative.* 3 vols. University of Chicago Press, 1984–88. For the three forms of mimesis, see especially chapter 3 of volume 1.

Rorty, Richard. *Consequences of Pragmatism.* Brighton: Harvester, 1982. Cited as CP.

——. *Philosophy and the Mirror of Nature.* Princeton: Princeton University Press, 1979.

——. "The Pragmatist's Progress" in *Interpretation and Overinterpretation.* Cited as PP.

Rosenblatt, Louise. *The Reader, The Text, The Poem.* Carbondale: Southern Illinois University Press, 1978.

Ruskin, John. *The Stones of Venice.* See vol. 3, ch. 2, para 8.

Saussure, Ferdinand de. *Course in General Linguistics.* Ed. C. Bally and A. Sechehaye. Trans. W. Baskin. New York: McGraw-Hill, 1966.

Sayers, Dorothy. *Three Great Lord Peter Novels.* London: Victor Gollancz, 1978.

Schleiermacher, Friedrich D. E. *Hermeneutics: The Handwritten Manuscripts of F. D. Schleiermacher.* Ed. Heinz Kimmerle. Trans. J. Duke and J. Forstman. Missoula: Scholars Press, 1977).

Scholes, Robert. "The Fictional Criticism of the Future." *TriQuarterly* no. 34 (Fall, 1975), 233–47. Cited as FCF.

——. *Textual Power: Literary Theory and the Teaching of English.* New Haven: Yale University Press, 1985. Cited as TP.

Scruton, Roger. "Public Text and Common Reader" in *Reconstructing Literature,* ed. Laurence Lerner.

Searle, John. "Reiterating the Differences: A Reply to Derrida," *Glyph* 1 (1977), 198–208.

Shakespeare, William. *Measure for Measure: A New Variorum Edition of Shakespeare.* Ed. Mark Eccles. New York: Modern Language Association, 1980.

Smith, Steven B. *Reading Althusser: An Essay on Structural Marxism.* Ithaca: Cornell University Press, 1984.

Steiner, George. "Text and Context" in *On Difficulty and Other Essays.* Oxford: Oxford University Press, 1978. Cited as T&C.

——. "To Civilize our Gentlemen" in *Language and Silence.* London: Faber & Faber, 1967. Cited as TCG.

Sturrock, John, ed. *Structuralism and Since.* Oxford: Oxford University Press, 1979.

Taine, Hippolyte. *History of English Literature.* 4 vols. Trans. H. van Laun. Edinburgh: Edmonston & Douglas, 1873.

Tallis, Raymond. *The Explicit Animal: A Defence of Human Consciousness.* London: Macmillan Academic and Professional, 1991. Cited as *EA*.

——. *Not Saussure: A Critique of Post-Saussurean Literary Theory.* London: Macmillan, 1988. Cited as *NS*.

Taylor, Charles. "Interpretation and the Science of Man," *Review of Metaphysics* 25 (September 1971), 3–51.

Thoms, Keith. "The Past in Clearer Light, A Beacon on Our Future," *Times Higher Education Supplement,* December 2, 1988, pp. 13, 16.

Thurley, Geoffrey. *Counter-Modernism.* London: Macmillan, 1983.

Todorov, Tzvetan. *Introduction to Poetics,* trans. Richard Howard. Minneapolis: University of Minnesota Press, 1981.

Warner, William Beatty. *Reading Clarissa: The Struggles of Interpretation.* New Haven: Yale University Press, 1970.

Watts, Cedric. "Bottom's Children: The Fallacies of Structuralist, Post-Structuralist and Deconstructionist Literary Theory" in Laurence Lerner, *Reconstructing Literature.*

Weimann, Robert. *Structure and Society in Literary History.* Charlottesville: University of Virginia Press, 1976; Baltimore: Johns Hopkins University Press, 1984.

Wellek, René. "The Fall of Literary History" in *The Attack on Literature.* Chapel Hill: University of North Carolina Press, 1982. Cited as FLH.

——. "Literary History" in *Literary Scholarship.* Ed. Norman Foerster. Chapel Hill: University of North Carolina Press, 1949. Cited as LH.

——. "Six Kinds of Literary History" in *English Institute Essays* for 1946. New York: Columbia University Press, 1947. Cited as SKLH.

Wellek, René and Austin Warren. *Theory of Literature.* New York: Harcourt, Brace, 1949.

White, Hayden. "New Historicism: A Comment" in *The New Historicism.* Ed. Harold Veeser. London: Routledge, 1989. Cited as NH.

——. "The Problem of Change in Literary History." *New Literary History* 7 (Autumn, 1975), 97–111. Cited as PCLH.

Wimsatt, W. K. "Genesis: An Argument Resumed," *Day of the Leopards: Essays in Defence of Poems.* New Haven: Yale University Press, 1967. Originally published in *The Discipline of Criticism,* ed. Peter Demetz, Thomas Greene, and Larry Nelson. New Haven: Yale University Press, 1968.

Wimsatt, W. K. and Monroe Beardsley. "The Intentional Fallacy," *Sewanee Review,* 54 (Summer 1946), 468–88.

Wittgenstein, Ludwig, *Philosophical Investigations.* Trans. G. E. M. Anscombe. New York: Macmillan, 1953.

Index to Terms

Terms are indexed only where defined or substantively discussed.

Index of Names

Names that appear in a mere list have been omitted; names that appear in notes have been cited only where the person has been quoted.